THE LAW OF THE SEA

*A publication of the Law of the Sea Institute
and the Mershon Center for Education in National Security*

EDITED BY LEWIS M. ALEXANDER

THE LAW
OF THE SEA

Offshore Boundaries and Zones

The Ohio State University Press

FOREWORD

The Law of the Sea Institute was established at Kingston, Rhode Island, in February, 1965, for the purpose of exchanging ideas and information on matters relating to the control and use of the sea. As its first project, the Institute sponsored a week-long conference at the University between June 27 and July 1, 1966. It was attended by over one hundred persons from the fields of law, marine science, business, government, and the social sciences. A second conference is planned for June of 1967, and it is anticipated that one will be scheduled in each year thereafter.

The papers presented at the first conference are printed in this volume. Following each group of papers, or panel, there was considerable discussion from the floor. Rather than reproduce the discussions verbatim, it was necessary, in the interests of space, to reduce the material to a summary of the salient points for each morning and afternoon session.

Support for the first conference was received from the Office of Naval Research, the Bureau of Commercial Fisheries, and the Environmental Science Services Administration. The Institute is indebted to these organizations for helping to make possible the 1966 conference. It also is grateful to the Mershon Social Science Program of the Ohio State University for its assistance in the publication of these *Proceedings*.

Present members of the executive committee of the Law of the Sea Institute are William T. Burke, Francis J. Christy, Jr., John A. Knauss, Dale Krause, and Lewis M. Alexander.

LEWIS M. ALEXANDER
University of Rhode Island

PREFACE

Rhode Island is the most watery of all the United States on a percentage basis. Of our total area of 1,214 square miles, 156 square miles—not counting the offshore waters—are presently under water. There are 384 miles of shoreline, which is pretty good for a state of such small size.

Rhode Island also has a nautical tradition which makes its selection for this meeting even more appropriate. Newport was one of the major seaports of this nation in the eighteenth century, leading at one point in its history both New York and Boston. Oliver Hazard Perry was born near where we are today in South Kingstown. Another hero of the War of 1812, James DeWolfe, was born in Bristol. And our Narragansett Bay is one of the largest deep-water harbors in the North American continent. It has been estimated that all the Allied fleets of World War II could have been comfortably moored, at one time, in our own bay.

This is, indeed, a timely occasion for Americans—and I understand we have a few guests from abroad, from Russia and from other countries—to be discussing the Law of the Sea. As you may know, on June 15, 1966, the Senate passed a bill to establish a contiguous fishing zone beyond the territorial seas of the United States to a limit of twelve miles. Also in the Senate last week my own Sea Grant College bill was reported out of the full committee and went to the floor of the Senate. We are waiting for a companion bill which we hope will come over shortly from the House. We are not sure that we will get it through this session, but we are going to do our very best.

It is timely also to hold this conference because the newspapers brought out last week an example of what might be called "double piracy." The pirate radio station in the Thames estuary off England was seized by pirates. I don't quite know what "double piracy" means, but I should think this would be an interesting subject for one of the talks. I think we will see more and more of problems of this sort developing. I know that as I have worked on my Sea Grant College legislation, which calls for the practical exploitation of the knowledge of the basic research that we have, one could see the problems that will arise—the man-made islands that will be created way outside the continental limits; the mining settlements that will exist under the seas where people will be living for months on end. What happens in these areas if murder is committed? What kind of law prevails? These are the kind of questions that are absolutely without answer as of now, and it is a conference like this that can create a climate and a direction that will set the tone for the answers that will come. I saw the effect of a conference like this just about eight months ago, when the Southern New England Marine Science Association, (SNEMSA), held its meeting in Newport calling for practical legislation to develop the knowledge of the seas we have. It is really out of that conference that a lot of the support for my Sea Grant College bill developed, and it is in great part thanks to that conference that we have been able to get it as far as we have.

The United States has the most extensive nautical coastline, almost 13,000 miles, of any nation. Russia has, as I guess Russia is more fully aware than I, a longer coastline, but a great deal of the coastline touches on the Arctic Sea. But we maintain that we have the longest navigable coastline of any country in the world. Foreign fisheries are aware of the riches on our shores and are coming to exploit them in ever increasing numbers. Ten years ago we could expect only about one hundred foreign vessels off our shores during the summer fishing. Now, at the height of this summer season, 1966, we can expect a huge fleet of more than twelve hundred ships, more than twelve times the number. These foreign vessels keep moving in closer and closer to our own coast. At the moment not many of them fish within twelve miles of the mainland. Still it is a good time to be setting the twelve-mile limit before they do move in and establish a historic fishery.

As you are aware, too, all but twenty-five coastal fishing nations have already extended their fishing jurisdiction to twelve miles and many have gone far beyond. Those that have gone further include the South American nations and Guinea in Africa. But we accept the twelve mile limit of such countries as the United Kingdom, France, West Germany, and Norway, and they would accept our twelve-mile limit if we established one. The basic reason that we have all joined together in this twelve mile fisheries limit is not just for conservation of fishery resources; what is more important, we are trying to give protection to the coastal fleets of small fishing vessels against large foreign ships which can force them off their ground. Larger fishing vessels use very different techniques; for example, they may trawl across the surface where smaller boats will be conducting stationary fishing and thus literally make it impossible for the smaller boats to operate. I understand that last year alone, 1965, there were sixteen separate verifiable incidents, in which sixty-five units of fishing gear owned by U.S. fishermen were destroyed by foreign trawlers. The world's fisheries have grown, as we all know, into a much larger operation than they used to be. I remember in the middle of World War II when I was given the responsibility of the rehabilitation of the Sicilian fishing industry that we went in there and found the job was really very simple. That fishery consisted of corrals that stretched out into the sea to catch the fish as they went along and were attracted by the fishermen's fires or bright lights. All we had to do was to provide a few lines, a few hooks, and just very basic materials indeed.

But now when foreign fisheries are becoming so mechanized, it requires far more complicated and advanced techniques and more capital than before. Although the twelve mile limit will not solve all the problems of foreign interference currently facing our fishermen and those of other nations, it is a fair, necessary, and beneficial step in the right direction. Perhaps the next move, and this may come in part as a result of your conference, would be to consider another Geneva-type conference on the law of the sea relating to fisheries rights and jurisdictions, such as those that took place in 1958 and 1960. A very useful exercise here would seem to me to be some sort of recommendation as to when such a conference should occur, where it should occur, and with what problems it should be concerned. This would be very beneficial not only for our nation but for all the countries of the world, and I would hope might be one of the results of this conference.

There are various interesting ideas to be examined here too. I was particularly struck by the idea that our offshore fisheries limits should not be set on a longitudinal but on a depth basis such as the 100-fathom line. I'm not sure whether this could work practically; it might be worth examining in this conference. And I am sure it probably will be.

As the nation with the longest fishable coastline, it would be fitting for the United States to take the lead in urging the United Nations to address itself again to this question of fishing rights and jurisdictions off the coastal states. Many are familiar with this problem that we face in the Congress concerning the continental shelf. What resources, basically fisheries, belong to the country that adjoins the shelf, and what belongs to the "first come first served"? I remember we had a very complicated debate in the Senate one time, and it finally developed that, under the continental shelf theory, oysters would belong to the country to which they adjoin, but crabs or lobsters that leave the surface of the sea bed would not. They belong to anybody who comes and catches them.

We are faced with another problem too. When speaking in the Senate I am also very conscious that I am a senator from a strong Navy, as well as fisheries, state. We have a very real interest on the one hand in enlarging our fisheries interests but on the other hand in making sure that the territorial limits in the sea are kept as narrow as possible. With a strong Navy we want to make sure that the waters of the world are as free as possible to our ships. One would find, if one stretched the three-mile limit to six or twelve miles that many waters which at present are considered open to the use of the world would become closed. Many straits would become closed, including Gibraltar and those in Indonesia. So we are torn here. On the one hand, we ought to keep the limit as narrow as possible for the commerce of the seas, and, on the other hand we want to extend it from the viewpoint of fisheries resources. It seems to me that we are trying to get the best of both worlds when we say that there should be a longer fisheries limit than there is a territorial one. But this is natural because it is in line with our own interests. I would think, too, that the Soviet Union, which is developing a strong Navy and also has its own fishing industry to consider, would not feel too different from us in this view.

I note that on today's agenda it is planned to take a new look at the 1958 Geneva Conference, and I hope that from this look and from examining some of these problems that I have mentioned, you may come up with positive recommendations. Already today there is considerable international co-operation in ocean affairs. As oceanologists know, some of the most productive international programs today are in the ocean science fields and in conservation. The International Maritime Consultative Organization, IMCO, at whose original meeting I had the honor of representing the United States as a delegate appointed by President Eisenhower, has faced up to the problems of merchant marine sanitation, pollution, and safety. But I think that IMCO could be a great deal more active. One of your recommendations might well be that IMCO, along with its Committee on Merchant Marine Safety Standards, might also concern itself with some of the problems of international law.

In this way all the problems of the law and the problems of the sea would be basically in one particular place. Because the sea is international, no one nation can use or exploit it without regard to the needs, the practices, and the historical claims of others. Most nations recognize this; some do not, but the outlook in general is hopeful. I think it is possible that the nations will solve the difficult problems of conflicting interests in the global sea long before full peace and harmony are achieved on land.

And in conclusion, I would like to say a word about the legal obstacles we Americans face with our expanding ocean technology. It is vital in this conference that experts like you focus on this problem with all your imagination and sagacity. Incidentally, the Sea Grant College program that I have been working on with the help of many of you in this room should provide an increasing flow of skilled manpower and scientific innovation to boost this technology. Since technology has not yet reached the stage that deep-sea mining is feasible these questions of who owns the sea and what law applies are doubly important. If we wait until the problems actually arise then we will be guided by the situation of the moment—by what each individual nation's local concern and immediate self-interest is—but if we examine these problems ahead of time perhaps we can have a more objective viewpoint. This is somewhat in line with the idea that the reason we senators are elected for six years is that we are perhaps able to handle problems that come to us a little more objectively than if we have the heat of an election every two years. And I think it is for this same reason that these problems of international law could best be examined before the heat builds up and before the actual crisis has arisen.

It seems likely, too, at least now, that public opinion is ready for any kind of recommendations or thoughts along this line. I think that as Dr. Horn said earlier, there is a general realization that we must learn to live together or hang separately; and there is a willingness, particularly in areas where vital national interest is now concerned, to accept law—international law—international reason, and international order. So, for all these reasons, I wish this conference well and believe that out of these various subjects that will be discussed, and particularly the one or two thoughts that I have advanced here, will come recommendations that will lead perhaps to a quick reconvening of another conference on the international law of the sea. From this conference may also come some definite recommendations for our own State

Department and our own government about what shall be our policies in the field of international law—some conclusions concerning how we can have the best of two worlds with a wide fishing limit and a narrow territorial sea. As you wrestle with these problems I wish you good luck, and I'm very glad to welcome you all to my state. Thank you.

THE HONORABLE CLAIBORNE PELL
Senator from Rhode Island

CONTENTS

FIGURES

TABLES

THE LAW OF THE SEA

Myres S. McDougal

Chapter One:

INTERNATIONAL LAW AND THE LAW OF THE SEA[*]

Unhappily, I find myself in disagreement with some of the points Senator Pell has just made. I am not at all sure that it is either in the interest of this country or in the common interest of mankind that this country should claim a twelve mile contiguous zone for fisheries. I think it may take a hundred years for the law of the sea to recover from the last two international conferences which dealt with it, and I would regard the immediate call of another conference as an unmitigated disaster. Let me say, also, that the very function of the law of the sea is to protect and secure the common interests of the peoples of the world. Its entire purpose is to serve the common interests, both inclusive and exclusive, of the different communities and to reject all claims of special interest. This is indeed the function of law in any community, national or international. Thus, when one contraposes international law and the vital interests of states, one is creating an apposition that we simply cannot live with. International law is established and maintained only because it secures and protects the vital interests of states.

The task assigned to me is to get back to fundamentals. I am instructed to talk about the interrelations of international law and the law of the sea and to suggest something of the broad framework of policies which should guide and control the making and application of the law of the sea. As I reviewed some of the recent literature, much of it written by members of this audience, it struck me that I should emphasize that more than a framework of guidelines is involved in our inquiry. The larger processes of world effective power do in fact impose severe constraints. There are limits within which those who clarify and implement the law of the sea must operate. It would appear a part of my task to emphasize some of these limits.

If we are to get back to fundamentals, it is necessary, first, that we consider the nature and role of law in any kind of a community; next, that we apply this understanding to observe the nature and function of law in the larger world community; then, that we mark out the special features of the constitutional or, more precisely "constitutive" processes of international law; and, finally, that we then come back and relate the main features of the public order of the oceans, or the international law of the sea, to this larger context.

Let us begin with the notion of law in any community. By a community we mean a territorial group in which there is interdetermination, reciprocal impact, interdependence. If we observe any community of this kind, we can see an effective power process in the sense the decisions are taken and enforced, whether people like them or not, by high indulgences and severe deprivations. Some of these decisions are of course taken by naked power, or by a mere calculation of expediencies, in the arrogant insistence on "sovereign" rights. Others of these decisions are, however, taken from perspectives of authority. Such decisions are taken by the people who are expected to make them, in accordance with community expectation about how they should be taken, in established structures of authority, and by authorized procedures. The people who make these decisions have enough effective control, enough bases of power, that they can put their choices into effect in a consequential number of instances. There is, thus, in any community a process of *authoritative* decision as well as a process of naked power. By "law" what we commonly mean, if pressed to comprehensive and realistic description, is *decision* that is taken in accordance with authority and that has effective control.

Whatever our purpose, law is, then, most usefully regarded as a conjunction of authority and effective control. Whether we are scholars, advocates, or decision-makers, we are not interested simply in rules or words—what is written in the books. The rules, the words, are often highly abstract or ambiguous and always travel in pairs of opposites. We are interested in the whole process of decision, how these rules, these policies, are made and continually remade and in fact applied in particular instances. We are interested not only in describing the past, but also in projecting into the future. We seek to understand the past, the conditions affecting past decisions, in order to anticipate and control the future. Our concern with the past is only for the more effective projection of policies for the more secure realization of basic community goals in the future.

Let us now transfer these perspectives to the international level, to the world arena. If we can take the point of view of the man from Mars, or the anthropologist, or the observer who identifies with the whole of mankind, I believe we can see in the larger earth-space arena today a community process that is entirely comparable to that which we have in the more mature national societies. It is of course largely an un-organized, decentralized process, but it exhibits the same kinds of inter-determinations, the same kinds of interdependences, as our national processes. If we look more closely into the social process, the inter-determinations, we can see that there is, similarly, a process of effective power. No state in the world today is free to do what it wants to do, not even the United States, Russia, or Communist China. We are all caught in the constraints of this effective power process; the network of continuing impacts, of potential reciprocities and retaliations, circum-scribes the globe.

When we realistically examine this world process of effective power, we can observe also that it includes, along with the naked power decisions, a process of authoritative decision. Decisions with transnational participation and of transnational impact are in fact made by the people who are expected to make them, in accordance with people's expectations about how they should be taken, and in established structures of au-thority, and by authorized procedures. Many of these decisions, further, are attended by sufficient effective power to be put into controlling prac-tice. The principles of the United Nations Charter, the laws of war, the law of the sea, the law of diplomacy—all these authoritative prescriptions of general community policy are honored in a very high degree in particular applications. We can also observe that these prescriptions, these policies, are continuously being made and remade.

What we mean by international law, when we speak comprehensively and realistically, is then this process of authoritative decision which transcends the boundaries of any single state. If we look closely at this most comprehensive process of authoritative decision, we can see that it is composed of two different kinds of decisions. First, there are the decisions which establish the process of authoritative decision—the constitutional or "constitutive" decisions. Secondly, there is the whole flow of particular decisions emerging from this constitutive process which establishes, secures, and protects the important features of the different community value processes and a public order. These latter decisions are those which regulate the production and distribution of goods and services, clarify and protect civil liberties or human rights, encourage the flow of enlightenment, protect health, and so on.

An example, familiar to most, may clarify what we mean by public order decisions. The principal function of what we call private international law has long been recognized as that of organizing the world into an international economy. This objective is sought, for increasing the production of goods and services for all mankind, by prescribing and applying principles, which both grant competence to particular states, such as the principles of jurisdiction—the principles of territoriality, nationality, protection of interests, impact territoriality, passive personality, and so forth—and principles which impose limits upon the competence, such as the traditional principles about the responsibilities of states—the Bill of Rights of international law—with provisions against expropriation and mistreatment of foreigners and for securing access to the courts and fair procedures in courts.

I have used this analogy of private international law because I think it relates to processes of decision most comparable with what we have in the law of the sea. The law of the sea is, from this perspective, a flow of particular decisions, projected by the larger constitutive processes of the world arena, designed to establish an ordered, economic, effective way for the peoples of the world most fully to exploit the oceans of the world in their common interest. International law as a whole is composed of the two kinds of decisions, both those that set up the process of authoritative decision and the particular decisions emerging from the process and establishing a public order. The law of the sea, as important as it is, is merely a part of these latter or public order decisions.

Let us now examine more carefully what I call the constitutive process of the larger, world arena. A complete exposition would describe how this process identifies appropriate decision-makers, clarifies basic community policies, establishes structures of authority, maintains bases of power, authorizes implementing procedures, and projects all the many different types of decisions necessary for the making and application of community policy. It is the features of this process which constitute the context that constrains your choices about the law of the sea and determines in large measure what you can and cannot do in creating and maintaining a public order of the oceans.

One striking feature of this constitutive process is that the most important decision-makers are still largely the officials of nation-states, with few third-party decision-makers whose writs are compulsory. There is of course an increasing, though still modest, role for the officials of international governmental organizations as in the United Nations, the specialized agencies, and the regional organizations, as well as for arbitral and judicial bodies. In some of the important types of decisions, political parties, pressure groups, private associations, even the individual human being, have begun, as we will see, to play significant roles.

When we turn to the basic policy objectives for which the effective elites of the world maintain this constitutive process, these can, I think, be most realistically described in terms of promoting the common interests of all peoples and of rejecting all claims of special interest. In the broadest sense, this is the function of law in any community: to maintain a uniformity in decision in clarifying and implementing common interest and to minimize arbitrary decisions, taken without regard to the consequences for others. The common interests which are sought to be protected can be conveniently categorized into two broad groups: first, the inclusive and, second, the exclusive. By inclusive interests I refer to demands and expectations about activities that have a high degree of collective impact, that have important consequences across community lines on a transnational or global scale. By exclusive interests I refer to demands and expectations about activities whose impact is primarily upon the peoples of a single territorial community.

From a global perspective, the inclusive interests of the peoples of the world certainly include the maintenance of minimum order—the minimization of unauthorized violence and other coercion. The various provisions of the United Nations Charter merely reflect the continuing aspirations of the peoples of the world with respect to this interest. It is the one interest indispensable to any community governed by law. Our very notion of law as uniformity of decision in accordance with community expectation is compatible with arbitrary decision by coercion. So conceived, minimum order has of course for some centuries been a basic goal of the public order of the oceans.

Beyond minimum order, however, the peoples of the world have more extensive interests in what we may call optimum order: the greatest production and widest distribution of all demanded values that can be obtained with available resources. You will recall that this is the basic goal we ascribed to private international law—the promotion of an international economy for increase in the aggregate of goods and services and fairness in the distribution of such aggregate. Of more immediate relevance, the same goal has long infused what we call the

7

law of the sea. For three centuries, the effective elites of the world have maintained a law of the sea, a constitutive process for the oceans, because they perceived that in this way the peoples of the world could produce more goods and services—a greater production and wider distribution of all values—for the whole of mankind. The history of achievement during the last three centuries also certainly documents the wisdom of this judgment. With the oceans of the world kept open for the shared use of all having the necessary capabilities and skill, and for the utmost specialization in skill and resources, the aggregate product has been greatly enhanced for the benefit of all.

By an exclusive interest, which requires protection as a common interest, I refer to interest with respect to which states share a common concern—because of the unique impacts of the activities involved—not precisely in the same modality. For example, every state of the world has an interest in protecting the community processes on its land masses from dangers and threats from the oceans. It has, thus, an interest in the waters closely proximate to it which will permit it to preserve the security, the minimum order of its own social processes, and to encourage an internal optimum order, the greatest productivity and fairness in distribution. No two states of the world have, however, precisely the same interest in proximate waters. Canada has different interests in the waters immediately off its coast from those we have in the waters off our coasts. Senator Pell rightly pointed out that because of the length of our coastlines we have most extensive interests of this kind, but many other states have comparable interests, even if in different degree. Because of this comparability in interest it has long been regarded as in the common interest of all states that every state be given at least a modest control of proximate waters.

By a special interest—the kind of interest that constitutive process is maintained to reject—I refer to a claim which is destructive in its impact upon others and bears no rational relation to a genuine exclusive interest which can be shared with others. Thus, the claims that some of our Latin American neighbors have made to expansive territorial seas are claims of special interest made without regard for their impact on others and with highly destructive consequences for the total production and distribution of goods and services. Such claims do not represent genuine exclusive interests because they cannot be made with promise of reciprocity. The only argument our Latin American friends have made to justify these claims is that if they can have an extensive

8

territorial sea they will sell the privilege of fishing and make money. Their chance for ultimate advantage, however, depends upon the assumption that everything else will remain the same. Should other states make comparable claims, there would be complete disintegration of the common interest and the Latin American states would suffer inestimable loss along with everybody else. Once states depart from the criterion of common interest, the only alternative is naked force. If a state makes a claim which it cannot make with promise of reciprocity to other states, it is inviting resort to coercion and violence. What we mean by a special interest is, then, this interest which is asserted against the community, irrespective of its impact upon all, and one of the principal purposes for which the larger constitutive process is maintained is to reject all these claims of special interest and to secure a public order based on common interest.

It is for these reasons that I am not sure, as indicated above, that it is in the common interest of all mankind, including ourselves, for us to claim a twelve mile contiguous zone for fisheries. It is not at all clear that a state can effectively control, conserve, and harvest fish with any kind of a contiguous zone, even one that embraces a whole continental shelf. As I am presently informed, fish just don't move, breed, or live this way. Hence, what we make is not only a claim of special interest, but an ineffective one. Further, we set a bad model to the rest of the world—a model that our Latin American neighbors and others may emulate. We should not make claims that cannot be documented in terms of the scientific facts of the fishing industry to be in the common interests of all mankind. I'm not now suggesting a dogmatic judgment on this, I'm merely trying to indicate the kinds of considerations which should be taken into account, in the light of the best, up-to-date information that can be obtained.

The structures of authority, the arenas of decision in constitutive process within a nation-state are commonly described in terms of executive, legislative, judicial, and administrative. On the global level, I believe it is better to talk in terms of diplomatic, parliamentary-diplomatic, parliamentary, adjudicative, and executive. The structures of international law do not fit the neat categories inherited from Montesquieu and others. The great bulk of interaction in the global authoritative process of decision is still foreign office to foreign office. This is what we mean by diplomatic. Occasionally, such interactions are parliamentary-diplomatic, as in great multilateral conferences, such as the recent conferences on the law of the sea or the earlier conferences on the laws of war. The parliamentary institutions are more continuous, such as in the General Assembly or the Security Council of the United Nations. The adjudicative include the International Court of Justice and the thousands of arbitral tribunals. The executive include the secretariats of international governmental organizations—general, specialized, and regional—and perhaps some of the interactions of executives from within nation-states. The general community policies sought with respect to institutional structures are, of course, those of adequacy and economy, as well as of openness in access and compulsoriness in jurisdiction. The movement toward these policies of adequacy, economy, openness, and compulsoriness is perforce slow.

Among the bases of power which the general community puts at the disposal of decision-makers for sanctioning purposes, the most important in international law, as in national law, is authority itself: people's expectations about who is authorized to make and enforce what decisions. In addition to authority, in this sense of community expectation, we may also observe a broad global distribution of other bases of power, such as in effective control of the military instrument, or of wealth, enlightenment, skill, health, or other values. Both authority and the values which affect control are distributed inclusively in the organized general community and exclusively among the different nation-states. For realistic orientation we need to know the distribution, inclusive and exclusive, of authority in the sense of the expectations of the peoples of the world about who is authorized to make what decisions. We need to know also their expectations about control, what they think will actually happen if decisions are taken in accordance with authority. Finally, we need to know the distribution of capabilities in fact. Unfortunately, even the established decision-makers may not have accurate perspectives of either their authority or control.

The basic policy being sought on the global level in the organization of bases of power is, of course, that of putting enough authority and control into inclusive decision-making—into the United Nations and other intergovernmental organization and even into unorganized inclusive decision-making, such as from foreign office to foreign office—to identify and protect inclusive interests but not in a degree to permit a monopolization of power or domination over the different territorial communities. Most of us continue to believe in a pluralistic world, composed of a large number of territorial communities with equality in access to authority. We do not want a monolithic, centralized superstate. We also demand, I am sure, that one of the basic policies for which constitutive process is maintained is to make certain that the different territorial communities do have enough authority and enough capabilities to secure their independence and to preserve a modest pluralism and experimentation in world social process.

The strategies that are authorized by constitutive process for both inclusive and exclusive use in the making and enforcing of decisions are those which political scientists describe as the diplomatic, the ideological, the economic, and the military. We can observe their unilateral or combined use, and their general or regional use. Sometimes they are employed persuasively, sometimes coercively. The general community preference in maintaining the process is, again, to emphasize persuasive use, as against the coercive. Most of us do not demand the maximization of coercion even in governmental processes. The more common emphasis is upon communication—the use of diplomatic and ideological instruments in the formulation of policies and rules. What we call legal process is largely an ideological exercise in which community policies or prescriptions—the so-called rules—are projected into the community in an effort to affect the expectations of people and the character of their interactions. Hence, the tremendous contemporary emphasis is on the importance of communication, the employment of the diplomatic and ideological instruments. Unfortunately, our experience in our national communities suggests that the coercive employment of the economic and military instruments cannot be entirely eliminated. Expectations of control must be made to accompany expectations of authority if government is to be effective. Movement toward putting effective control of the economic and the military instruments in the hands of inclusive decision-making has, however, been minimal. We must still rely upon voluntary commitments from the different states, the different territorial communities.

The different kinds of decisions taken within the constitutive processes of nation-states are commonly described as legislative, executive, and administrative. As indicated above, these terms, however, refer more to structures of authority than to types of decisions. The most general notion is that of the making and application of law. If we expand this notion into a comprehensive, detailed picture, we must talk of a variety of types of decisions, or authority functions.

First, there is an intelligence function—the acquisition, processing, and dissemination of the information that can guide rational decision. This is a function whose improvement is, for example, badly needed

11

with respect to the law of the sea. We just don't begin to have the information about fish, the riches of the sea bed, or contemporary security problems which can guide rational choice in distinguishing between common and special interests and in making plans for the better securing of common interests.

Next, there is a "promotion" or recommending function, which includes the formulation of demands, the mobilization of support, and the propagation of demands. The question is who takes effective initiative to get policies projected as authoritative community prescription. This is a function in which international governmental organizations, pressure groups, political parties, and the individual human being all play important roles.

Most importantly, there is the prescribing or "legislative" function: the projection into the future of community policy which is both authoritative and controlling. Its proper performance includes the exploration of relevant facts and possible policies, the detailed clarification and choice of policy, and the communication of expectations of authority and control. Historically, this function has been performed both deliberately, through multilateral agreements and the resolutions of international governmental bodies, and implicitly, through the creation of expectations by co-operative behavior. The basic policies sought have been those of comprehensiveness and dependability in the exploration of facts and possible policies, of rationality in the choice of policies, and of effectiveness in communication.

Another important function is that of invocation, the provisional characterization of facts in terms of community prescription and the setting in motion of the processes of decision. In one arena or another— international or national—most participants in the processes of effective power have access to this function. The basic policies sought include promptness in initiation, dependability, and minimization of provocation.

The function of putting community prescriptions into controlling effect in particular instances is commonly referred to as that of "application." This includes, in the minimum, the examination of potentially relevant facts and policies, a final characterization of the facts and a choice of policies, and enforcement measures. Since facts are always potential and community prescriptions, such as in the law of the sea, commonly travel in pairs of opposites, there are often great difficulties both in the final characterization of the facts and in the interpretation and integration of prescriptions for relation to the facts in ultimate

12

choice. The basic policies sought include promptness in the anticipation of crises, comprehensiveness and realism in the examination of facts, conformity of decision to basic community policies, and effectiveness in enforcement measures.

Another indispensable function is that of "termination," that of putting an end to prescriptions and to arrangements effected under the prescriptions being terminated. This requires assessment of the facts alleged to condition the need for termination, the cancellation of the prescription or arrangement, and the adoption of measures designed to ameliorate the damages done by termination. The basic community policies sought include promptness in initiation, comprehensiveness and dependability in assessment, conformity of cancellation to basic community policies, and effectiveness in amelioration.

A final function of "appraisal" includes the gathering, assessing, and disseminating information about the actual operation of the whole decision process. The same participants in effective power process who play an important role in the intelligence function obviously have a comparable role in appraisal. The basic policies sought include impartiality, comprehensiveness, credibility, and persuasiveness.

Such, then, are the main features of the comprehensive constitutive process of authoritative decision established and maintained by the effective elites of the world for securing their common interests in all aspects of world public order. It is this process which makes and applies what we call the international law of the sea. If we had the time, we could review, spotlight, and emphasize the features of this process that are particularly significant for the problems of making and applying the law of the sea. One obvious feature, for a quick recast, is in the still primitive decentralization of the process—in the fact that nation-state officials still make most of the important decisions in relatively unorganized arenas and, hence, that all such decisions must be made with a promise of reciprocity and mutual tolerance for the other participants. One state cannot effectively claim what it is not willing to concede to others in comparable situations.

It may require emphasis also that in the larger community, as in the component national communities, the ultimate sanctions of law are in the predispositions of human beings—the perspectives of the effective elites. To be effective one has to affect these perspectives. Resources, military hardware, raw materials—all these are important only as they affect the perspectives of living, breathing, human beings, the members

13

of audiences which are sought to be persuaded or controlled. The principal task in sanctioning, in securing conformity, is to affect the predispositions—the demands, identifications, and expectations—of people and to cause them to want to clarify common interest and to reject claims of special interest.

Another obvious feature (and this accounts for my animus against conferences) is that historically most international law has been made by custom—by people creating expectations in each other about the requirements for future decision by simply co-operating or engaging in collaborative activities. Such co-operation creates expectations about the uniformities in decision that are expected and required. The great bulk of our inherited prescriptions in the law of the sea had their origin in this way, and when the community achieves legislative prescription of this kind there is some guarantee of its rationality. That the same persons—nation-state officials—must be both claimants against the community and decision-makers offers some safeguard against exaggerated, inflated claims. If what I claim I must concede to you, and if I am, in turn, a judge as well as a claimant, there is, the history of the law of the sea suggests, a chance to clarify common interest. In the present posture of world affairs, when a great conference is called and the representatives of the states gather around the table, they come with *all* of their perspectives, with instructions about the total policies of their states, the policies that relate not only to the law of the sea but to other things. Thus, a change in the customs duties charged by the United States on copper, the peculiar difficulties in relation to the Gulf of Aqaba, and a great variety of cold war issues are, all, alleged to have had impacts upon decision in the most recent conferences upon the law of the sea. The point is that when statesmen sit down at these great conferences, the total policy of all the major participants is at stake and a conference on the law of the sea is not the best place to dispose of, and reconcile, the total policies of such participants. There are so many intrusions of considerations that have no relation to the law of the sea that even the people who are most competent to make the law of the sea are not allowed to do so. Hence, until we can, by traditional customary processes, secure a greater consensus, a greater degree of clarity about what the common interests of peoples of the world are in relation to the important contemporary problems in the public order of the oceans, I think we should go very slow in encouraging a call for more conferences.

14

Let us return now to your primary interest and examine more closely the main features of our inherited international law of the sea. As some of you know, Professor Burke and I, in the long book with which I hope you are familiar, suggested that any realistic consideration of this subject must begin with the peculiarities of the social or community process by which the seas are exploited and enjoyed. There are in fact very great peculiarities in this process. The sea—in much higher degree than the land masses—is an easily sharable resource. It is tremendously vast—its expanses are great. Most of its resources that we presently know are renewable, flow resources. Similarly, where one ship has just been, another, with proper roles of accommodation, can soon come. There are tremendous numbers of the peoples of the world who are capable of exploiting this resource, peoples who have the skills and other bases of power to make an effective contribution. There is a great range of objectives that can be satisfied from the exploitation of the seas. Familiar items are transportation, communication, and the production of food. Every value that we cherish in a free society may be affected by the use of the oceans, and scientific knowledge may disclose still new uses. The strategy in the use of this resource may be co-operative, non-competitive: what one gets, others may also get. For three centuries the important outcome of this co-operative enjoyment of the oceans has been a tremendous production of goods and services for distribution to the whole of mankind.

It is from this community process in the enjoyment of the oceans that claims are made to the world constitutive process for the settlement of disputes and management of problems in co-operative use. For the better clarification of basic community policies—for sharpening our distinction between common and special interests and for the more economic accommodation of inclusive and exclusive interests—it is indispensable that we sharpen our categories of the claims that are made to processes of authority about the enjoyment of the sea.

It is most convenient to think roughly in terms of three broad categories of claims. First, there are claims to access—to use and enjoyment. Secondly, there are claims to competence, to jurisdiction. By this reference I include both the making of law and the application of law with respect to activities on the oceans. It is necessary to keep quite distinct the making and applying of law to activities on the ocean from the comparable functions with respect to other activities in world community process. Finally, there is the claim to resources.

15

These three different types of claims may be made with respect to any of the waters of the globe. They are made with respect to what we call internal waters. They are made with respect to what we call the territorial sea. They are made with respect to what we call the contiguous zones and more recently with respect to continental shelves or equivalents. They are also made with respect to what we call the high seas.

You will observe my caution in using these words: internal waters, territorial sea, contiguous zone, continental shelf, and high seas. These are normative, ambiguous words. They refer both to facts and to legal consequences. They purport both to describe and to state preferences. It is better to think simply in terms of the geographical distribution of these types of claims to waters. The labels are too often merely reasons, justifications, that are given for different types of decisions or choices among competing claims.

When we begin our task in clarifying basic community policies we can observe that for every state of the world, the exclusive interests are greater the closer one is to the shore. The farther one moves out from the shore, the more the inclusive interests predominate; and in the light of several centuries of highly successful co-operative enjoyment of the oceans it would appear that we should begin with a strong presumption in favor of the inclusive interest. Where there are many people capable of engaging and willing to engage in production, where the resource is sharable in high degree, and where the utmost production can be had from the sharing, we should begin with a presumption in favor of sharing. This does not mean, of course, that exclusive interests should be totally disregarded. What we require for rational decision is a way of balancing the exclusive interests of the coastal states in proximate waters and the inclusive interests of all the states in the utmost enjoyment of all waters which will take due account of differences in context. What Professor Burke and I have suggested is that we try to identify more sharply the change in exclusive interest as we move in successive stages out from the shore.

If we begin closest to the shore—with what are called internal waters—I believe we can observe that the state has much the same interest in controlling activities in these immediately proximate waters as it has on its land masses. Even the control of access is commonly regarded as arbitrary. Incidentally, this has not always been so. Many of the founding fathers of international law believed in freedom of access; remember that Vitoria wanted freedom of access to the Indians in order to convert them to Christianity. I know, however, of only one recent decision, the Saudi Arab–Aramco Arbitration, in which the court has held that there is a customary right of access, independent of explicit consent, to the internal waters of a state. The control of resources is also put largely in the hands of the coastal state, and the coastal state is honored in an assertion of exclusive competence, if it chooses, to make and apply law to any activities within these waters.

Still I must remind you that this competence of the coastal state in internal waters is not absolute. Even on the land masses a state must make and apply its law subject to certain limitations imposed by international law. It is forbidden to abuse diplomats or to violate the law for the protection of aliens, the principles about responsibility of states. When questions are raised about the law of the sea, it is well to remember that states are confined to an inclusive, shared competence even on the land masses. This inclusive, shared competence is easily demonstrated with respect to internal waters. Many states of the world honor a large competence in the state of registration to control activities on board a ship, even when within internal waters. There are activities which affect the internal constitution of the ship. Ships, like nation-states in the larger community, have their own internal constitutive process. By and large these activities are left to the control of the state of registration. There are other activities which involve interactions with other people around the world—the making of agreements, the imposition of deprivations, and such like. The control of such activities is widely diffused by the traditional principles of jurisdiction. Competence may be accorded on the basis of territoriality to the coastal state. But it may also be accorded to the state of registration, or to the states of the nationalities of the actors, or to the states upon which the activities have impacts. This again is a widely shared competence. Other activities may uniquely affect the social process on the coast, on the land masses. It is agreed that the coastal state may control, may make and apply its law, to any such activities.

When we move out from internal waters to the territorial sea, exclusive interest is still high but the inclusive interest begins to be more insistent. The principal modification is in relation to access. The ships of other states are said to have a right of innocent passage, but within this geographic zone the burden is put upon such ships of proving their innocence. The competence of the coastal state otherwise is

17

comparable to what it has on the land masses and within internal waters, but states seldom in fact exercise such competence in the same degree of comprehensiveness.

When we move beyond the territorial sea to contiguous zones, coastal states, which regard themselves as uniquely affected or uniquely threatened by specific activities on the oceans, may assert a competence to make and apply law in control of such activities, even though they are the activities of the nationals—the ships—of other states. In such geographic zones, however, the burden is put upon the coastal state to justify the reasonableness of what it does. The demonstration of reasonableness—of unique impacts and potential harms—requires a complete contextual examination of who is doing what to whom, under what circumstances, with what instrumentalities, with what assertions of authority, and with what alternatives for minimizing loss. Though it is impossible to outline briefly all the relevant indexes of "reasonableness," it may be emphasized that the requirement imposes the exact opposite of arbitrary decision. The disciplined, systematic examination of all the features of the context is designed to facilitate a fair and economic accommodation of all the exclusive interests of the coastal state in protecting itself with the inclusive interests of all states in the enjoyment of the oceans.

The concept of the continental shelf, in terms of its contemporary legal significance, had its origin simply as a way of allocating to the coastal state the resources of the proximate ocean bed. From the way the Dutch are now using this concept, as I gather from the papers I have seen by some of you, it would appear that an effort is being made to generalize it to embrace a more comprehensive set of legal consequences. It would seem that the Dutch are really claiming a large portion of sovereignty over the continental shelf. This is a complete perversion of the original notion. The original notion accorded priority to the inclusive interest in all uses of the ocean waters other than for exploitation of the minerals, the riches of the sea bed. The concept of a contiguous zone could very easily have protected the interests of the Dutch which you describe. The difficulty may have been caused by certain recent restrictive attitudes toward the availability of contiguous zones. It may be recalled that some English writers give little explicit recognition to contiguous zones. The English employ the concept but don't like to admit it. Similarly, the Convention on the Territorial Sea and Contiguous Zone purports to put an arbitrary twelve mile limit on contiguous zones and greatly to limit the purposes for which they may be employed. Hence, the Dutch may have felt that under such highly limited interpretations of our past experience, they had no recourse for stopping attacks from the outside other than by inflation of the continental shelf device. It could be a minor tragedy that they did not, instead, adopt a more rational conception of contiguous zones.

When we get out to what are called the high seas, the assumption is that the inclusive interest prevails. It is commonly agreed that states have complete equality of access, with none being able to bar the others; that each state makes and applies law to its own ships; and that no state can apply its unilateral competence to the ships of other states except for violations of international law. The intellectual task is largely that of balancing and accommodating potentially conflicting inclusive interests. We do this in many ways—both by customary prescriptions defining reasonableness and by conventions of all kinds, such as those establishing the rules of the road.

In this emphasis upon an areal organization of claims I have left out certain important types of claims which relate to the demarcation of such areas. The first problem is that of fixing the limits of internal waters. The criteria by which such limits should be fixed depend of course upon what difference it makes how we fix them. In the light of our discussion above, such criteria must require a careful balancing of inclusive and exclusive interests. If one extends internal waters far out into the oceans, one only increases exclusive interest—the control of the coastal state—to the detriment of inclusive interests. Unfortunately, some provisions in the 1958 conventions, in extending internal waters out beyond any previous conception, do just this. The *Norwegian Fisheries* case, of course, had set a model for this parochial arrogance. On its facts and closest reasoning, the *Norwegian Fisheries* case was perhaps not too much subject to criticism. The essential policy established was that if a coastal state can show a unique exclusive interest in the management of certain immediately adjacent waters, then it can assert and protect this interest. In other words, a state is authorized to run a line for demarcating internal waters in the general direction of its coast if there is a history of exclusive fishing, if there are rocks and bays and other configurations which affect internal security, and if there is special economic need. This decision was, however, much

19

inflated in the 1958 conventions. It has been even more inflated in subsequent claims. The consequence has been a tremendous damage to inclusive interests.

The next type of demarcation claim relates to the width of the territorial sea. I remain a diehard on this. It seems to me that if our experience upon the oceans has demonstrated anything, it is that it is in the best interests of the peoples of the world to have the narrowest possible territorial sea. I sometimes tell my class that this should be the low-tide mark. There isn't any need even for a three mile territorial sea. I say this for two reasons. First, in terms of military security, the width of the territorial sea is today almost wholly irrelevant. Secondly, it is probably no less irrelevant for fishing; if the habits of fish are such as are commonly described, the control of a territorial sea has very little to do with the rational exploitation of a fishery. The one function then that a territorial sea might serve in the contemporary world is that of protecting a very petty minimum order. It might assist in protection against small intrusions—such as violations of the immigration laws, or of customs and health regulations, and so on. It is possible, however, that a flexible concept of contiguous zones could offer even better protection against such intrusions. In fact, an appropriate balancing of inclusive and exclusive interests might suggest that there is today just no rational ground for a territorial sea at all.

The next claims relate to the width of the contiguous zone and the continental shelf. What are the contemporary limits on these traditionally very rough and flexible areal delimitations? During World War II, when our purpose was the protection of military security and neutrality, we claimed as far as 1,300 miles. Other states have also made extensive claims. For customs, I believe there are statutes on our books making claims for as much as 150 miles. I wonder if these statutes have been repealed by the enactment of the 1958 Convention. It seems to me utterly incredible that anybody could ever have voted for a twelve mile limit on contiguous zones. We are not living with such a limit; we couldn't live with it! I don't know any major state which could live with it. It does not, furthermore, make matters any better that "security" was omitted from the 1958 Convention as a permissible purpose for contiguous zones. The suggestion was made at the 1958 Conference that states don't need contiguous zones for security because they can employ self-defense anywhere. It should need little argument, for anyone who has followed the discussion on Vietnam or

Cuba, that self-defense, with its requirements of necessity and proportionality, is a much more difficult concept than that of contiguous zone, which requires a showing only of reasonableness.

With specific reference to the continental shelf, as we all know, the geographic configurations around the world are very, very different; but here the geographers and lawyers are in great disagreement. The achievement on this was of course the highlight in brilliance of the 1958 conventions. What was the provision: to a depth of 200 meters or as far as one can dig? How far one can dig, if one can trust the *New York Times*, is apparently changing every few minutes. This is again the kind of legislation which emerges from these great conferences. The important tasks in the accommodation of inclusive and exclusive interests are left to the future.

The final type of claim is that which relates to the nationality of ships. The whole structure of authoritative decision about which we have been talking is, as was noted, a highly decentralized, unorganized structure, in which the laws are made and applied by the officials of states. Such a structure will work only if there are certain simple rules by which everybody abides. There have been a few such rules, cast in both positive and negative form, which have made this process work for three hundred years. The most important is, as suggested above, that every state has complete freedom of access to the high seas and that no state can preclude the ships of any other state from access. A second is that each state may make and apply law to its own ships—that is, to the internal constitution of its ships—and that no state may make and apply law to the ships of other states except for violations of international law. The linch-pin in this simple system has been the further rule that no state may question the competence of another state to confer its nationality upon a ship. If a ship has acquired one nationality, it cannot acquire another or be treated as having another until it loses the first.

This system worked very well prior to the 1958 Conference on the Law of the Sea. The conferees, however, took from the *Nottebohm* decision the mysterious concept of genuine link, which has never been defined and clarified even with respect to individual human beings, and purported to apply it to ships. Human beings can go up on a land mass and circulate in the different territorial communities; ships, ordinarily, cannot. The concept of "genuine link" must perform a very different function when related to the human rights of the individual human beings and when related to effectiveness in the enjoyment of the oceans. It would appear quite arbitrary to borrow the concept from the one context for application in another, especially when it had not even been appropriately tested in the first. Nobody has ever suggested any empirical idexes, or policy relevance, of what the words "genuine link" could mean as applied to a ship. The traditional policies that nation-states have employed in conferring nationality on ships have little or nothing to do with the international enjoyment of the oceans. The only rational policy about the nationality of ships in the international arena, must be that which promotes the effectiveness, the harmonious functioning, of our inherited law of the sea. Should one state be given the competence to question, on any ground, another state's competence to charter ships for the enjoyment of the oceans, there would be grave risk of subverting the whole process. A premium would be placed upon naked power, rather than authority, in the maintenance of access to the oceans.

The most general theme which I suggest to you as a framework for guiding your inquiries about the various problems in the law of the sea is, then, that of the necessity for relating all your considerations and recommendations to the basic policies for which the peoples of the world maintain a comprehensive constitutive process of authoritative decision: to clarify and secure their common interests and to reject all claims of special interest. Your task is to relate the claims of states, about every particular problem, to their inclusive and exclusive interests and to recommend solutions which will both accommodate and integrate such common interests and reject all claims of special interest, which do not admit of reciprocity and shared enjoyment. The adequate performance of this task will require of you a systematic and disciplined examination of the larger context which affects every particular problem. Precisely who is claiming to do what to whom, for what objectives, in what domains, by what strategies (of what degrees of coerciveness), and with what value consequences? Who claims injury and a right of response, with respect to whom, and so on? What competence to make and apply law is asserted on each side? What is the relation of the claims on each side to basic community interests, inclusive and exclusive? What are the alternatives open to a decision-maker, identified with common interests, for accommodating the claims and ameliorating injuries? The problems become no easier when posed in such a contextual framework, but the mere asking of the relevant questions may point us toward more appropriate solutions and encourage the gathering of the kind of information necessary for such solutions.

It does not escape me that this basic policy criterion of securing and protecting the common interests of all mankind in the shared enjoyment of the oceans is likely to have a hard time in the calculable future. The conditions of interdependence or interdetermination and the fantastic improvements in global communication do of course work toward the better securing and clarification of common interest. Unfortunately, however, the public order of the oceans is deeply affected by the more comprehensive models of world public order demanded by the effective elites of the world, and we do not today have a single projected world public order—embodying only the values of human dignity or a free society—but rather a number of contending world public orders, all aspiring to be universal, but honoring the values of security, freedom, and abundance in very different degree. The kind of future public order of the oceans we can achieve must of necessity be a function of the outcome of this larger struggle. When it is added that even the proponents of a public order of human dignity—both rich and poor, North and South—can sometimes mistake their long-term common interests and make claims of special interest, your task can be seen to become even more formidable.

I suppose, however, that few of us would be here if we were wholly pessimistic. My predecessor at Yale, Professor Edwin Borchard, had a saying that a man is an optimist who thinks the future is uncertain. The future public order of the oceans would not yet appear completely foreclosed for claims of special interest and monopoly. You would appear still to have opportunity to influence it. I wish you and your conference the greatest success in doing so.

---

* A transcription. The basic themes here discussed are developed in more detail in McDougal, Lasswell, and Reisman, "The World Constitutive Process of Authoritative Decision" (a chapter in Black and Falk, *The Future of the International Legal Order*, to be published late in 1967, with separate publication in the *Journal of Legal Education*, Vol. XIX, Issues 3 and 4, 1967) and McDougal and Burke, *The Public Order of the Oceans* (1962).

Discussion of McDougal

1. *Why is precision necessary in regard to nationalities of ships at sea but not so necessary in terms of boundaries?* The function of nationality is to insure all people freedom of access to the sea; if you permit anybody to question someone else's competence to confer nationality on a craft, then freedom of the sea is gone. But in many boundary problems precision is undesirable until you're sure first what a particular line is for, and second that within a short space of time it may not be necessary to change it in the light of new developments.

2. *Has not the development of technology meant that freedom of the seas is no longer a valid rule?* Under conditions of complete freedom, the technologically advanced countries of the world are going to rapidly deplete the resources of the sea. We've got to evolve from the principle of freedom of the seas to a principle of common interest for mankind in a regulated high sea, carried out by some general international organization.

But the major states of the world are not going to put control over the sea's resources in the hands of an international organization. And it is possible that more benefits can be obtained through give and take than through dictation from above. The development of the resources of the high seas will not take place in a vacuum, but rather under the laws of the particular states which are doing the exploiting. Rather than systems of regulation, the important question will be what are the reasonable indexes of effective control over these resources?

3. *From the viewpoint of economics, does not freedom of access to a resource lead to economic waste in the future?* Not in the case of space extension resources, where the principle use is communications or travel. And for other resources, waste may be part of the price for the achievement of total goals—social as well as economic. Even the

concept of maximum sustainable yield must be viewed within the context of the existing socio-economic conditions within an existing area. By utilizing the criteria of flexibilty and reasonableness the principle of maximum freedom of the seas can be made to work.

4. The Geneva Conventions resulted in considerable expansion at the expense of the high seas. The acceptance of the straight baseline regime, the twelve mile contiguous zone, the ambiguity of the outer limits of the continental shelf—such principles are eroding away the extent of the areas which remain free to all nations.

Chapter Two:

THE CONVENTION ON FISHERIES AND CONSERVATION OF LIVING RESOURCES: ACCOMPLISHMENTS OF THE 1958 GENEVA CONFERENCE

The subject of international law confuses and baffles most laymen, since the procedure by which it is developed, although having some similarities to the formulation of domestic law, has even more dissimilarities. International law of fisheries has been developing at an increasing pace during the past several decades to reach a climax—at least a temporary climax—in the 1958 Geneva Fishery Convention. I shall attempt to review the events which led to this convention, its principal contents and something of their significance. I hope that this will shed some light on the interests, influences, and procedures which go into the development of international law—at least of international law on fisheries.

The 1958 Fisheries Convention had its genesis in the developing international fishery situation of the late forties and fifties. During these years certain problems affecting fishery jurisdiction had been brought to the United Nations and referred to the International Law Commission, which was charged with the study of Law of the Sea. This Commission in its annual sessions had labored on these problems and had embodied its conclusions, which at this stage might be construed as preliminary and tentative, in reports which were circulated to governments for comment. For reasons I shall presently mention, at that time U.S. officials concerned with fisheries paid little attention to the reports of the International Law Commission.

The United States, beginning with the Fur Seal Convention in its first limited form, later in the forties and fifties through the Halibut and Salmon Conventions, and finally, the Inter-American Tropical Tuna Convention, the Northwest Atlantic Fisheries Convention, and the North Pacific Fisheries Convention, had acquired considerable experience in the development and operation of fishery conventions dealing with conservation and in determining how they might be made effective. In the light of this experience the early International Law Commission proposals seemed directed backward toward the situation of the thirties rather than forward to the developing problems of the fifties and sixties. For this reason, it did not seem likely that these proposals would lead to conclusions that would be very helpful in contemporary or future fisheries situations or that they would enlist much support from interested countries. At this time, also, the United States was having considerable difficulty stemming from the efforts of certain countries to impose by force on United States fishing vessels operating on the high seas off their coasts, their extreme claims to jurisdiction. These countries generally argued that their claims were justified by the requirements of conservation, that jurisdiction was necessary in order to prevent the destruction of resources by the long ranging fishing fleets of other countries (also ecosystems and biomes). They refused to consider as the solution of the conservation problem the accepted procedure of international co-operation in research and joint regulation.

Early in 1954, it occurred to some of us in the Department of State that instead of taking a negative attitude toward the work of the International Law Commission it could be more productive to get this Commission to consider some of the newer concepts evolving from experience with the several international fishery commissions. Such action would stimulate the development of a forward-looking legal system which would serve the growing needs of the international community. This question was discussed repeatedly in meetings of the Department's Fishing Industry Advisory Committee where it was viewed with considerable mistrust as leading into an area beyond our control and initiating developments that would be disadvantageous to us. There was a widespread conviction that when the United States became involved in broad international deliberations we usually lost more than we gained. After considerable debate, the opposition to the proposed procedure was quieted to the extent that opposition and support were at an approximate stand off. In this situation we decided to proceed with caution in sounding out the international support we might enlist on such a project.

We first consulted with officials of a number of countries, particularly those of the United Kingdom and Canada, to sound out their reaction toward promoting a world conference with the objective of incorporating in a broad international convention some of the principles we had found useful in bilateral and multilateral conservation conventions. We reasoned that unless some effective international rules on fishing and conservation were agreed upon, unilateral actions would create increasing chaos. The officials of both countries, after several discussions and a careful review of the situation, were in substantial agreement with the proposed objective.

In the fall of 1954 the United States placed on the agenda of the United Nations the proposal to convene a joint technical and legal conference to seek to develop agreement on international rules for dealing with conservation of high seas fishery resources. The United States proposed that because of its technical nature the item be referred to the Economics Committee. However, this proposal was viewed with some suspicion by the United Nations legal experts and was shifted to the Legal Committee of the United Nations. The international lawyers were not inclined to allow the technical people to intrude upon their world of international rule-making. The Legal Committee gave short shrift to the proposal for a joint meeting of technical and legal experts to consider international law on fisheries. However, after much discussion, maneuvering and lobbying by those interested in including scientists and administrators in a conference dealing with international law and conservation, agreement was finally reached that the United Nations would convene an international technical conference on living resources of the sea. The United Nations resolution specifically provided that the conference was "to make appropriate scientific and technical recommendations and shall not prejudice the related problems awaiting consideration by the General Assembly" and "Decides to refer the report of the said scientific and technical conference to the International Law Commission as a further technical contribution to be taken into account in its study of the questions to be dealt with in the final report which it is to prepare pursuant to resolution 899 (IX) of 14 December 1954." We considered it highly desirable to convene the conference at a very early date to forestall attempts at development of fragmented or regional international law. Although conference experts advised that it would take at least a year of preparatory work, the United Nations in December, 1954, agreed to convene the conference at Rome in April, 1955.

A committee of international fishery experts was convened by the United Nations staff on short notice in mid-December, 1954, to work out an agenda for the conference. It completed its work prior to the Christmas recess. A number of background papers were solicited from experts in the field to be available prior to convening the conference.

The United Nations Technical Conference on Living Resources of the Sea was convened by the United Nations in Rome on April 18, 1955, with the FAO playing host (but not sponsor). Forty-five countries sent representatives and six sent observers. This included practically all countries with a sea coast and a number that were landlocked. Many of those countries, which at the United Nations had strenuously opposed having technical experts join with legal people in considering international law regarding fisheries, were represented by their legal experts. Most of the fishing nations, particularly the European and North American nations, were represented by their principal fisheries people with many of the leading fishery scientists of the world included as advisers. So in point of fact we had achieved a conference of scientists and legal experts, which had been an original United States objective. Klaus Sunnana of Norway, a well-known fisheries administrator, was elected Chairman, and Francisco Garcia-Amador of Cuba, Chairman of the United Nations Legal Committee and a member of the International Law Commission, was elected vice-chairman.

In the early stages of the conference the issue of coastal countries' jurisdiction, without regard to realistic conservation requirements or co-operation of the fishing countries, played a dominant role. However, as the conference progressed the influence of the scientists became an increasingly important factor in defining the kind of scientific information required for effective conservation of high seas resources and the extent of international co-operation needed to achieve this objective. In the course of the three weeks plus of the conference wide agreement was reached regarding the definition of conservation and the principles and policies that would lead to effective international co-operation in conservation programs.

Following the termination of the Rome conference the results were taken to the meeting of the International Law Commission in Geneva (which convened about a week after the Rome conference closed) by Dr. Garcia-Amador, vice-chairman of the Rome Conference, and were used as the basis for a new set of articles on fisheries. Understandably, it came as a shock to most of the International Law Commission members who had not been involved in the United Nations and Rome activities that they should throw out the fishery articles on which they had been working for several years and consider a new approach to the problem. However, as those members came to understand that serious consideration of the International Law Commission proposals by the United Nations was unlikely unless they took into account the conclusions of the Technical Rome Conference, they accepted the new draft as the basis for their further deliberations.

Several of the technical people who had attended the Rome Conference moved on to Geneva so that they would be available for consultation by members of the International Law Commission. Perhaps they played a part in convincing some members of the realities of the situation.

The conclusions from the 1955 sessions of the International Law Commission were circulated and the comments of governments solicited. The proposals, influenced by the Rome conference, had evolved substantially toward the ideas we had in mind when the United Nations operation was initiated. The United States government examined the International Law Commission report and made a point of commenting at length on the further changes that we considered essential and the reasons therefor. Other interested governments did likewise. At its 1956 session the International Law Commission reviewed its 1955 draft in the light of the comments received. Once again a number of fishery experts were on hand for consultation as needed. After extensive debate and drafting, a new report was completed and circulated to governments for study and comments.

The 1956 report of the International Law Commission was substantially in line with the objectives of the United States and of the other countries interested in conservation which had joined with the United States in encouraging the work. The United States then took the lead in the United Nations in proposing a world conference to be convened at Geneva in 1958 to seek agreement on fisheries as well as other Law of the Sea matters. The principal background material for this conference was to consist of the report of the International Law Commission, together with the comments of governments.

Prior to the convening of the 1958 Geneva Conference, United States experts spent considerable time consulting with the officials of other countries, particularly in the field of fisheries, to develop agreement on objectives and co-operation in working for their attainment.

This was the principal preparatory background which contributed to the fisheries work of the Geneva Conference.

The United Nations Conference on the Law of the Sea convened at Geneva, Switzerland, on February 24, 1958, and closed on April 27, 1958. Eighty-six countries were represented (the family of nations had grown somewhat since 1955). The basic work of the conference was divided among four committees: First Committee—Territorial Sea and Contiguous Zone; Second Committee—High Seas: General Regime; Third Committee—High Seas: Fishing; Conservation of the Living Resources; Fourth Committee—Continental Shelf. I shall comment primarily on developments in the Third Committee which dealt with fisheries.

The countries which played an active role in the Third Committee might be divided into three groups based on their general attitudes toward high seas fishing. The first might be termed conservatives, since their interest was primarily in maintaining the past freedoms to fish with the minimum of restrictions on such activities; the second group might be termed radicals or extremists since their efforts were directed toward completely overturning the established order for the purpose of securing maximum control by coastal states over the fishery resources in waters adjacent to their coast (regardless of the extent to which they were utilizing these resources or the likelihood that they would utilize them in the foreseeable future). A third group, which I shall term moderates, sought some modification of the established order primarily for the purpose of securing a sound and practicable international conservation system that would assure the continued productivity of the resources of the high seas. As the issues became clear and delegates became convinced of the need for an effective world conservation system, the group of moderates increased somewhat in number. This was encouraged by the conclusions of some of the more reasonable conservatives and extremists that they could not secure adequate support for their preferred objectives and that they had better settle for a sound conservation system in preference to nothing (or chaos).

The United States fishing industry includes important fisheries on the high seas off foreign shores as well as off our own coast, and this helped us to work out a United States position which to a considerable extent represented a blending of the interests of the overseas and coastal types of fishing. Thus, the United States interests lay with the moderates and

31

the generally united backing of our fishing industry helped to make it possible for the United States representatives to play an important role in leadership of the moderate faction.

As the conference developed, it became clear that the various delegations were principally concerned with three issues: (a) the kinds of limitations on freedom of fishing on the high seas, (b) the obligations which fishing nations have with respect to conservation measures for the stocks of fish they are harvesting, (c) the special interests of the "coastal states" over the resources off their coasts. Another lesser issue, finally settled on the basis of the Rome conference conclusions, was the definition of conservation.

From the above issues, a number of intense controversies developed, outstanding among which was the drive for additional jurisdiction by "coastal states." The coastal states justified their claims on various grounds, great emphasis being placed on the argument that only in this way could conservation be assured, that only the coastal states were sufficiently concerned with conservation to enforce the necessary restrictions on fishing. (Pseudo-scientific arguments based on ecology did not impress many delegations.) The opponents of the jurisdiction proposals maintained that effective conservation could be achieved only through the co-operation of all concerned countries in an effective research and management program.

The second area of contention evolved from the first; most of the moderate group and finally some of the conservatives were prepared to concede the special interest of the coastal states in conservation of the fish stocks off their coasts and the special rights that derived from this, provided these rights were strictly related to the needs of conservation and could not be used to discriminate against foreign fishermen. These delegates were much concerned to prevent abuses by the coastal states of any new powers that might be agreed upon and as a practical matter could not agree upon these new powers unless adequate safeguards were included.

Out of these needs came the proposal for technical and scientific criteria to assure that the special authority of the coastal state would be properly used. Many of the "fishing states" were concerned that these criteria might not be strictly observed, while on the other hand the coastal states were concerned that the generally superior research facilities of fishing states would be devoted primarily to demonstrating that strict limitations on fishing were unnecessary. This controversy led to the development of a procedure for settlement of disputes regarding the interpretation of the scientific and administrative evidence bearing on the need for conservation measures and the kind of measures to be adopted. The development of this procedure, spelled out in articles 9, 10, and 11, made it possible finally for most of the fishing states to agree upon the new powers for the coastal states and for most of the coastal states to accept the strict criteria which would prevent abuse of these new powers.

The three principal issues I have mentioned above are reflected in the fisheries convention as follows: Freedom to fish is covered in Article 1, paragraph 1; Obligations of Fishing States are covered in Article 1, paragraph 2 and Articles 3, 4, and 5. Special interests of coastal states are covered in Articles 6 and 7. Definition of conservation is included in Article 2.

Since the special powers of the coastal states could be accepted by most of the conservatives and many of the moderates, only with the protection provided by the arbitral procedure, the committee agreed that these articles must be accepted or refused as a whole. This requirement is included in Article 19 which stipulates that no reservations can be made to Articles 6, 7, 9, 10, 11, and 12. Finally, the draft articles were put to the vote which was 45 in favor, 1 against, and 18 abstentions. Representatives of the Soviet Union and other bloc countries expressed support for all of the articles except the provisions for obligatory settlement of disagreements. They abstained in the voting.

There was one other important proposal submitted by the United States and Canada, the "abstention" principle or procedure. This principle, incorporated in its essentials in the North Pacific Fisheries Convention, was described in the United States-Canada submission to the 1958 Geneva Conference as follows:

The "abstention" concept, as described above, relates to situations where Coastal States have, through the expenditure of time, effort, and money on research management, and through drastic restraint on their fishermen, increased or maintained the productivity of stocks of fish, which without such action would not exist or would exist at far below their most productive level. Under such conditions and when the stocks are being fully utilized, that is, under such exploitation that an increase in the amount of fishing would not result in any substantial increase in the sustainable yield, then States not participating, or which have not in recent years participated in exploitation of such stocks of fish, excepting the coastal States adjacent to the waters in which the stocks occur, should be required to abstain from participation in such fisheries.

The abstention procedure takes into account the fact that under the conditions stated above, the present, the continuing or the growing productivity of the stocks of fish is the result of and dependent on past and current action of the participating States, and that the participation of additional States would result in no increase in the amount of useful products. Rather than increasing production the advent of additional States is almost sure to stimulate the deterioration or stagnation of such conservation activities through removing the incentive for maintaining the conservation programmes.

In recognition of a "special interest" on the part of a coastal State, the adjacent coastal State should be excepted from the operation of the rule regarding abstention. Strict and precise criteria should be laid down in the qualifications of a fishery for the rule, and questions arising as to qualifications referred to the arbitral procedure contemplated by International Law Commission articles 57–59.

After considerable discussion the Fisheries Committee approved this proposal as a resolution, by more than a two-thirds vote. However, when it came before the plenary session it became involved with other issues (the Israel-Arab controversy) and failed to obtain the two-thirds majority required for adoption by the conference. (However it obtained a good majority vote.) This was the only important United States proposal on fisheries which we were unsuccessful in having adopted by the conference.

Prior to the Law of the Sea Conference in 1958 there was very little that one could conclude with respect to accepted rights and duties bearing on conservation of fish. (The Rome Conference in 1955 began the process of formulating world-wide agreed-upon practices.) The Geneva Fisheries Convention was the first to develop an international code respecting fisheries. The United States has ratified the convention which came into effect in March, 1966, when the Netherlands provided the twenty-second ratification. However, the convention cannot be considered to represent international law, at least in total, until substantially more ratifications are obtained. Nevertheless, even prior to its effective date, the convention has done much to provide precedents and standards for bilateral and multilateral agreements. There is no doubt that should there be disputes between countries regarding certain of the rights and duties spelled out in the convention, and the dispute taken to the World Court, that court would give great weight to the provisions of the convention.

Now, eight years since the Geneva Fisheries Convention was negotiated, we must admit that much of the world has not yet caught up with its provisions, in practice at least. With this in mind the United States has recently begun to talk up a proposal that the FAO convene a World Fishery Conference that would consider, among other fishery matters, how the convention could be most effectively implemented and encourage more ratifications. Such a conference could also consider auxiliary procedures, such as the development of joint enforcement measures, which would make the provisions of the Geneva Fisheries Convention more effective. However, those interested in conservation will have to be on the alert to forestall attempts to muster support for modifications which would reduce the effectiveness of the convention. It is unfortunately true that while amendments to an agreement can make such an agreement more effective, they can also serve to weaken it.

William R. Neblett

Chapter Three:

THE 1958 CONFERENCE ON THE LAW OF THE SEA: WHAT WAS ACCOMPLISHED

I. *Introduction*

In preparing this paper, I confess to a point of view based on the interests of United States commercial fisheries, particularly the domestic shrimp fishery. It has been to the interest of the shrimp fishery to accent the doctrine of freedom of the seas for fishing[1] because the shrimp fishery is classified in part as a distant fishery, as is also true with tuna. This position also explains in advance the apprehension of this fishery as to attachment to any continental shelf doctrine. Despite this concern, it is still possible to speak objectively on the influence of the several Law of the Sea conventions on developing international law.

This paper is scheduled to follow a presentation made by William C. Herrington, the man I consider most eminently qualified to discuss the 1958 Geneva Convention on Fisheries,[2] so I confine this discussion to other topics at Geneva in 1958 and 1960: (1) the Territorial Sea and Contiguous Zone, (2) the High Seas, and (3) the Continental Shelf.

II. *Preparatory Work—The International Law Commission*

For eight years preceding Geneva, 1958, the International Law Commission studied, debated and formulated what they considered to be the traditional law of the sea. The conventions here under discussion show generally no radical departure from the commission's recommendations. Without the commission's "stirring up the waters" and providing a springboard, it is doubtful that any accord could have been reached in 1958.

Some writers have criticized the work of the commission as too stylized, or vague, or lacking imagination.[3] It appears that the commission did not conceive of itself as a legislative body. The report ended in being an annotation of majority and minority views with some attempt to balance the equities.

I am an admirer of Dr. Francisco Garcia-Amador, chairman of the commission, whom I first met at Havana during the negotiation of a convention between the United States and Cuba for the conservation of shrimp.[4] I also consider his book, *The Exploitation and Conservation of the Resources of the Sea,*[5] a must reading on that subject.

In my own preparation for the 1958 Conference, I am also indebted to Professor S. A. Bayitch of my alma mater, the University of Miami School of Law, who provided me with his *Inter-American Law of Fisheries*[6] while it was still in manuscript form.

III. *What Makes Them Vote as They Do?*

The topic assigned is "What Was Accomplished," but in relating to some extent "How It Was Accomplished," we should show the action and interaction that took place then in a condensed fashion within a short time, but which continues to bubble in a more leisurely manner around the world today.

To a neophyte like me, this world conference had some revelations. One was the mass of A/CONF documents ground out endlessly by duplicating machines.[7] These reflected the patent moves, countermoves and positions of individual states or blocs. There was the constant attempt to lobby certain delegates concerning certain points. There was Lesson Number One: That the real reason for a state voting in a certain fashion must be learned if one would become proficient in the grim game of estimating how that state would vote on hypothetical proposals.[8] Number Two: How did you slightly alter your pet proposal to make it inviting to more voters?

Then there were the blocs; the Europeans, the Latin Americans, the Africans. There were the peacemakers, principally the Indians, who sought harmony for the sake of harmony. The international lawyers of renown outnumbered the scientists, and many important decisions were decisions for reasons of state. These reasons were varied. Some were internal policy of the particular state, and many were grounded on national pride. Not enough, for my liking, were truly based on science; yet it must be admitted that the sciences of fisheries and oceanography are infants.

The same action and interaction go on today. You cannot move in this area from any narrow point of view, whether it be legal, economic, or scientific. You need a combined and broad view plus an inner view of the self-interest of each state involved.

Geneva, 1958, was a real step forward in the Law of the Sea, despite the unresolved matters remaining. First, in certain areas it codified existing law and by large majority votes put an end to speculative and argumentative theories. Second, it focused attention on other subjects and crystallized thinking to a sharp point by the interaction of opposing theories in debate. Third, often where full accord was not reached, it provided some weight of authority by actual votes recorded as greatly in favor of certain premises and opposed to others. Fourth, the enunciating of principles has made it easier for later bilateral and multilateral agreements between states. Fifth, it has placed restraints upon states who would move against the principles enunciated, whether or not those states ratify the respective conventions.

Let us examine a few of the positive accomplishments of the 1958 Conference.

IV. *The Regime of the High Seas*

Of all the 1958 Conventions at Geneva, the one on the High Seas contained more "codification" than any other. We fishermen especially note the preservation of the principle of the right to fish;[9] then the definition of piracy; anti-pollution measures; protection of cables; the right of states without sea coasts to use the seas freely. I recall the most troublesome matter as being concerned with flags of convenience, and the strong language of Article 5 of this Convention: "There must exist a genuine link between the state and the ship; in particular, the state must effectively exercise its jurisdiction and control in administrative, technical and social matters over ships flying its flag." It does appear that this well-intentioned language is a step forward, but it cannot be said that genuine results have followed the exhortation.

38

V. *The Territorial Sea and the Contiguous Zone*

This convention helped to crystallize international law in the confused area of "straight baselines," a matter which had been greatly stirred up by the recent Anglo-Norwegian Fisheries case decision in 1951.[10] This is no dead issue today. Canada's recent unilateral move to a twelve mile fishing sea is partially cloudy because of uncertain baselines and because of claims to historic bays, another item on the Geneva agenda.

The conference denied the extreme claims for special baselines for archipelagoes advanced by Indonesia and the Philippines. It set reasonable distances for determining bays as historic waters and devoted a great deal of attention to the serious subject of innocent passage. The Territorial Sea Convention defined low-tide elevations as distinguished from islands.

While the idea of a Contiguous Zone was not new, and states had previously declared such zones for sanitation or antismuggling, this convention provided a measurement of twelve miles seaward from the baseline by which the territorial sea was measured and the conference gave effective recognition to the outward reach of coastal states for fishery reasons, although failing by one vote in 1960 to reach a final decision, of which more later.

One triumph at Geneva, 1958, was in keeping separate the subject matter of the four conventions. There were strong moves in the Fishery Committee, and even in the Committee on the Continental Shelf, to delay decisions and even activity pending the resolution of the vexing problems of the Territorial Sea and Contiguous Zone. Although some problems are interrelated, the separation of subject-matter allowed many accords to be reached which would otherwise have been irreconcilable.

Following the failure of the 1958 Conference to reach accord on the problem of the territorial sea and contiguous zone,[11] some states took a vigorous approach to the problem. In 1958, the Canadian and United States positions were quite divergent. In 1960, Canada came armed with "The Canadian Proposal,"[12] and toward the end of the 1960 conference, the United States and Canada joined hands and submitted a proposal based on three major points:

1. A territorial sea of six nautical miles, measured from applicable baselines.

39

2. A contiguous fishing zone consisting of an additional six miles.

3. Preservation of historic rights for those states previously fishing in the area with a gradual phasing out in ten years.

The coastal states were not happy with this formula's standing alone; so prior to the final vote on the United States–Canadian proposal, an amendment was adopted giving the coastal states further preferential fishing rights in any areas of the high seas adjacent to their exclusive fishing zone when it could be scientifically established that a special situation or condition made the exploitation of the living resources of the high seas in that area of fundamental importance to the economic development of the coastal state or the feeding of its population. This amendment was accepted as a desperate do-or-die conciliation by the United States and Canada and was subsequently disavowed by the United States as a separate principle. Nevertheless, the disavowal was not heeded by the coastal states, who continue to hang their hats on this as a principle.

Despite the adoption of the amendment, the main proposal failed to get two-thirds majority required for approval in plenary session by *one* vote, there being 54 in favor, 28 against, and 5 abstentions.[13]

It appears that the following principles, having obtained substantial support, may be said to represent a majority view:

1. A territorial sea of six miles is acceptable.

2. A coastal state may seek extension of exclusive fishing rights to twelve miles.

3. A coastal state may have an interest in fishing for specific reasons in adjacent areas farther removed than twelve miles from its baselines.

4. When nations have traditionally fished in waters whose regulation is proposed, their rights to continue doing so must be recognized.

5. Wild and unsubstantiated claims for exclusive jurisdiction over fisheries is not countenanced by world opinion.

VI. *Present Moves in the United States*

The uproar now in the United States is over the near approach of large fleets of modern factory fishing vessels from Japan and the Soviet Union. There is a clamor in the northwest and in the northeast for more protection for United States-based fisheries. Committees in Congress are considering legislation to establish a twelve mile fishing sea.[14] It appears that because of the movement of fishery stocks very little protection is gained by domestic fisheries in moving to twelve miles.[15]

The matter in the United States is further complicated by the fact that it is known that large stocks of fish[16] which are not now usable commercially in the United States are available in areas adjacent to our own coasts. It does not appear that foreign fishing fleets are actually depleting those stocks of fish which form the present basis for the livelihood of United States fishermen;[17] however, in the absence of full scientific information on the ecology of these fisheries and their possible interdependence, alarm is felt that either (a) the foreign fleets will deplete commercial stocks fished by United States fishermen, or (b) the taking of large tonnages of adjacent fish may disturb nature's balance and result in a detriment to United States fishermen. Further, the awakening realization of the importance of the food resources of the ocean in the face of a growing population gives rise to the feeling that it should be a matter of national concern to look ahead and preserve these nearby fishery resources. This concern is illustrated by Senate Joint Resolution 29, introduced recently by Senator Magnuson and others to authorize and finance a crash scientific study of these adjacent stocks of fish. This appears to be tailored to meet the Geneva formula that claims beyond twelve miles should not be made in the absence of scientific information and the establishment of a need by the state claiming especial interest in the resource. There is a new awareness that the living resources of the sea are not inexhaustible.

In this connection, it is noted that fishery products benefit mankind in more than one way; first, as a direct nutritive food; second, as an industrial product needed for the fertilization of land crops or the feeding of domestic animals destined for human consumption. In addition, there has recently evolved an overwhelming interest in oceanography and marine technology which has served to focus attention and interest on ocean products. In this atmosphere, whatever principles are recognizable as such in connection with the law of the sea become increasingly important.

VII. *The Move to Increased Jurisdiction*

Many states have moved unilaterally to larger territorial and contiguous fishing zones (see Table 1). In March, 1958, the Secretariat of the

United Nations prepared a draft synoptical table,[18] at the request of the First Committee (Territorial Sea and Contiguous Zone). This indicated the territorial, customs, and fishing seas claimed by various states. The changes since then are extensive. Many of the European states, the Middle Eastern states, the British Commonwealth states, and several Asian states have increased their territorial or fishing seas to twelve miles. I have counted twenty-three such extensions[19] and find that most of the emerging states of Africa have joined the trend. The movement toward establishment of twelve miles is obvious, and technology is now seeking answers to those problems posed by the use of zones larger than twelve miles that may very well influence future developments.

TABLE 1

TERRITORIAL AND CONTIGUOUS FISHING ZONES
CLAIMED BY STATES

	Conservative Position	Middle Position	Radical Position
States holding territorial sea, including fishing, from 3 to 10 miles	19	..	..
States adhering to the 12 mile territorial sea, including fishing	..	26	..
States adhering to the territorial sea of 3 to 10 miles but claiming 12 miles for fishing	..	29	..
States claiming beyond 12 miles	..	..	12
Total	19	55	12

VIII. *The Continental Shelf*

It is probable that no new doctrine of international law has received universal recognition so rapidly as has that of the continental shelf. Its being an extension of the border endeared it to nationalistic pride, a matter evidenced by the hours spent in discussing the nature of sovereignty or jurisdiction, which ended by according the state "sovereign rights" over the natural resources. These were further defined as being exclusive and unshared rights.

As in the matter of the territorial sea, the area of control was difficult to define, and it is probably only a matter of time before technology triumphs over the 200 meter depth for exploitation purposes. If there was legislation at Geneva, this convention may be said to be new law created, although several unilateral declarations preceded Geneva.

There is a hangover fisheries connection with the continental shelf which really should no longer exist after the distinctions made in Geneva in 1958. The United States bears some guilt because in the Truman Proclamation of September 26, 1945,[20] a policy was enunciated with regard to "coastal fisheries." We fishermen do not like to miss any opportunity to point up the need for additional national concern with fisheries. Mr. Truman spoke of fish in these terms:

> . . . having due regard to conditions peculiar to each region and situation and to the special rights and equities of the coastal state and of any other state which may have established a legitimate interest therein.

However, the association of fish with the continental shelf grieves me, in view of the particular emphasis on the sea bed and subsoil, and the careful language of the convention itself, which states:

> Article 2, paragraph 4. The natural resources referred to in these articles consist of the mineral and other non-living resources of the seabed and subsoil together with living organisms belonging to sedentary species, that is to say, organisms which, at the harvestable stage, either are immobile on or under the seabed or are unable to move except in constant physical contact with the seabed or the subsoil.

This language is no accident.[21] Yet, there remain a few states which continue a fish-shelf association, which actually connotes a widespread control area for the state fortunate enough to have a large shelf, but which is at odds with the other concepts upon which there is general agreement.[22]

The exploitation of the sea bed and subsoil is receiving serious attention at this very moment. The Marine Technological Society is even now meeting in Washington in a three day conference studded with speaker-luminaries and backed to the hilt by large United States corporations ready to go. It is fortunate that there are some international guidelines in the 1958 Convention on the Continental Shelf, and we have long had domestic legislation in this area in the Submerged Lands

43

Act[23] and the Outer Continental Shelf Lands Act.[24] Persons seeking treasure-trove in wrecked Spanish galleons in my home state of Florida are having some trouble with ships lying outside the three-mile limit.

One very clear use of the above-quoted Article 2, paragraph 4, of the Convention on the Continental Shelf occurred recently when the burgeoning king crab industry of Alaska was disturbed by the trawling activities of Japanese and Soviet fishing fleets. An artificial twelve mile fishing zone would afford little or no protection to this valuable industry. It was found, after scientific investigation, that the king crab, at the harvestable stage, is in constant physical association with the continental shelf, and thus classifiable, as the oyster, sponges, coral, conch, and the sacred chank of India and Ceylon, as a part of the shelf. The other states involved have accepted this interpretation as a resolution of an intricate and sore controversy.

IX. *Conclusion*

It is evident that although we progress slowly in the field of the law of the sea, there are definite gains from sitting down to the conference table and going over these many problems with our neighbors in the community of states. Bilateral and multilateral agreements have been facilitated because of the guidelines set forth in the Geneva Conventions. Fourteen European states have amicably resolved a number of problems in the North Sea. It seems likely that further international discussions concerning fishery matters will be held not later than 1968 at a conference to be hosted by the United States, the avowed purpose of which will be to give implementation to principles already enunciated at Geneva in 1958. We can never overstress the importance of having some indicia of international agreement as the basis from which to argue and settle, rather than finding ourselves speaking in different tongues.

1. Neblett, "Freedom of the Seas—For Fishing," *U.S. Naval Institute Proceedings,* LXXXV, No. 2, 85–87.
2. Arthur Dean, Chairman of the U.S. Delegation referred to the Convention of Fisheries as "the first comprehensive international legislation, complete with arbitral procedures, on the subject." (Dean, "The Geneva Conference on the Law

of the Sea: What Was Accomplished," *Am. J. Intl. Law,* LII, 607 [1958].) See also *Columbia Law Review,* LXII, No. 7 (Nov., 1962), 1206–29, for Professor Bishop's comments.

3. McDougal and Burke, *The Public Order of the Oceans,* Yale University Press, 1962, p. 8.

4. Signed at Havana August 15, 1958. Department of State, *Treaties and other International Acts, Series 4321,* Government Printing Office, Washington, D. C.

5. Second Edition, Leyden, A. W. Sythoff, 1959, addendum, 1963.

6. Published for Inter-American Law Program, School of Law, University of Miami, by Oceana Publications, Inc., New York, 1957.

7. Later available in bound copies as *Official Records of United Nations Conference on Law of the Sea,* Volume I–VII, A/CONF.13/37 through 13/43.

8. The evaluating of prospective votes was most important and affected substantive matters as well as phrasing. The various blocs also had periodic meetings in private rooms, and it was sometimes possible for delegates not members of such groups to appear before them persuasively.

9. *Convention on the High Seas,* UN Doc. A/CONF.13/L.53, Art. 2: "The high seas being open to all nations, no State may validly purport to subject any part of them to its sovereignty. Freedom of the high seas is exercised under the conditions laid down by these articles and by the other rules of international law. It comprises, *inter alia,* both for coastal and non-coastal states: . . . (2) Freedom of Fishing . . . These freedoms . . . shall be exercised by all States with reasonable regard to the interests of other States in their exercise of the freedom of the high seas."

10. I.C.J. Rep. 116.

11. Neblett, "The Territorial Waters Dispute and the Shrimp Industry," *Proceedings of the Gulf and Caribbean Fisheries Institute,* Eleventh Annual Session, November, 1958, pp. 10–14. Marine Laboratory, University of Miami.

12. *The Law of the Sea—A Canadian Proposal,* The Queen's Printer and Controller of Stationery, Ottawa, 1959.

13. "Though formally unavailing, this vote of fifty-four nations is proof at least of widespread international acceptance of a six-mile territorial sea and of a twelve-mile exclusive fishery zone measured from the same baseline."—Johnston, *The International Law of Fisheries* (New Haven: Yale University Press, 1965), p. 244.

14. S.2218. Senators Bartlett, Magnuson, (E.) Kennedy. Hearings May 17, 1966.

15. Comment of Senator Warren G. Magnuson at hearing on S.J. Res. 29, April 19, 1966: "The Senator from Alaska and I have a 12-mile limit bill. That doesn't solve it at all."

16. The term "stocks of fish" is used as a fishery concept denoting the management and control of a fishery, the population and ecology of which are subject to determination. There is a variance of habit and travel between species and even between the same species in different locales. Where a fish population is preserved virtually intact and its breeding, feeding, and other vital statistics can be determined, it can be managed, that is, reasonable regulations can be made for the exploitation and conservation of that particular stock. There are practically no stocks of fish which receive protection by an artificial mileage limitation. Protection of spawning, nursery areas, or whatever should be required by scientific analysis should be wherever the fish are found.

17. At hearings on S.J. Res. 29, April 19, 1966, before the Subcommittee on Merchant Marine and Fisheries of the Committee on Commerce, Donald L. McKernan, Director of the Bureau of Commercial Fisheries, testified as to the Soviet fishing fleets: "There are obviously heavy concentrations along the edge of the Continental Shelf, the 100 fathom curve, and this is where the Russians have concentrated their initial fishing." (Page 18 of Hearings.)

18. UN Conference on Law of the Sea, A/CONF.13/C.1/L11, March 20, 1958.

19. To twelve miles since 1958: Belgium, Denmark (including Greenland and Faroe Islands), France, Iceland, Iran, Ireland, Israel, Italy, Libya, Morocco, New Zealand, Norway, Pakistan, Portugal, Sweden, Syria, Thailand, Tunisia, Turkey, Union of South Africa, United Kingdom, Uruguay, and Venezuela. The Dominican Republic went from twelve to fifteen miles; Korea from an announced fifty to a 20–200 mile fishing sea.

20. 59 Stat. 884. Presidential Proclamation No. 2667.

21. Marjorie M. Whiteman: "Conference on the Law of the Sea: Convention on the Continental Shelf," *Am. J. Intl. Law,* Vol. LII, No. 4, October, 1958, pp. 638–41. This is an outstanding treatise on this Convention. Miss Whiteman, an Assistant Legal Adviser to the Department of State, was the U.S. spokesman in Committee IV.

22. Notably Argentina, Cambodia, Korea, Nicaragua, Panama. Tunisian sea follows the 50 meter isobath for part of the coast (maximum 65 miles). In the U.S., Congressmen Pelly and Wyatt have introduced bills (H.R. 14961 and 15011) to establish U.S. jurisdiction to seaward boundary lines drawn following the 200 meter depth contour.

23. 67 Stat. 29, 43 U.S.C. 1301–15.

24. 67 Stat. 462, 43 U.S.C. 1331–43.

Robert L. Friedheim

Chapter Four:

FACTOR ANALYSIS AS A TOOL IN STUDYING THE LAW OF THE SEA[*]

As Quincy Wright has pointed out, international law as an intellectual discipline has reached the crisis stage. The concepts of traditionalists are obsolete, and replacements worked out by modernists may be "premature."[1] Efforts have been made recently to modernize and change international law to fit contemporary circumstances. But the substance of law can itself be subject to conflict, although many lawyers think of it as the chief means of settling conflict.

Negotiations at the two UN Law of the Sea Conferences, 1958 and 1960, are a case in point. At Geneva, traditionalists and modernists alike worked assiduously to mold the conference results—in the form of conventions—to their liking. But the results were conventions fully satisfactory to no one. Failing to settle the key problem—breadth of the territorial sea and contiguous zone—the conferences left a critical gap in the law of the sea. But more important to those who wanted to link the new concepts of the law to the old was the attack on traditional concepts by the "dissatisfied" states at the conferences. This attack, in the opinion of many Western delegates who were themselves eminent traditional international lawyers or trained by them, if continued in the future, will destroy the very foundations of the law.[2]

If international law is to be salvaged, not only might it be necessary to restructure the law but tailor it to the particular economic, political, and social context in which it might be expected to operate. The past and the present should contain some useful clues on what might be appropriate for the future.

The purpose of this paper is to examine the conflicts over law which arose at the two United Nations law of the sea conferences. These conflicts, once analyzed, should demonstrate not only the substantive conflict patterns which developed, but also the position of states thereon. With this analysis as a basis, we can then make reasonable assumptions about why the states took the positions they did, and the likelihood of the positions they would take on the conflict issues in the same or different contexts in the future.

I.

Since we are discussing the attempt to create law in what is essentially a parliamentary-diplomatic setting, we have in the proceedings of the conferences a ready-made body of analyzable data.[3] The eight published volumes of documents faithfully record the debates, discussions, and arguments of delegates, and their votes when a roll-call vote was requested. In addition, many delegates often gave an explanation or apology for their vote and made clear what they thought the vote of their opponents represented. Two methods now in fairly common use in the behavioral sciences seem appropriate in looking for conflict patterns in this large body of materials: factor analysis of the roll-call votes and content analysis of the debates.

Since roll-call votes were usually requested only on contentious issues —both procedural and substantive—the voting records supply a wealth of material on conflict. Because of their compact form and availability, and because there is ample precedent in the analysis of United Nations voting, this paper will attempt a factor analysis of the votes at the UN law of the sea conferences.[4]

Factor analysis is a statistical technique for clustering variables into groups according to their intercorrelations. Variables correlating high among themselves and low with other variables cluster together and are said to determine a single underlying factor. The particular factor-analysis technique used here, called R-analysis, uses the votes at the law of the sea conferences as the variables. In the factor pattern obtained, each vote is described in terms of underlying issues of conflict. Each conflict issue represents a cluster of votes on which particular nations and groups of nations manifest a similar voting pattern. Each cluster (factor) when interpreted should help us pinpoint the areas of conflict which arose at the conferences. By use of the factor scores (giving nations relative standing on each of the factors), we can determine the position that nations and groups of nations took on the issues.[5]

TABLE 2

ROTATED FACTOR MATRIX FOR CONFLICT ISSUES: UN LAW OF THE SEA CONFERENCES

VOTE NUMBER	ISSUE	1	2	3	FACTOR 4	5	6	7
36	U.S.: 6–12 plus historic rights	.86						
25	Vietnam: reverse order of voting	.86						
72	U.S.: reconsider 6–12 plus historic rights	.75						
20	Netherlands-Portugal-United Kingdom: innocent passage through straits	.75					.45	
78	U.S.-Canada: 6–12 plus historic rights	.71						
6	U.S.: Art. 3—territorial sea and contiguous zone	.71						
69	U.S.-Canada: 6–12 plus historic rights	.71						
16	Art. 24: innocent passage for warships	.66				.39		
68	Brazil-Cuba-Uruguay: modify historic rights	.64						
70	Ethiopia-Ghana-Liberia: fishing technical assistance	.62						
18	Ecuador: postpone consideration of Arts. 1, 2, 3, and 66	.59				.46		
61	Art. 68: continental shelf rights	.54						
4	Draft resolution: compulsory jurisdiction and arbitration	.51		.57				
24	Portugal: territorial seas, access to foreign ports	.51		.41				
52	U.S.-Greece-Pakistan: criteria for dispute settlement	.49		.41				
63	Art. 73: settlement of disputes	.48		.57				
27	Canada: 6-mile territorial sea	.46						
50	Greece-U.S.: compulsory settlement of fishery disputes	.44		.64				
60	U.S.: exclusive continental shelf rights	.41		.54				
12	Cuba: no reservation on fishing articles	.40		.66				
75	Iceland: preferential fishing rights for "overwhelmingly" coastal state	.39	.69					
47	Ceylon: separate votes on draft resolution and ILC Art. 48	−.40	.49			−.74		
46	Mexico: hot pursuit	−.46						
66	Committee of the whole: fishing rights of "overwhelmingly" coastal state	−.48		−.40			−.59	
22	Art. 18: innocent passage	−.49						
43	Poland: "bound to refrain" from acts affecting others	−.51					.51	
23	Mexico: innocent passage	−.51				−.60		
21	Mexico: innocent passage defined as obeying coastal states' regulations	−.52		−.45				

TABLE 2—Continued

Vote Number	Issue				Factor			
		1	2	3	4	5	6	7
62	India: no defense installations on continental shelf	—.53				—.60		
5	First Committee: fishing-contiguous zone	—.54	.64					
76	Argentina: amend U.S.-Canada historic rights to 30 years	—.56	.52				—.47	
41	Poland: no naval maneuvers to interfere with navigation	—.59				—.53		
19	Latin American states: no violation of coastal state interest	—.63		—.38				
30	Chair rule not allowing Ecuador to change vote	—.73						
32	Colombia: appeal chair rule	—.75						
8	U.S.S.R.: 3–12 territorial sea	—.78						
29	India-Mexico: territorial sea up to 12 miles	—.79						
7	Eight power: 12–12 territorial sea	—.80						
71	Eight power: 12-mile territorial sea until another conference is called ...	—.80						
74	Eighteen power: 12-mile territorial sea and contiguous zone	—.82						
26	Ghana: vote on Canadian proposal in 2 parts	—.82						
40	Morocco: move to adjourn	—.84						
31	U.S.S.R.: 3–12 territorial sea	—.85						
39	Mexico: move to adjourn	—.85						
35	Canada: divide U.S. proposal into 2 parts ...	—.86						
33	Colombia: 12-mile territorial sea	—.87						
34	Mexico: divide U.S. proposal into 3 parts ..	—.89						
37	India: revive India-Mexico proposal	—.90						
54	Iceland: fishing rights of "overwhelmingly" coastal state		.91					
56	Iceland: proposal as a whole		.91					
58	Iceland proposal: second reading		.89					
10	Iceland: Art. 60a—fishing and coastal rights		.88					
57	U.S.-Canada: abstention on fishing		.79					
28	Canada: par. 2—12-mile fishing and contiguous zone		.74					
44	Peru: coastal rights in definition of freedom of the seas		.73					
73	Eight power: 12-mile sea until another conference is called		.72					
49	Five power: conservation after due regard for coastal interest		.72					
51	Ecuador: amend U.S.-Greece-Pakistan proposal		.72				—.43	
75	Iceland: preferential fishing rights of "overwhelmingly" coastal state	—.39	.69					

TABLE 2—*Continued*

Vote Number	Issue	Factor						
		1	2	3	4	5	6	7
5	First Committee (Canadian proposal): fishing contiguous zone	−.54						
77	Guatemala (amend U.S.-Canada); fishing under historic rights		.64				−.48	
67	Iceland: eliminate "historic rights"		.58				−.62	
9	Arts. 49–50: fishing and conservation		.56		−.44			
76	Argentina (amend U.S.-Canada): define historic rights as 30 years	−.56	.54					
42	Mexico: definition of freedom of the high seas		.52			.52		
46	Mexico: hot pursuit	−.46	.49	−.40			−.47	
1	Continental shelf: define exploitability		.46					
53	Art. 54, par. 1: special fishing interests of coastal states		.44		−.54			
55	Iceland: compulsory settlement	.40		.70				
12	Cuba: no reservations on fishing articles	.44		.66				
50	Greece-U.S.: compulsory settlement of fishing disputes	.48		.64				
63	ILC Art. 73: ICJ settlement of disputes	.51		.57				
4	Draft article: compulsory jurisdiction and settlement	.41		.57				
60	U.S.: exclusive rights of continental shelf	.49		.54				
52	U.S.-Greece-Pakistan: dispute settlement criteria	.51		.41				
24	Portugal: territorial sea and access to foreign ports			.41				
2	Continental shelf, crustacea, etc.			.37				
19	Latin American states: no violation of coastal state interest	−.63		−.38				
46	Mexico: hot pursuit	−.46	.49	−.40				
21	Mexico: innocent passage definition as obeying coastal states' regulation.			−.45				
15	Art. 9: buoyed channels	−.52		−.52				
9	Arts. 49–50: fishing and conservation		.54		−.44			
11	Draft: special coastal rights and fishing				−.50			
53	Art. 54: coastal states' fishing in adjacent waters		.44		−.54			
14	Art. 5: straight baselines				−.75			
59	ILC: definition of continental shelf				−.79			
48	U.S.-United Kingdom: draft resolution on pollution of the high seas					.79		
13	Credentials committee: Hungarian credentials					.64		

TABLE 2—*Continued*

VOTE NUMBER	ISSUE	FACTOR						
		1	2	3	4	5	6	7
42	Mexico: define freedom of the high seas		.49			.52		
45	Panama: nationality of ships					.48		
18	Ecuador: postpone consideration of Arts. 1, 2, 3, and 66					.46		
16	Art. 24: right of warships to innocent passage	.59				.39		
41	Poland: no naval maneuvers to interfere with navigation	.66				−.53		
43	Poland: states "bound to refrain" from acts affecting others	−.59				−.60		
62	India: no defense installations on continental shelf	−.51				−.60		
47	Ceylon: separate votes on ILC Art. 48, draft resolution	−.40				−.74		
78	U.S.-Canada: 6–12 and historic rights	.71					.45	
73	Cuba: protocol to fishing resolution—coastal states to limit catch		.72				−.43	
76	Argentina (amend U.S.-Canada): define historic rights as 30 years	−.56					−.47	
77	Guatemala (amend U.S.-Canada): fishing under historic rights in "lawful manner"		.58					
66	Committee of the whole: fishing rights of "overwhelmingly" coastal state	−.48					−.48	
67	Iceland: eliminate historic rights		.56				−.59	
65	Switzerland: moderate proposal for landlocked rights						−.62	−.70
3	Switzerland: fifth committee recommendation for landlocked states							−.87
	Miscellaneous:							
17	Cuba: resolution to convene new conference							
38	Colombia: definition of sovereignty	No loadings exceeding + or −.37 on these factors.						
64	Hungary: definite convention for landlocked states							
	Roll-call variance accounted for by factor (eigen values) λ =	23.38	12.36	5.52	2.94	5.23	2.68	2.09

We are here trying to determine the underlying issues of conflict by first finding an "unrotated" factor pattern matrix by the principal component method. This matrix was then rotated both orthogonally and obliquely in an attempt to approximate the best "simple structure" solution.[6] The ideal simple structure solution is one in which each variable loads on only one underlying factor. However, with a large number of variables (in this case seventy-eight votes) and only a few factors, it is unreasonable to expect every vote to be explainable in terms of only one underlying factor. For example, our analysis (as will be shown later) indicates that one underlying factor is clearly related to the East-West conflict while another factor concerns the voting on the North-South issues. However, on several votes both an East-West conflict and a North-South conflict were involved; hence, although ideally these votes should be the result of a single underlying dimension, obviously because of the nature of these votes, their interpretation depends on two dimensions.

The completed unrotated, orthogonally rotated, and obliquely rotated factor matrices were examined, and it was decided that the orthogonally rotated matrix provided the best description of the underlying dimensions in terms of the voting record. The first two factors in the unrotated matrix were interpretable, but because most votes loaded highly on one or both of these first two factors ($\lambda_1 = 32.99$; $\lambda_2 = 11.61$) the remaining factors were difficult to interpret. The oblique rotation gave us results very similar to those obtained from the orthogonal rotations, but for reasons of succinctness (the factors are independent), it was decided to use the orthogonal solution.

All of the 78 votes at the conference were used to construct the principal factor matrix. Selection of certain key votes was not necessary.[7] Nor was elimination of unanimous votes necessary because there were only two unanimous roll-call votes at the conferences, and the factor they defined provided significant data. Only one other roll-call vote even approached unanimity. Of the 78 votes, 67 were substantive votes while 11 were procedural. Results of a subanalysis demonstrated that there were no distinctly different dimensions of conflict for procedural and substantive votes. In fact, the procedural votes factored directly into the clusters on substantive issues.[8] Another way of putting this is that the delegates were using procedural motions to fight out substantive issues on other grounds.

Essential for the success of the factor analysis is the conversion of the nominal voting categories (yes, no, abstention, and absence) into

53

some meaningful ordinal relationship. The ideal ordinal scale would have a no vote at one end of the continuum, a yes vote at the other extreme, and an abstention or absence somewhere in between. Other investigators[9] elected to give a no vote a rank of 0, a yes vote a rank of 2, and both an abstention and absence a rank of 1. While the scale thereby constructed does provide the desired relationship between voting categories, the author did not feel it adequately reflected the significance of a nation's vote with regard to all other votes cast on the same ballot. If, for example, in an assembly containing eighty members three nations vote no and the remaining seventy-seven nations vote yes on a particular issue then quite probably the issue has considerable significance for the three nations voting no. In spite of a sizable majority favoring the issue these three nations felt strongly enough about the question to vote against this majority. Even if the issue is a trivial one, examining why the opposing nations took the stand they did could reveal important information about the voting policy of these nations. Since we are relying on the factor analytic procedure to sort out the important issues underlying a large number of ballots, it is crucial that the ordinal ranks assigned to these votes do reflect the significance of the votes to each nation. Therefore, we would do well to assign our ranks in a manner such that nations which do take "extreme" positions in the face of a sizable majority (on a particular vote) do receive more "credit" for their stand on the vote in question. A convenient method for assigning ranks which provides the desirable properties described above is presented by Alker and Russett in their book, *World Politics in the General Assembly*. The method for assigning ranks outlined below is similar (but not identical) to the one employed by Alker and Russett.

Originally, each yes vote was assigned a rank of 9, each no vote a rank of 1, and each abstention a rank of 5 (absences will be discussed later). Notice that an abstention was considered to be halfway between a yes vote and a no vote, and hence no more negative than positive on a particular question. For each ballot, the voting categories are replaced by the ranks assigned above. These ranks are summed for all nations voting on a particular ballot and this sum is divided by the number of nations voting to determine the average rank. Deviate scores are found for each nation's vote by subtracting this mean rank from the original assigned rank. Since for this analysis no assumptions were made concerning the position of an absent nation on a particular ballot, absent nations were given a "neutral" rank equal to the mean rank. The

54

standard deviation for these deviate scores now including absent nations (with a deviate rank of 0) was determined and standardized voting ranks were finally obtained by dividing the deviate scores by the standard deviation.

A short example will illustrate that this method of ranking has accomplished what we desired and gives "credit" (in the form of larger deviate scores) to nations which take extreme positions.

Let us suppose that on a particular vote in our hypothetical assembly consisting of 80 members we have: 60 who vote yes; 10 who vote no; 5 who abstain; and 5 who are absent. Then,

The mean rank = ... 7.67
The deviate scores for those voting yes = ... 1.33
The deviate scores for those voting no = ... —6.67
The deviate scores for those who abstain = ... —2.67
The deviate scores for those who are absent = ... 0.00
The standard deviation of the deviate scores = ... 2.73
The standardized voting ranks for those voting yes = ... 0.48
The standardized voting ranks for those voting no = ... —2.71
The standardized voting ranks for those abstaining = ... —0.98
The standardized voting ranks for those absent = ... 0.00

Notice that the neutral point of our scale, the rank of an absent vote, is 0. Therefore, any rank above 0 can be considered a vote in favor of the issue (obviously yes will always be greater than 0 and no always less than 0), and any rank below 0 can be considered a vote against the issue. The significance of the vote to the voting nation is indicated by the distance of the standardized voting rank from 0. The greater the deviation from 0, the greater the significance of a particular vote to a nation. In the above example, the ten nations voting against the issue took their extreme stand possibly because of some vital characteristic of the issue important to them. Note that the size of the voting rank of those voting no (—2.71) reflects this extreme position compared with the size of the rank of the nations voting yes (.48). Note also that an abstention in the face of a large majority voting yes received a negative rank (—.98) implying that for this ballot an abstention is not a neutral position but one that does indicate some opposition.

55

The validity of the above assumptions concerning the significance of a vote to a particular nation is certainly open to question and the author is not implying they apply in every circumstance. There is no implicit ordinal "significance" scale isomorphic to a nation's assigned voting rank when the rank is based only on the relationship between that vote and all others cast on the same ballot. In addition, there are a number of motives other than "significance of the issue" that may cause a nation to take an extreme stand (bloc affiliation, swapping votes, political reasons, and so forth). However, regardless of the inaccuracy of the ranking system or the motives of the voter, the above schema for assigning ranks can provide some rough quantitative information about the relative importance of a particular issue to a nation. With the help of the factor analysis, even these rough estimates will serve to illuminate some of the basic issues underlying the conferences.

II.

From the rotated factor matrix seven clusters or factors were selected for analysis. Each represented a significant conflict issue or issues which arose at the conferences. They are: (1) a North and West versus a South and East struggle (plotted for convenience as East-West in Figure 1) primarily on the territorial sea and contiguous zone; (2) a North versus South conflict on the fishing rights of coastal states; (3) a clash on supranationalism; (4) a conflict over legal theory interpreted as a sign of discontent of "legal conservatives"; (5) an East-West struggle over direct cold-war issues; (6) a second conference contest over the rights of coastal states to control fishing in their contiguous zones and adjacent seas; and (7) a muted quarrel over how to solve the problem of landlocked countries' right of access to the sea. These clashes are described in Table 2.

The dominant struggle of the conferences was principally over what settlement to make of the question of the breadth of the territorial sea and contiguous zone. No hard data is needed merely to identify this issue as the key issue of the conferences. Our data verified this appraisal of many participants, observers, and commentators. But it also did more. This issue was not only the critical one, but the statistically dominant one. The first cluster in the rotated matrix, containing the territorial sea, contiguous zone, and related votes, had an eigen value of $\lambda = 23.38$.

While this dominance shows up in the rotated matrix, as we have seen, it is even more obvious in the unrotated matrix. In addition, the line-ups on the territorial sea and contiguous zone questions importantly influenced the voting on a number of allied issues.

The highest loadings in the cluster—both positive and negative—were on votes in which a proposed breadth of the territorial sea was tied in the same proposal with a proposed contiguous zone. None of these proposals received the two-thirds majority vote needed for passage and inclusion in the Convention on the Territorial Sea. The probable reason for the failure of any proposal to receive a requisite majority was in the very attempt to combine two distinct issues in hopes of compromises. The territorial sea, while it has many legal ramifications, was viewed at the conferences by many states principally as a security zone in which the coastal state exercises complete sovereignty. The contiguous zone, on the other hand, is supposed—for states with a narrower territorial sea—to provide control of fishing rights in a belt adjacent to the territorial sea without giving the coastal state full sovereign control. Doubtless it was hoped by those who wanted to keep the breadth of the territorial sea at a minimum that a contiguous zone would satisfy a number of states who wanted to expand their sea frontiers for primarily economic reasons, that is, to gain firmer control over offshore fishing. The combined proposals succeeded only in allying against it opponents of both measures: those whose concern was fishing thought the limitation stated in most of the contiguous zone clauses too restricting; those whose concern was security would still accept no breadth less than twelve miles.

As Figure 1 shows, the struggle on this question was basically between the Soviet bloc, the "neutralists," the Arab group, and about half of the Latin American states at one pole, and the United States, a heterogeneous collection of U.S. friends and allies, the conservative European group, and the remaining Latin American states at the other.[10] Because of the consistent Soviet bloc position, the negative factor scores represent an East vote. Juxtaposing factors 1 and 2 in Figure 1 helps us interpret the meaning of these clusters. Since the Soviets voted consistently "North" or with most of the states with high fishing or shipping capabilities in factor 2, it seems probable that their votes in factor 1 were directed toward the creation of a sea security zone of maximum breadth. With low factor scores on factor 2, it is also probable that the Arab group had more of a security than economic basis for their votes. This

57

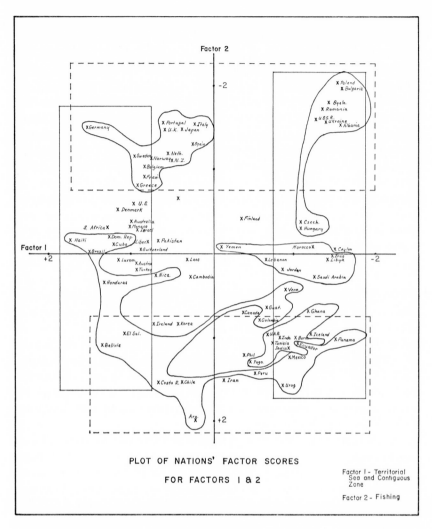

PLOT OF NATIONS' FACTOR SCORES

FOR FACTORS 1 & 2

Factor 1 - Territorial Sea and Contiguous Zone

Factor 2 - Fishing

FIG. 1.—Plot of nations' factor scores. Factor 1: East-West, territorial sea and contiguous zone. Factor 2: North-South, fishing.

is not the case for the leading neutralist and Latin American states, which had high negative scores on factor 1. Given the fact that they also loaded "South" on factor 2, it is probable that economic considerations were of considerable importance on their high loadings on factor 1. Thus the states with negative scores on factor 1 comprised an East and South grouping. Notice in Table 2 that these states supported proposals for a twelve-mile territorial sea and adamantly opposed any attempt to set a uniform breadth at any lesser distance. They also opposed compromises in a number of related areas. With a twelve-mile territorial sea within which the coastal state would have been able to exercise complete control—including control over fishing—no contiguous zone was necessary (except in vote 33 where Colombia proposed to give the coastal state a territorial sea of twelve miles and a fishing contiguous zone of another twelve miles beyond the territorial sea). For those who opted for less than a twelve mile sea (not that any would be likely to), the broad-sea advocates would allow a twelve mile contiguous zone measured from the same base line. While appearing to compromise, actually this group was adamant.

The opposing coalition, a West and North grouping, supported U.S.-led compromise packages on the territorial sea and contiguous zone, and opposed South and East attempts to legitimize recent coastal states' attempts to increase their control of extensive water areas off their coasts. Most of this group voted North on factor 2, and the chief proposal they supported—a relatively narrow territorial sea and a fishing contiguous zone hedged with limitations—had both security and economic elements. A narrow territorial sea had extremely important security connotations for those states with surface navies or those who were depending upon transoceanic U.S. support. In addition, states with large merchant navies also had economic grounds for preferring a narrow territorial sea; they did not wish to see many traditional sea lanes swallowed up in enlarged territorial seas of coastal states. Some of these states were willing to compromise on fishing rights off the shores of other states, but they still had important economic interests at stake and would not surrender them completely.

The factor scores of those states who supported the proposals loading positively on factor 1 and opposed the proposals loading negatively also illustrate a frequent dilemma of a state that proposes compromise measures. This trap is offering something to everybody, and not enough to anybody. This is precisely what happened to the United States when it attempted to play a leadership role at the conferences. Its offer of a six mile territorial sea was more than its more conservative allies preferred, and less than what its opponents would accept. The contiguous zone in the U.S. proposals had a clause which allowed other states to fish in the outer portion of the coastal state's contiguous zone for a stated period of years. Its opponents referred to this pejoratively as "historic rights." Because the privilege was only temporary, U.S. friends were not fully committed to it. The result was consistent opposition to U.S. compromise measures by opponents of these measures, and only inconsistent support from U.S. friends. While the Western coalition could count on support of the more conservative European states in opposing East and South proposals, it could not always count upon these states to support U.S. compromise proposals.

The second most important conflict at the conferences, having an eigen value $\lambda = 12.36$, was a straight North-South conflict over the right of coastal states to control fishing off their shores. More precisely, it was a conflict between developed states with large distant-water fishing fleets that traditionally fished far from home—often off the coasts of underdeveloped states—and underdeveloped states with primitive short-distance fishing fleets, some of them with rich fishing grounds anywhere from several to several hundred miles off their coasts, sometimes exploited by developed states.

All of the votes on factor 2 directly or indirectly concerned fishing. The various mutations of the Icelandic proposal, loading above .88 on the factor, served as a symbol for what the supporters of the South position wanted. The Icelandic proposal would have given a coastal state the right to limit other states' catch of fish in fishing grounds off its coast when its people "is overwhelmingly dependent upon its coastal fisheries for its livelihood or economic development."[11] In a world of shrinking resources, this would have assured a number of states living in dire poverty that well-equipped fishing states would not exhaust their last under-utilized food resource. But while the South states feared exploitation by others, they were not always capable of exploiting these resources themselves. Nevertheless, the "rights" of coastal states became an article of faith for them; preferably stated as vaguely as possible so as not to cut down on their tactical mobility.

Consistent supporters of the South position had positive factor scores (Figure 1). They were drawn mainly from leading Neutralist states and the Latin American group. The opponents, with negative factor scores, were European Community states and members of the Communist bloc. Between these two extremes, with both low positive and low negative factor scores, were the Arab group, the U.S., and a heterogeneous collection of U.S. friends.

The reasons for the extremes are obvious. The Europeans and the Soviet Union had important distant-water fishing interests, while a number of the South states had rich coastal fisheries. The position of the states between the extremes is more interesting, since they might in the future either throw their votes one way or the other or attempt to reconcile the extremes. The former seems more likely, because attempts at the latter, principally by the United States, were made and failed.

This can be seen as well in factor 6, which clustered together the votes at the second conference on fishing questions. Although the second conference was called only to solve the problem of the breadth of the territorial sea and contiguous zone, all fishing problems were again aired. The compromises that went into the United States proposal on the contiguous zone and the decisions made concerning fishing at the first conference were soon under attack (factor 6, Table 2). This attack was led by the entire Arab group, with factor scores ranging from —2.44 to —.99, a few leading neutralists, and a number of Latin American states. The outstanding defenders of the compromises, with high plus factor scores, were Canada and the remaining Neutralists, and Latin American states. Defenders of the compromises did not include many of the states that were active in proposing compromises or who had important fishing interests. Thus the compromises seemed not to be particularly satisfactory to the great states of the world.

Since these fishing matters were not finally resolved at the second conference, they may well be opened again. Those interested in learning from past failures should look at the voting pattern of the Arab group in this instance. At the first conference, the Arab states did not show a significant interest in coastal rights of fishing states (factor 2, Figure 1), nor were they committed with more vociferous Latin American states to rejecting third-party solutions to disputes over fishing rights (factor 3, Figure 2). In fact, they showed mild support for supranationalist settlement means. Their position hardened at the second conference. I do not know why.[12] But if it increases support for additional coastal states rights, and the great fishing states show as much reluctance to compromise in the future as they did at the conferences, fishing problems may become even more intractable when they come up for settlement again.

61

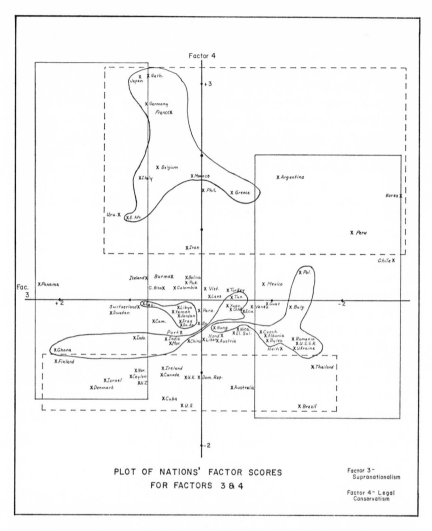

Fig. 2.—Plot of nations' factor scores. Factor 3: supranationalism. Factor 4: legal conservatism.

Another voting pattern displaying a significant conflict dimension concerned supranationalism. This is defined here as the willingness of states to bind themselves in advance to third-party settlement of disputes which might arise. It also means a willingness to defend rights common to all through law rather than support proposals which would increase the scope of national sovereignty. Unlike Alker's work on supranationalism, which found a supranationalist element spread across several factors, we have found supranationalism defined by a single factor (factor 3, Table 2).[13] This factor, with an eigen value of $\lambda = 5.52$, indicates that supranationalist votes accounted for a significant amount of variance in voting. Supranationalist settlement of conflict of states is still a popular nostrum among those with a legal point of view. Sadly for those who would like to depend on such means of settling disputes, most states represented at the conferences were not willing to put too many of their security or economic eggs in this basket. Figure 2 shows the relative standing of states on this factor. Factor 3 was plotted East-West, because most of the West states had positive factor scores, while the Communist bloc had negative factor scores. Consistent support for supranationalism was forthcoming only from a relative handful of major Western states, European neutrals, Scandinavians, and Neutralists. Consistent opposition came from the Communist bloc and those states—mostly Latin America—who wanted no control at all over their attempts to dominate fishing off their shores. Most states fell in the middle, with low positive and negative factor scores. It is difficult to interpret the future of supranationalist measures from this plotting. Pessimists could point to the fact that the United States, the United Kingdom, many major European states, the Arabs, and some Neutralists, were not here willing to commit themselves clearly to supranationalism. On the other hand, optimists could say that it might be significant for the future that many otherwise vehemently nationalistic new states now trying to find their place in the world did not take a strongly *anti*-supranationalistic stand. They could even point to the fact that the Arabs and most Neutralists had positive factor scores, possibly indicating some support for supranationalism.

Factor 4, Table 2 shows a dimension, related particularly to fishing, but distinct in itself. It is called here legal conservatism. Two types of votes were involved. (1) Compromise measures which accorded coastal states a minimum degree of their demands. These were usually unspecific as to particular rights, broad generalizations, and in general without teeth. (2) Proposals involving possible threats to the ideal of freedom of the seas. Frequently the two overlapped.

63

As factor 3, Figure 2 shows, the major European states with very high positive factor scores were the legal conservatives. They would have none of the attempts to give coastal states what the compromisers thought were harmless rights if such compromises upset their theory of the freedom of the seas. They would not even concede that the continental shelf concept should be brought into the contemporary law of the sea. These votes on seemingly innocuous issues also aroused some ardent supporters of the rights of coastal states—Uruguay, the Philippines, Iran, Argentina, Korea, Peru, and Chile. They too had high positive factor scores, but unlike the European states who were protesting that the conference had gone too far, were saying that it had not gone far enough. They were not satisfied with a statement of vague rights; they wanted strong and specific coastal states' rights written into international law.[14]

On the other hand, the archetypical supporters of these measures were the United States, the United Kingdom, "White Commonwealth," and Scandinavian states. Indicating that they would accept these general coastal rights, but without enthusiasm, were states with low negative factor scores, principally Arab, Neutralist, and Communist states.

No multilateral conference in the contemporary international system is complete without a direct U.S.-Soviet clash on a wide range of issues. The law of the sea conferences were no exception. Factor 5, with an eigen value of $\lambda = 5.23$, picked up the variance accountable to the cold-war clash across the seventy-eight votes. The votes that loaded high on the factor typified the struggle between the bipolar giants. Almost all of these direct cold-war issues fought out at the first conference had important security implications.

The major arena in which the great cold-war adversaries and their allies used the law to defend their own vital interests and attack those of their opponents was the Second Committee, which was charged with considering the regime of the high seas. A critical question vigorously debated was the use of the high seas for testing atomic weapons or as a dumping ground for atomic wastes. In particular, the United States and the United Kingdom were concerned with Article 48 of the International Law Commission draft, which would have required states to draw up regulations to prevent atomic pollution and also would have required states to co-operate in drawing up regulations to prevent pollution of the high seas from atomic "experiments." The Anglo-American

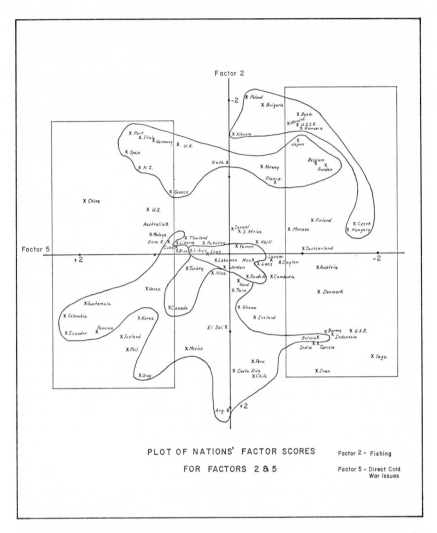

Fig. 3.—Plot of nations' factor scores. Factor 2: North-South, fishing. Factor 5: East-West, direct cold-war issues.

states counterattacked, proposing that these provisions be deleted and a non-binding resolution be substituted. Even though this proposal was accepted, the Communist bloc states and some of the major Neutralists

65

did not let the West have an easy victory. They sponsored vaguer proposals which would have accomplished the same thing as did Article 48 (e.g., the Polish proposal requiring states to be "bound to refrain from acts on the high seas affecting others") and also proposals prohibiting naval maneuvers from interfering with navigation and prohibiting defense installations—Texas towers, etc.—on the continental shelf. The bitterest fight, however, was over the U.S.-sponsored proposal that the conferences not take any position on the credentials of the Hungarian delegation—the tail-end of a persistent United States harassing tactic stemming from the Hungarian revolution.

Figure 3 shows a different pattern from the previous figures. Most notable was the inability of the United States to hold onto the votes of its European friends—allies and neutrals alike—when the issues had cold-war implications. The United States record was not as bad as Figure 3 indicates, since the factor scores here include more than the votes that loaded particularly high on factor 5; nevertheless, her record of attracting the votes of allies on cold-war related issues was not good. While the United States should not have expected support from Japan—given her understandable sensitivity on atomic questions— more consistent support from France (who was absent from votes 47 and 48), NATO members from Scandinavia and the Low Countries, and a number of European neutrals might have been hoped for. If these direct cold-war issues had gone against the United States, she would indeed have been embarrassed. But the United States received support on these and other votes with cold-war implications from a group which had on other issues vehemently opposed her: Latin America. Of the Latin American states, 13 had positive factor scores on the fifth factor; 7 had very high positive factor scores. Among those who rescued the United States on cold-war questions were states such as Colombia, Ecuador, Panama, Venezuela, Uruguay, and Mexico, all among her bitterest opponents on coastal fishing rights, the territorial sea, and contiguous zones.

As might be expected, the East position had as its core the Communist bloc, and those neutralist states usually associated with the anticolonial caucusing group in the General Assembly.

The spread in the factor scores of the Communist block is interesting. A certain amount of divergence in the structure of the bloc can be seen from the votes with cold-war implications. On votes loading high on factor 5, no bloc member voted against the bloc on direct cold-war issues, and only Poland abstained (once). But on votes that did not load as high, there was divergence within the bloc. Both Czechoslovakia and Hungary were more "Soviet" than the Soviets; Czechoslovakia has always been noted as a faithful bloc member, and Hungary probably was "behaving" to demonstrate loyalty two years after her abortive rebellion. Because Albania's absence rate was high for a Communist state (12.8 per cent), we cannot tell whether her deviance was significant for policy (the difficulties with Moscow had been brewing since 1956, but there was no open break until 1960). But the low factor scores of Poland ($-.25$) and Bulgaria ($-.42$) may indicate that there were some real differences over policy within the bloc.

The seventh and final factor, a muted dispute over the rights of landlocked countries, demonstrates that factor analysis can reveal conflict situations even in certain unanimous votes. There were only two votes here, both on the Swiss proposal for landlocked countries' rights to use and have access to the seas, taken at two different times. A moderate proposal, this generally affirmed only those rights of landlocked countries that were already widely accepted. It was accepted over an eighteen-power proposal which went much further to give landlocked states stronger rights of transit to the sea across the territory of coastal states. (The stronger proposal was rejected because of the lack of support from a combination of coastal states and powerful maritime states.) While the Swiss measure was adopted by what was called under conference rules a unanimous vote because no state voted against it, nine or ten states abstained once or both times. Among the abstainers were both landlocked countries who felt the measure was too weak, and coastal states who were afraid it granted the landlocked too many rights. While the conference was able to paper over these differences, mainly because the problem was a highly specialized one, it did not come up with a solution fully satisfactory to either interest.

III.

Factor analysis, like any other analytical tool in the growing repertoire of social scientists, cannot solve the substantive problems of those concerned with constructing policy. Factor analysis cannot foretell what a better or perfect international law of the future will or should be. But it

67

can provide an international lawyer with a better understanding of why past attempts at getting nations to agree have broken down. This may result, on the one hand, in providing him with the basic data necessary to make proposals to reconstruct the law that will be tactically successful and strategically wise. On the other hand, it may provide him with data that would indicate to him that the problem was insoluble and that no solution would be adopted in circumstances similar to those where other proposals failed.

This is not to say that without a technique like factor analysis the substantive specialist cannot by carefully reading the documents, for example, derive a tolerably accurate picture of the issues and alignments. But more precise techniques like factor analysis give the investigator more precise results. Factor analysis simply can give us a better profile of the issues that states perceive as similar and therefore vote upon in a consistent pattern. For example, it would have been easy to overlook the different coalitions which were formed on the two parts of the Canadian proposal on the territorial sea and contiguous zone without the aid of factor analysis. When voted upon separately, the six-mile territorial sea clause showed up in factor 1 (vote 27, loading .46) indicating another alignment. Thus, although Canada intended this combined proposal to solve one over-all problem, the delegates chose to deal with it as two separate and distinct issues, and two separate and distinct groups of nations formed.

Since factor analysis groups together the votes of states that vote a similar pattern, we have a better starting point for investigating the depth of a state's commitment. My own previously published comments, based on an analysis of the debates, pointed out that the European "conservatives" were very vocal about any modification of the law of the sea which would have eroded a basic commitment to the concept of the freedom of the seas.[15] But this could be explained, as it was by many Latin American, Asian, and Soviet-bloc detractors, as a mere smoke screen to cover European fears of losing real rights and privileges. But factor 4, where the Europeans consistently voted against compromise measures which would have stripped them of very few actual rights, belies this interpretation. The commitment of the Europeans to an ideal was deep and abiding.

Finally, because factor analysis is quantitative, it can tell us which issues and alignments were dominant, which were secondary. At the law of the sea conferences the basic alignment was East-West (even though many "West" states were not as consistently "West" as they might have been), since it showed up in factor 1—the factor with the highest eigen value—and factors 3 and 5. The North-South alignment was the most important secondary alignment.

Because the United States government may soon begin preliminary discussions on reopening some of the issues which the United Nations law of the sea conferences did not solve or solve satisfactorily, perhaps a prognosis of the chances for such an effort is in order, however unscientific.

Unless there are some unique new solutions that will not arouse old hostilities, or unless states have softened their stands within the last six years, the voting data does not foster optimism. While the East-West conflict may have to a large degree subsided, the territorial sea is still considered an important security problem by both U.S. and U.S.S.R. If this emphasis continues to dominate, it will affect a whole host of allied issues. On the North-South quarrel, the present data indicate that the struggle has gone beyond real interests into the realm of the symbolic. If the South states take fishing rights as synonymous with economic development, and the European states continue to see concessions as abandonment of an ideal theory, this conflict may remain insoluble. Finally, the failure of "splitting-the-difference" compromises (particularly U.S. proposals on the territorial sea and contiguous zone, and fishing) bodes ill for any new attempts to compromise.

* The consulting assistance of Richard M. Fenker, Jr., is acknowledged with gratitude. This research has been supported by the Department of Political Science and the President's Fund, Purdue University.

1. *The Study of International Relations* (New York: Appleton-Century-Crofts, 1955), p. 233.

2. For a detailed discussion of this point see my "The 'Satisfied' and 'Dissatisfied' States Negotiate International Law: A Case Study," *World Politics* XVIII:I (October, 1965), 32–39.

3. United Nations Conference on the Law of the Sea, *Official Records,* 7 vols. (A/CONF.13/37-A/CONF.13/43); Second United Nations Conference on the Law of the Sea, *Official Records,* (A/CONF.19/8).

4. For the application of factor analysis to UN voting see: H. R. Alker, Jr., *World Politics in the General Assembly* (New Haven: Yale University Press, 1965); H. R. Alker, Jr., "Dimensions of Conflict in the General Assembly," *American Political Science Review,* LVIII (1964), 642–57; H. R. Alker, Jr.,

"Supranationalism in the United Nations," Peace Research Society *Papers*, III (1965), 197–212; B. M. Russett, "Discovering Voting Groups in the United Nations," *American Political Science Review* (June, 1966). For a detailed exposition of factor analysis see: Harry Harmon, *Modern Factor Analysis* (Chicago: University of Chicago Press, 1960).

5. For a good definition of "Factor Score" in this context see: H. R. Alker, Jr., and B. M. Russett, *World Politics in the General Assembly*, pp. 33, 34, 38.

6. *Ibid.*, p. 36.

7. As, for example, in *Ibid.*, p. 27.

8. See Table 2, particularly Factor 1.

9. B. M. Russett, "Discovering Voting Groups in the United Nations."

10. The solid and dotted line boxes were drawn to assist the reader. These boxes are merely illustrative and serve to characterize the nations loading on the extremes of the factors.

11. Doc. A/CONF.13/C.3/L.79/Rev. 1.

12. The reason might be a fear of allowing Israel to fish near their shores or in any manner use the Gulf of Aqaba. The delegate from Lebanon, Mr. Fattal, was quite explicit on this point. Second United Nations Conference on the Law of the Sea, *Official Records*, p. 28.

13. H. R. Alker, Jr., "Supranationalism in the United Nations," p. 202.

14. The results of a further factor analysis using the Q-technique (with the nations as variables) on the same voting records showed even more clearly that there was a legal conservative group of nations operating at the conference. The group of nations voting similarly on the legal conservatism issues defined by our R-analysis formed a bloc in the Q-analysis. The conservatives in the Q-analysis were: Netherlands, Japan, Germany, France, Belgium, Italy, and Monaco. Q-analysis was particularly useful because it also identified the opposing group on the same issues, the "legal progressives." They were: Mexico, Venezuela, U.A.R., Chile, Indonesia, Saudi Arabia, Ecuador, India, and Tunisia.

15. "The 'Satisfied' and 'Dissatisfied' States Negotiate International Law . . .", p. 35.

Lewis M. Alexander

Chapter Five:

OFFSHORE CLAIMS OF THE WORLD

An idealized diagram of the pattern of national control in offshore waters would involve the delimitation of three zones: the high seas which are free to the use of all nations; a narrow territorial sea over which coastal states have sovereignty, subject to the right of innocent passage by foreign vessels; and internal waters, over which national sovereignty is absolute. But the diagram if it conforms with reality, should also portray two additional truths: first, that states are far from agreed as to the method for measuring the extent of the internal and territorial waters off their coasts; and second that many states have claims to control in the waters beyond territorial limits. This paper attempts to summarize the nature of claims in offshore waters throughout the world.

As a geographer I am concerned primarily with the extent of the territory involved in a nation's offshore claims, with the particular characteristics of the water areas which are claimed, and with relationships existing between the communities lying along the coast and the offshore waters over which a coastal state may seek control. One country, for example, may press its demands for a twelve-mile territorial sea, and yet possess only ten miles of seacoast, while another, holding to the three-mile breadth, may border on the ocean for thousands of miles. The sea areas involved in offshore claims can vary widely in importance. Some may include rich fishing grounds or be located at strategic straits, while other areas, for the present at least, are of little economic, military, or political significance. Finally, the nature of land/sea interaction may be of consequence in cases where coastal states seek special rights in their offshore waters on the grounds of peculiar economic interests. Such variations from place to place throughout the coastlands of the world have had a significant, though frequently underrated, place in the literature on the law of the sea.

There are in the world at present 135 independent countries. The exact number may vary according to one's definition of "independence'" but this figure will be taken to form the basis for subsequent statistics. Of the 135 national states, 28 are land-locked, while 107 border on the

TABLE 3

OFFSHORE CLAIMS OF THE WORLD
ARRANGED ACCORDING TO BREADTHS OF THE TERRITORIAL SEA

	Length of Coastline*	Fishing Limits (in Nautical Miles)	Other Limits
Three miles:			
Argentina	2,120	10	Continental shelf
Australia	15,091		
Belgium	34	12†	
Brazil	3,692	12	
Canada	11,129	12†	
Cuba	1,747		
Dahomey	65	12	
Denmark	686	12†	
Dominican Republic	325	15	
France	1,373	12†	
Gambia	38		
Ireland	663	12†	
Ivory Coast	274		
Jamaica	280		
Japan	4,842		
Jordan	5		
Kenya	247		
Liberia	290		
Malaysia	1,853		
Malta	50		
Morocco	863	12	
Muscat and Oman	1,005		
The Netherlands	198		
New Zealand	2,770	12	
Nicaragua	445	200	Continental shelf
Pakistan	750	12	
Poland	241		
South Vietnam	865	20 km.	
Taiwan	470		
United Kingdom	2,790	12†	
United States	11,650	12	
West Germany	308		
Four miles:			
Finland	735		
Norway	1,650	12	
Sweden	1,359	12†	

TABLE 3—*Continued*

	Length of Coastline*	Fishing Limits (in Nautical Miles)	Other Limits
Five miles:			
Cambodia	210	12	Continental shelf to 50 meters
Six miles:			
Cameroon	187		
Ceylon	650		Right to conservation zones to 100 miles offshore
Colombia	1,022	12	
Greece	1,645		
Haiti	584		
India	2,759	100	
Israel	124		
Italy	2,451	12†	
Mauritania	360	12	
Senegal	241		
Spain	1,494	12†	
Thailand	1,299	12	
Tunisia	555	12	To 50 meters isobath
Turkey	1,921	12	
Union of South Africa	1,430	12	
Uruguay	305	12	
Twelve kilometers:			
Honduras	374		
Nine miles:			
Mexico	4,848		
Ten miles:			
Albania	155	12	
Yugoslavia	426		
Twelve miles:			
Algeria	596		
Bulgaria	134		
China (the mainland)	3,492		
Cyprus	290		
Ecuador	458	200	
Ethiopia	546		
Ghana	285		Conservation zone out to 100 miles
Guatemala	178		
Indonesia	19,889		
Iran	990		

73

TABLE 3—*Continued*

	Length of Coastline*	Fishing Limits (in Nautical Miles)	Other Limits
Iraq	10		
Libya	910		
Malagasy Republic	2,155		
North Korea	578		
North Vietnam	382		
Panama	979		Continental shelf
Rumania	113		
Saudi Arabia	1,316		
Sierra Leone	219		
Soviet Union	23,098		
Sudan	387		
Syria	82		Plus a 6-mile "supervision" zone
Tanzania	669		
Togo	26		
United Arab Republic	1,307		
Venezuela	1,081		

Fifty kilometers:

Chile	2,882	200	

One hundred thirty miles:

Guinea	190		

Two hundred miles:

El Salvador	164		

No specified territorial limits:

Costa Rica	446	200	
Iceland	1,080	12	
Lebanon	105	6	
Maldive Islands	251	6	
Peru	1,258	200	
Portugal	398	12†	
South Korea	712	20–200	Continental shelf

No information available:

Burma	1,230	
Congo (Brazzaville)	84	
Congo (Leopoldville)	22	
East Germany	191	
Gabon	399	
Guyana	232	
Kuwait	115	
Monaco	3	

74

TABLE 3—*Continued*

	Length of Coastline*	Fishing Limits (in Nautical Miles)	Other Limits
Nigeria	415		
The Philippines	6,997		
Singapore	28		
Somali Republic	1,596		
Trinidad and Tobago	254		
Western Samoa	241		
Yemen	244		

Landlocked countries:

Afganistan
Andorra
Austria
Bhutan
Bolivia
Botswana
Burundi
Central African Republic
Chad
Czechoslovakia
Hungary
Laos
Lesotho
Liechtenstein
Luxembourg
Malawi
Mali
Mongolia
Nepal
Niger
Paraguay
Rwanda
San Marino
Switzerland
Uganda
Upper Volta
Vatican City
Zambia

* In nautical miles. Statistics are taken from *Sovereignty of the Sea*, Office of the Geographer, U.S. Department of State, Bulletin No. 3, April, 1965.
† Historic rights provided for.

sea. Although only the latter group have offshore areas to which they can claim control, the land-locked countries may also be involved in such claims; first, because they too have interests in the use of sea and, second, because they may be represented at international law of the sea conferences. A dozen land-locked countries, for example, had delegations

75

at the 1958 Geneva Conference and were given the opportunity to discuss and vote on the breadth of the territorial sea and other aspects of offshore control.

Each of the independent countries of the world is, in a sense, unique—in terms of its historical development, its political and legal systems, and its commitment to and dependence on the resources of the sea. If a cartographer were able to portray such national diversities graphically, he would have a highly complex map of the world's land areas. To this map he could then add the diversities of the marine environment, such as length and configuration of the coast, breadths of the continental shelf, and the distribution of living and non-living resources of the sea. It is against such a background of diversities that the problems of offshore claims must be considered.

The two Geneva conferences attempted to bring order out of chaos, and while recognizing geographic, historic, and other differences throughout the world, to provide uniform procedures governing national rights in, and use of, the marine environment. The high degree of success achieved by the first conference has been well publicized. But in the years since 1958 national claims have continued to encroach on the high seas. As the areal extent of these claims becomes ever greater, the extent of the free seas of the world diminishes. More important, perhaps, the marginal seas, to which these claims are advanced, are often of greater economic or strategic value than are areas of commensurate size in mid-ocean. For the sake of discussion we shall divide offshore claims into two types—those involving territorial waters and those concerned with extraterritorial rights.

The extent of a country's territorial sea depends both on the breadth which is claimed and the position of the baselines from which the breadth is measured. Turning to the latter problem first, we may note that the 1958 Convention on the Territorial Sea makes rather complete provisions for the delimitation of "normal" baselines, following the tidelines, but that complications arise in the use of straight baselines. Article 4 of the convention lays down certain guidelines, both for determining when the straight baseline regime may be adopted and for delimiting individual baselines, but in both cases the language is imprecise. How, for example, can one determine the cut-off point at which islands along a coast do not constitute a "fringe" or when economic interests peculiar to a coastal region do not justify liberal baseline delimitations? Such imprecision may give rise to sweeping claims to straight baselines along rugged coasts or coasts fringed with islands, with little regard paid to whether or not the sea areas lying within the lines are sufficiently closely linked to the land domain to be subject to the regime of internal waters. Certain it is that the straight baseline regime, adopted originally for a peculiar situation in northwest Europe, may lead in time to the closing off of extensive areas of the marginal sea as internal waters.

The Geneva conventions made no mention of straight baselines in archipelagoes, but here again claims have been made to extensive inter-island water areas as being internal in nature. By analogy perhaps the sea areas enclosed by straight baselines in archipelagoes should be so linked to the land domain as to be subject to the regime of internal waters, but such a requirement has received little legal attention. And the Geneva conventions themselves are silent as to what the actual criteria are for justifying an internal waters regime. Claims to straight baselines in archipelagoes may be held as contrary to international law, and other states need not recognize them. But foreign ships operating within what a coastal state maintains are its own waters run the risk of arrest, fines, and confiscation of catch or gear. How often in the present world community can conditions be permitted to exist in which warships of a protesting country stand guard over the ships of their nations which are operating in disputed inter-island waters? A point worth noting is that most of the colonial territories on the mainland of the continents have become independent, and now it is the island territories which will be achieving self-rule. In many cases island groups are administered as one political unit and, when attaining independence, will continue as unified countries. But some of these island groups are spread across thousands of square miles of ocean. Will they, too, demand that their inter-island waters be treated as internal?

Straight baselines may also be used to close off historic bays. Again the Geneva conventions are silent on the bases of claims to historic waters, but such claims exist and seem likely to grow in number. An interesting point here concerns the newer states of the world whose former mother countries never considered their colonies' coastal indentations as being uniquely a part of the national territory. After how many years of independence may such a former colony be in a position legitimately to advance its claims to certain offshore waters as belonging to it historically?

Where, specifically, are the sea areas of the world which are claimed as internal, and are closed off by straight baselines from territorial waters? I know of no single map or series of maps yet compiled which show the global extent of internal waters, although I feel that such maps would be highly meaningful to law-of-the-sea studies. The maps probably should show two categories: those waters which would be recognized as internal, according to the Geneva conventions, and those "gray" areas where unilateral claims have been made which do not conform to the Geneva articles.

From baselines and internal waters we turn to the breadth of the territorial sea. In 1950, Dr. Boggs, then Geographer to the Department of State, compiled a list covering sixty-one independent countries, which showed the breadths claimed for their territorial sea. Of these sixty-one countries, forty claimed three miles, three claimed twelve miles, and the remaining eighteen claimed between three and twelve miles. A list, compiled by this author, covered eighty-five coastal states. Of these, thirty-two claimed three miles, twenty-six claimed twelve, and twenty-four had territorial breadths between three and twelve miles, sixteen of the breadths being fixed at six miles. In addition, there was one claim each of 50 kilometers, 130 miles and 200 miles. No data was available for the territorial claims of the remaining twenty-two coastal countries of the world.

Let us look more closely at the changes which have taken place in territorial claims since 1950. The number of three-mile countries declined from forty to thirty-two, although it is interesting to note that many of the great maritime powers, such as Britain, France, the Netherlands, Japan, and the United States have continued to adhere to the three mile principle. Thirteen of the three mile countries in 1950 have now gone to greater breadths, ranging from six to 200 miles.

The growth of the twelve mile bloc from three in 1950 to twenty-six in 1966 has been occasioned in part by the rise of newly independent states, many of which were the former colonies of the traditional three mile countries. Since the end of World War II, some sixty-two new states have come into existence, forty-eight of which border on the sea. A dozen of these new states now claim twelve miles as their territorial limits although another dozen of the new ones opted after independence for retention of the three mile breadth. One can hardly speak of a head-long "rush" to the twelve mile limit, particularly after the demise of the 1960 Geneva Conference, if even today only one-quarter of the coastal states of the world have claims to that breadth.

Two related questions are: first, how long are the coastlines of the countries which claim three miles, twelve miles, or some other distance; and, second, do some of these claims place important straits or channels entirely within the regime of territorial waters? Figures for coastline lengths range from over 23,000 miles for the Soviet Union to three for Monaco and five for Jordan. The accompanying table gives figures for the lengths of coastline for the coastal countries of the world, and from this one may estimate the amount of high seas areas which would be involved, for example, in a country's extension of its territorial limits from six to twelve miles. But such computations would not take into account whether or not rich fishing grounds are involved in this extension, or whether the move would place an important strait entirely within territorial waters. It is less than twenty-four miles, for example, across the entrances to the Persian Gulf, the Red Sea, and the Baltic Sea, and between Hainan Island and Mainland China. Again, the most meaningful way to relate territorial claims to the narrow seas would be by a series of maps showing the actual location of territorial waters claimed throughout the world.

Beyond territorial limits are the various special use zones. We pass over the contiguous zone, provided for in the Geneva conventions, as well as the problem of national rights to the resources of the sea bed and subsoil of an adjacent continental shelf. The most important extra-territorial claims are those involving fisheries control.

There are two separate aspects of an extraterritorial fishing zone to be considered; the geographic extent of the zone, and the type of control which is claimed for it. Some countries have zones which are delimited from the same baseline as the territorial sea, and extend three, six, nine or more miles seaward of the territorial limits. For other countries, the fisheries zones are not only greater in breadth than the territorial sea, but are measured from different baselines—generally straight baselines which themselves may be considerably seaward of the low water line from which the territorial zone was measured. Since the Geneva articles made no provisions for extraterritorial fishing zones (with one exception, to be noted later), countries are not bound by any set procedures in delimiting these zones.

A variation in delimiting fisheries zones is the designation of certain depths as the outer limit: as, for example the 50-, 100-, or 200-meter isobaths. Some countries refer merely to the "continental shelf" as marking the zone over which their rights extend. Presumably such references imply that the 200-meter isobath marks the outer edge of the shelf. There is a possible distinction here between the continental shelf as viewed by the fishermen, and the shelf as it appears to lawyers or mining engineers. The Geneva definition of the shelf is that it extends to a depth of 200 meters, or beyond that limit to where the depth of the superjacent waters admits of the exploitation of the natural resources of the said areas. As the outer limits of this "legally-defined" shelf move into deeper and deeper waters would the fishermen expect their shelf to expand accordingly, or might governments eventually find themselves talking about *two* continental shelves?

On our maps of internal and territorial waters of the world we should now add extraterritorial fisheries zones, taking note to distinguish, first, whether the restrictions in these zones apply to all countries or only to certain ones; and, second, what the particular restrictions on freedom to fish are. Certain countries may agree among themselves to adopt restrictions on their fishing effort within a particular offshore area, but such restraints are not binding on non-signatory powers. It seems probable, in years to come, that more and more bilateral and multilateral agreements will be made concerning fishing activities and the problem of compliance by non-signatory states may become an extremely serious one.

There are various types of control a coastal state may seek to exercise in an extraterritorial fisheries zone. The most drastic claim is to exclusive fishing rights, a claim which may be tempered by the recognition of the historic rights of certain other countries to exploit the fisheries of the zone. Thirty countries of the world, out of eighty-five with specific territorial breadths, have extraterritorial exclusive fisheries zones, with or without the recognition of historic rights. Of these, twenty-four countries, with territorial breadths ranging from three to ten miles, claim exclusive fishing rights out to twelve miles. Two other countries, with no clearly defined territorial limits, also claim exclusive fishing rights out to twelve miles. If we add to these the twenty-six countries with twelve mile territorial belts, we find that foreign fishermen are generally forbidden to come within twelve miles of the coasts of fifty-two countries, or nearly half the coastal states of the world, either because of territorial or exclusive fisheries limits. In addition, foreign fishermen must stay more than twelve miles from the coasts of eleven other nations.

A coastal state may not only recognize certain countries' historic rights, but go even further and permit entry into the fisheries of the extraterritorial zone by all nations, subject to the licensing regulations of the coastal state. By issuing licenses this state can still control entry by foreigners into its offshore fisheries and thereby maintain what it feels to be a rational management program. But there may be genuine disagreement among governments as to what constitutes a "rational" management program for those particular offshore waters. From this, two questions arise: for what purposes is the management program intended and on which party or parties rests the burden of proof of the need for and efficacy of the program?

Limiting foreign entry into offshore fisheries may be done primarily to protect the economic interests of the coastal state's fishermen; it may also be done for biological reasons, that is, in an effort to achieve maximum sustainable yield. In either case the restrictions which are placed on the operation of foreign vessels have generally not, up to this time, applied equally to the operations of the coastal state's nationals. Later on in this conference we shall hear more concerning the need for rationalizing the ocean fisheries of the world through large-scale management programs. Such programs would, for the most part, exist without regard for the fixed boundaries marking the outer limits of a coastal state's fisheries zone. Our purpose in this paper is not to conjecture about future management programs but to describe what exists in practice. The North Pacific fisheries treaties do indeed place restrictions on the freedom to fish certain species throughout a wide expanse of ocean (although even here certain territorial boundaries still exist) but the more common form of fisheries protection involves restraints on *all* fishing within a specified geographic area.

The least drastic of the extraterritorial fisheries claims is contained in the Geneva Convention on Fishing and Conservation of the Living Resources of the High Seas, whereby a coastal state has the right to unilaterally adopt conservation measures in the waters beyond its territorial limits. Such measures must not discriminate against foreign fishermen, but must be adhered to by foreigners, under a set of carefully phrased conditions which, among other things, permit the foreigners to appeal to an international body. This represents a far more rational approach to the world fisheries problem than are unilateral proclamations of exclusive (and often ineffective) fisheries zones, although the latter situation appears to be on the increase rather than decline.

There are, of course, examples of other types of extraterritorial claims, such as those of neutrality zones extending several hundred miles out from the coast, or the reserving of certain ocean areas for a

81

specific length of time for military or scientific testing. Our point here is not to catalogue all the unusual types of claims, but rather to ask, in the light of the various seaward expansions of national control which have been cited in this paper, whether or not our original diagram, showing the high seas, a narrow territorial belt, and the internal waters, is still a valid one?

As an idealized model, I believe that it still has validity. It conforms closely to the provisions of the 1958 Geneva Convention, except that it should also note the contiguous zone and the fisheries conservation zone, noted above, which lie beyond the territorial limits. But these two zones are not what the political turmoil is about.

There may be situations in which the idealized diagram might justifiably be modified. For instance, the zones of a particular country's sovereignty might be enlarged due to peculiar geographic or historical conditions or because of biological or economic need a coastal state's special rights to fisheries control beyond territorial limits might be extended. But such situations should be the rare exception, rather than the rule, and the burden of proof of the need for such rights should rest with the nation which seeks them not with the world community. We must avoid such rigid adherence to the "free seas" concept that in the light of changing conditions the law of the sea, as it now stands, becomes hopelessly outmoded. Every year sees the creation of new independent states, new technological advances in the use of the sea, new additions to the world's population, and new demands by segments of that population for a better way of life. As a political reality the law of the sea cannot remain static; but we must also avoid the haphazard partitioning of the oceans into a mosaic of national zones of control.

We hear, for example, the pleas of certain countries for special rights in their offshore waters on the basis of "overwhelming dependence" or "peculiar economic interests." Much attention has been paid to unique cases of land/sea interaction, or "marine orientation" as the process is coming to be called, in the coastlands of northwestern Europe. But if demands in other parts of the world grow for the recognition of special rights on the basis of unusual dependence on, or commitment to, the resources of the offshore waters, it seems clear that more precise guidelines will have to be worked out for determining what constitutes an unusually strong case of marine orientation. We may, of course, claim that under no conditions should such special rights be allowed, but with the growing complexities of the world they will certainly be proclaimed. Might we be helping to prevent anarchy if we tried to establish certain conditions under which such claims to special rights might at least be considered by the world community?

One of the problems arising for students of the law of the sea is to gain a perspective of the world as it is—of the various oceans and seas, each with its own unique characteristic, of the great variety of countries bordering on these oceans and seas, and of the pattern of national claims to offshore control around the globe. Maps will help, but maps alone cannot provide perspective. If one adopts a world view of the law of the sea, interesting concepts may emerge. For example, it soon becomes apparent that most of the historic fishing countries and fishing grounds lie north of the Tropic of Cancer, that is 23½° north latitude. Yet if the traditional grounds of the Northern Hemisphere are in danger of becoming overutilized, at least in terms of currently desirable species, there are productive grounds in the Southern Hemisphere that have considerable opportunities for exploitation. And for the past several years the leading fishing nation of the world has been a South American one. The sea may represent the world's last frontier, but frontiers also exist within the sea itself.

Another concept involves marine regions, such as the Northwest Atlantic, or the Caribbean/Gulf of Mexico area. Within such marine regions, countries may have certain interests in common in the use of the sea, and multilateral agreements may be worked out among the governments interested in the region. The idea of regionality is not new, but I would suggest within these regions that one try looking at the land areas from the sea; that is, consider what exploitable resources there are available there, what countries are engaged in the free use of the region's resources. Looking landward from the sea has proved highly effective in several geographic studies relating to law of the sea matters.

A third approach, for want of a better term, might be called a "geopolitical" one, emphasizing the dynamic nature of the various countries and groups of countries which border on the sea. What economic, military, or other problems do these countries face which might in some way affect their use of the sea? Are multinational blocs likely to form in order to seek special regimes for certain water areas? What colonial territories are scheduled for independence? Remember that at a future

83

law of the sea conference, it is theoretically possible that 130 or more delegations may be in attendance. How might these delegations line up in voting blocs?

"The pursuit of the global view is the geographer's intellectual adventure," one of my colleagues once wrote, but the need for such a perspective is not limited to geographers. The encroachment of national claims out into the high seas concerns all of us; only by perceiving the marine environment as an interacting world-wide phenomenon can we appreciate the impact any single claim or group of claims is likely to provide.

Discussion of Herrington, Neblett, Friedheim, and Alexander

1. Despite the failure of the abstention principle to be adopted at the 1958 Geneva Conference, it continues to be the policy of the United States to recognize this principle, and a provision to this effect was attached to the treaty of ratification of the Geneva conventions.

2. The means by which some of the Latin American states effectively control foreign fishing in their extraterritorial waters is by harassing certain fishing vessels, and the resultant economic loss to the fishing fleet acts as a deterrent to other vessels.

3. *Are countries such as Ecuador, Peru, and Chile violating international law by protecting what they feel to be their special interests in extraterritorial waters—interests which they feel are necessary for their economic life?* The criteria for their actions, some speakers held, are not based on scientific evidence, but are an attempt to extend sovereignty over these waters. Jurisdiction is a part of sovereignty. What constitutes conservation is not the desire of one state to preserve something they have no scientific data on, but to act after the scientific data have been assembled—that is, after examination of the species has been completed, and there is proof that the species is being overfished.

Another view, however, was that the Declaration of Santiago cannot be interpreted as claiming sovereignty out to 200 miles, but had as its sole object the conservation of the fisheries resources for the benefit of the coastal countries. The theory of the freedom of the seas may be made to work for the advantage of countries with large navies, merchant marines, and fishing fleets.

4. Conservation, as presently defined, may be based on the principle of maximum sustainable yield, but in specific cases, such as that of the haddock fisheries on Georges Bank where there is evidence that more than the maximum sustainable yield was harvested during the past year,

what specific steps will be taken by the federal government in the direction of conservation?

5. *With respect to Professor Friedheim's paper, is there not a danger here of becoming too precise in setting down how countries behave, and are going to behave with regard to international law?* Not necessarily. The social sciences must project on the basis of the data and techniques which they have available. Obviously, if the data or techniques used are insufficient for the purpose, then unwarranted conclusions may be reached. Since men are fairly consistent in their thoughts and actions, one can have some idea, although not with mathematical precision, how they are likely to act in the future.

Why cannot a more precise method of evaluating voting patterns at a future international conference be obtained through a systematic analysis of what the individual country's interests are as regards security, the cold war, etc.? Because this system, even before you start your evaluations, gives you a range of states to look to as possible allies, possible opponents, possible fence-sitters. The system may also point up votes that you did not see as related to, or having a similar pattern to, some voting arrangement you are already intuitively aware of.

6. The United States and the north European countries sent lawyers and fisheries specialists to the Geneva conferences, while most of the other countries sent persons with General Assembly experience, who were specialists in negotiation. The two groups talked at, rather than to, each other. Within the former group, particularly, there tends to be something of a "bifocal" type of approach—considering matters both from the viewpoint of long-range ideals and of the immediate demands of national interest. But most delegates to international conferences, it was pointed out, support first and foremost the national interest.

7. Since many persons, particularly from the developing countries, fear for the future in terms of population explosion, or of the historic rights and technological developments of the more technically-advanced countries, international law does not hold the same place in their social values as it does for us. They have more concern for short-range problems. How then can reciprocity be made meaningful to them? Possibly by tying in some form of tangible benefits to their support of concepts such as freedom of the seas, even though such actions might be looked upon by some as a form of coercion.

Chapter Six:

FISHERY RESOURCES IN OFFSHORE WATERS

Two terms in the title given me to discuss are vague, and their vagueness illustrates the difficulty in dealing with the law of the sea and obtaining agreement on its parts. They are "Fishery Resources" and "Offshore Waters." It is necessary to define what I mean by each.

I. *Fishery Resources*

By fishery resource, I mean any living resource of the ocean capable of being harvested practically by man and used by him for food or other purposes.

In 1964, 45 million metric tons of such resources plus 73,194 whales were harvested by man from the world ocean. In 1954 this harvest had been 23.6 million tons plus 60,983 whales. Thus the marine harvest had approximately doubled in ten years. But in the same period, ocean research had indicated that of the kinds of living resources of the sea that some groups of men were harvesting, or of kinds as large and amenable to harvest and use as those, the ocean was actually producing about 2 billion tons per year. Thus in 1954 about 2 per cent of this potential was taken, and in 1964 about 4 per cent. The rest that the ocean was producing died and decayed back to the web of life in the ocean unused by man. As a matter of fact, the actual harvest, for which we have reasonably good records, is not as large as the probable error for the rather crude, and conservative, estimate of 2 billion tons per year of potential production from the ocean.

The point in mentioning this is to note that at present we are studying what to do about governing the harvest of the living resources of the sea on the basis of rather minimal knowledge of, and experience with, the kinds of resources available for harvesting, their distribution in time and space, their life histories and behavioral characteristics, their resiliency to fishing pressure, and the groups of people likely to need or desire to harvest and use them. This renders policy decisions on these matters at this time risky, and I, for one, am quite conservative about making changes in the present public order of the ocean that would affect the harvesting until we have more knowledge and experience of these matters.

II. *Offshore Waters*

By Offshore Waters, I mean the ocean waters in which these resources are found, or in which they migrate or move from, through, and to. Man, for his convenience, has split this water into five juridical categories: inland waters, territorial sea, contiguous zone, fishery jurisdiction zone, and high seas. The living resources, however, move through the whole ocean at will, suiting the convenience of their natural habits instead of that of man.

The salmons come down out of the streams and mix thoroughly in the ocean, those from Asiatic streams coming over close to the American continent and those from American streams moving over toward the Asiatic coast; those from New England and Scotland mix in the sea off Greenland. Albacore are born somewhere in the western central Pacific, migrate over to the California coast where they are fished by Americans who have tagged them. We have found that such tagged fish move to the Asiatic coast the next year, or the year after. They are fished there by Japanese, who catch some of those tagged off California. Skipjack tuna tagged off Mexico are caught off Hawaii; bluefin tuna tagged in the Bahamas are caught in the North Sea; those tagged in the North Sea are caught in the Mediterranean. The cod of the Arctic feed off Russia and spawn off Norway. Sable fish are tagged in Puget Sound and returned from Bering Sea. Etc., etc.

The point in mentioning this is that there is no line that can be drawn on the ocean that separates living marine resources into convenient spatial categories, either as to species or as to groups of species. The cyclic pulsing of warming and cooling of the eastern Pacific, for instance, which occurs at irregular intervals of seven to ten or eleven years, shifts whole ocean communities north and south by long distances, or draws them toward the equator.

The more we tag fishes and follow their migrations, and the more we study the climate of the upper mixed layer of the ocean, the more kinds of fish we find making long and complex migrations, and the more we find out about shifting boundaries between not only surface, but subsurface currents, in an irregularly cyclical fashion ranging in time intervals from diurnal to some hundreds of years.

It is not usually the case that fish spawn where they feed. They may only move out a few miles and deeper, or they may move some hundreds of miles, or they may move some thousands of miles for this purpose, as do salmons, tunas, freshwater eels, cods, sardines, hakes, fur seals, gray whales, sperm whales, etc.

III. *The Origins of Fishery Resources*

Increasing knowledge of the ocean and its processes has brought us to expect heaviest concentrations of fishable resources near where upwelling of subsurface ocean water is greatest. The nutrient rich water from currents which have been below the photic layer (and sometimes not so very deep or for so very long) fertilizes the surface waters anew, and where the nutrients come close enough to the surface to reach where the light of the sun has penetrated, there flourish the plants of the ocean —the phytoplankton. Upon the phytoplankton graze the animals of the sea, and upon them feed the carnivores. Upon the small carnivores feed the large carnivores, and so on up to the enormous sperm whale.

These areas of extraordinary production of this primary food are the centers out from which radiate the great volume fisheries. Adjacent to the areas of heaviest primary production are the greatest available volumes of usable resources. The western sides of continents and large land masses are areas where such prolific abundance of food production are typically found. The Humboldt Current, Peru Current, California Current, Benquela Current, Canary Current, West India and West Australia are examples.

But the mixing areas in the higher latitudes on the eastern sides of continents, where the cold currents from high latitudes brush against warm currents coming from the tropics with resultant turbulence and vertical circulation, are also areas of high productivity and heavy fish production. Examples are provided by the meeting of the Oyashio and Kuroshio in the Japanese island area, that of the Labrador Current and

89

the Gulf Stream over the Grand Banks, the Patagonian Current and the Brazilian Current off southern Brazil, Uruguay, and Argentina.

As the research ships and fishing vessels have moved offshore, areas of mixing of this sort have been found stretching across whole oceans, with consequent increasing food and fish production. Examples are found in the equatorial current systems of the Pacific, Atlantic, and Indian oceans, the convergence zone that completely surrounds Antarctica, the area south of the Aleutian Islands, and so forth.

Additionally, areas of eddies of a rather persistent nature are found well offshore where subsurface waters dome up into the photic layer and become substantial sources of productivity without breaking to the surface. Examples are provided by the Costa Rica Dome and the Angola Dome.

Where island groups or ocean ridges interfere with the broad and often infertile surface currents of the open ocean, some turbulence and vertical circulation occur. Examples are provided by the numerous arcs of islands in the central Pacific, the Windward islands of the Antilles, the Seychelles, the Laccadives and Maldives, the Andamans, and the great archipelago that is Indonesia. Downstream from these island groups is increased production of phytoplankton, and a little farther are concentrations of zooplankton and larger carnivores that are supported by it.

The continental shelves have been typically where great fisheries have developed. Not only do they occur where many of the above upwelling situations occur, but by trapping the nutrients up in, or near, the photic layer they contribute much themselves to the effective utilization of the enormous quantities of plant nutrients in the reservoir of the deeper ocean. They also participate in the whole process of turbulence, vertical circulation, etc., in ways that are not very well understood as yet. For instance, the edge of the continental shelf appears to be heavier than usual fish producers in many areas of the world. The processes that govern this are not at all well understood. There is some thought that their interference with the enormous internal waves typical of those areas is a factor as that results in turbulence which reaches close to the surface.

As fishing techniques have developed, more has been found out about the considerable fertility of the continental slope in many areas of the world ocean, and fisheries at depths of 200 to 300 fathoms are becoming less uncommon. Experimental fishing on the bottom in the eastern Bering Sea to depths of 500 to 600 fathoms have recently been initiated by the Russians with a good deal of promise.

The point in mentioning all of this is that the rapidly expanding knowledge and understanding of the ocean, its resources, the dynamic nature of each, and the relationships among them, are all changing our thinking about these things so rapidly that it is a little difficult to assimilate the new understanding into the old forms of human thought and action in this field.

The ocean is beginning to appear to be a welter of richly productive valleys, broad, open, reasonable productive plains, great stretches of almost sterile "deserts," oasis of high production in otherwise sterile areas, and similar situations. These terms taken from our land experience do not fit our beginning ocean experience well at all, because productivity in the ocean is three-dimensional, rather than two-dimensional as on the land. The areas of heavy productivity are not necessarily related to land masses. Where they are, they may be a few miles broad, or they may be several hundred miles wide.

The upshot of all of this is that the productivity structure of the ocean does not at all fit well the juridical structure we have constructed for the governance of the harvest of marine resources because the juridical structure to date has really risen from our land experience and from needs arising therefrom, not from ocean experience or needs.

IV. *The Fisheries*

Until this very generation man has gone about the harvest of the ocean by empiric means. Modern ocean science began only 100 years ago with the "Challenger" expedition. The International Council for the Exploration of the Sea is less than seventy years old. The fisheries work of FAO began only in 1945. The great growth in ocean knowledge is a thing of the past twenty years, and perhaps more has been found out about the ocean and its resources in the past ten years than in the previous history of man.

This new knowledge has begun to revolutionize the ocean fisheries since about 1950 and its force upon them in the past five years has been immense. This continues to go on and will so continue. Since we are still using only a few per cent of the ocean's productivity, and that has

91

been mostly in northern temperate waters until quite recently, we cannot estimate with any precision how the world ocean fisheries will develop. Our experience is too short and small. It can be said that modern technology is permitting fishermen increasingly to go where the fish are, wherever that may be, and the fishermen have become as migratory as the fish.

The Japanese initiated the use of this new knowledge rather crudely, but effectively, in the expansion of their long-line tuna fisheries on a fully world-wide basis since 1952. They built valuable fisheries of this kind everywhere there were tuna, and in many places where the nearest dry land was 1,000 miles away. They have continued to advance into other productive resource habitats also by other fishing means and by continually more sophisticated application of ocean science and modern technology to world-wide fishery development problems.

In the past ten years, the Russians have surged forward mightily with the most sophisticated and massive application of modern science and technology to ocean fishing that has yet been developed. They are seeking out and utilizing one by one these particularly fertile ocean areas on a world-wide basis. By different means the Poles, Rumanians, English, Norwegians, Germans, French, Spanish, Italians, Greeks, Americans, Canadians, Koreans, and Taiwanese and others are intensifying and expanding their long-range fishing capabilities.

From the volume standpoint, the greatest relative expansion of fishing effort has been by the developing countries coastal to the tropical and subtropical ocean. The prime example of this has been Peru, which came from being almost a non-fishing country in 1954 to the greatest fish producing country in the world in 1964, when it produced by volume about 20 per cent of the total ocean production. This general process is going on elsewhere in the developing world, appears to be accelerating, and the likelihood is that it will continue to do so under the increasing assistance from the United Nations family of specialized agencies and bilateral aid programs.

As these developing countries develop coastal fisheries, they trend almost at once into becoming longer and longer range fishermen as well, fishing off the coasts of other countries as a part of their necessary fishery economies just about as naturally and necessarily as the fish migrate for biological necessity. Examples are provided by Mexico, Panama, Ecuador, Peru, Chile, Guayana, Cuba, Senegal, Ivory Coast, Ghana, Pakistan, and Thailand.

92

V. *The Nature of Fisheries Juridical Problems*

The strong development of long-range fishing simultaneously with an even stronger development of short range fishing by riparian nations is going to continue for the reason that the whole world is short of animal protein to fill its needs or desires, and the ocean is full of underutilized resources of animal protein that are enormous in extent and susceptible of relatively cheap harvesting. It is obvious that the best general interest of man will be served by a set of conditions that will permit the greatest possible use of these needed resources. It is equally obvious that this strong and almost universal striving to develop the ocean fisheries will cause great strife among the nations. Conflict over ocean fisheries has been the cause of war among sovereigns for almost all of modern history; major conflicts just short of war have occurred in our generation; and there is scarcely a week goes by that armed force is not used, or threatened to be used, in fishery conflicts somewhere in the world. It can be confidently expected that these problems will increase in intensity, number, and variety before they become less.

The prime source of conflict is that the living resources of the high seas are the common property of all nations under present international law. Fish of the high seas become the property of him who first reduces them to his possession. Since this law was made by man it can be changed by him. The difficulty is that laws of nature which cannot be changed by him interfere with reaching a rational solution to these problems.

The chiefest of these are the laws of population dynamics. Every population of living things, including those of man, is governed by the same natural rules. The number and volume of living things in a particular population are governed by the dynamic relations among the number of new entrants into the population from each succeeding generation and their rates of growth, on the one hand, balanced off against the rate of mortality in the population, on the other hand.

This applies to fisheries in this manner: When a fishery is instituted on the population this is simply an increase in the rate of mortality as far as the population is concerned. Either the rate of growth or the rate of entry from new generations into the population must increase or the level of the population decreases.

In practice the rate of growth is not affected in a substantial manner by the introduction of a higher mortality (fishery). Neither does the

93

survival rate increase by enough to counteract the newly increased mortality rate. Always upon the inception of a fishery the total number and weight of fish in the population of fish decrease.

But the population does have natural resiliency provided by nature to deal successfully with the wide variability in natural mortality induced by fluctuation in natural conditions. The total number of the fish in the population, their total weight, their average size, and their average age decrease as the production of the fishery increases. This process continues until a certain point beyond which all of these things continue except the yield of the fishery, which beyond this point begins, also, to decrease no matter how much effort is put into the fishery. This is called the point of maximum sustainable catch. It is the point at which the resource is yielding the maximum amount of food or other product useful to man on a sustainable basis.

The existence of this immutable law of nature complicates man's governance of the harvest of marine living resources horribly. If a man, or a group of men, owned a particular resource he would manage its harvest ordinarily in such a manner that the economic yield from the resource would be maximized. The difficulty is that the resources are not so owned and that the economic systems of various of the multiple owners of these resources are so different that there is no common level of population strength in the resource which will yield equal economic yields to all of the sovereign owners. Thus maximum economic yield cannot be successfully used as the standard for managing international fisheries, and all major fisheries are international in character.

The nations, realizing this after extensive debate in the course of the 1958 Law of the Sea Conference, retired for agreement to the standard governed by nature—the point of maximum sustainable yield. It was agreed that the harvest of the commonly owned resources of the high seas would be governed in such a manner as would render possible the optimum sustainable yield from such resources so as to secure the maximum supply of food and other marine products. This is the definition of conservation in the 1958 "Convention on Fishing and the Conservation of the Living Resources of the High Seas," to which the United States is a party, and which is now in force. The convention further states that all nations have the duty to adopt, or to co-operate with other nations in adopting, such measures for their respective nationals as may be necessary for the conservation of the living resources of the high seas.

This does not at all solve the problems of conflict over the fisheries. It merely provides a framework in which the natural laws can be made amenable to this objective. But the nations, and their nationals, still have the problem of dividing the benefits that flow from such conservation activities. There is also the deeper-seated desire to block other nationals from the harvest of particular resources either to gain trade advantage, secure tax revenue, build local industry, or to satisfy general perverseness and cupidity. The fish so far have defeated these objectives by their variety of occurrence and migration as briefly hinted at above.

The nations agreed that certain waters of a coastal country, the internal waters, are the sovereign territory of the country in which the nationals of other nations have no right to fish without the consent of the sovereign. They have also agreed, for quite other purposes, that each coastal country has a band of territorial sea outside internal waters in which the coastal state also has unique jurisdiction over fishing and substantially everything else but the innocent passage by the vessels of other nations. But they have not agreed on what the breadth of the territorial sea is, other than it needs to be reasonably narrow and thus reasonably uniform. There is agreement by the vast majority of nations that the breadth of the territorial sea is between three and twelve marine miles and does not extend to a greater distance than that. This leaves most of the ocean as high seas, and the common property of all nations. This is nearly 70 per cent of the earth's surface.

It is also agreed that the coastal nation has special interest in the living resources of the high seas adjacent to its respective territorial sea and these interests are secured in carefully specified rights. This does not, however, give the coastal nation any right to adopt measures for the conservation of those resources which are, in form or fact, discriminatory against foreign fishermen engaging in the fishery for such resources.

Most living resources supporting major fisheries do not stay within a zone twelve miles broad from land, and practically none stay within three miles of land. Many important ones, such as salmon, freshwater eels, river herring, shad, shrimp, not only move farther than that offshore, but also penetrate beyond the territorial sea into the inland waters and are dependent in their life histories upon doing so.

The salmon are particularly annoying in this respect because they ascend rivers perhaps 1,000 miles from the sea to spawn, and then when the young come back to the sea they not only undertake migrations several thousand miles from the river mouth, but are dependent for life on being able to do so, and are readily captured by a commercial fishery in these long migrations away from the home streams (to which they normally return). To protect their welfare the nation with salmon streams must often interfere in a major way with its other use of the river. It feels, therefore, a proprietary interest in the salmon which it cannot protect when the fish gets into the ocean.

But the completely oceanic resources are not any more tractable to management through this system of narrow territorial sea. The Norwegian cod, which conducts the major part of its spawning in the internal waters of Norway, or at least within the territorial sea, moves out and is fished for throughout the Arctic, north of the Atlantic, wherever the water conditions are right.

The sardine, anchovy, saury, hake, bluefin, and albacore off the coast of Mexico and California typify the complexity that occurs off most coasts. Most of the spawning of sardine and anchovy in this region takes place well to sea offshore both countries, and the fish are available there for fishing, although most of the actual fishing to date is done reasonably close to shore. Presumably the anchovy do not make very long migrations, but the sardine may. The hake spawn in this area also, but apparently move north to feed and grow along the coast up as far as British Columbia. Although generally coastal and demersal, they do not always stay close to the bottom, and may often school at or near the surface. Also they can be readily caught off shore more than twelve miles. The jack mackerel form a large population, which is fished on mostly near the coast, but the spawning area extends at least 1,000 miles off the coast, and the fish can be caught out there if large adults are wanted. The saury are found all over the northern part of the North Pacific, and we know nothing of their population structure. It appears to be continuous across the ocean. The albacore spawn thousands of miles from Mexico and California in the west central Pacific, and after coming over to where we can fish them off our coast, go back over to Japan where they can be fished there. The bluefin tuna are commonly caught in the territorial sea of Mexico and California but do not spawn in the eastern Pacific at all. They spawn south of Japan and north of the Philippines, and individuals tagged off Mexico are captured the other side of Japan, in the Sea of Japan. Fur seals feed off California and sometimes as far south as northern Mexico. Their nearest breeding ground is the Pribilof Islands in the Bering Sea. Gray whales pass through the territorial sea of southern California proceeding to their calving grounds in the internal waters of the lagoons of northern Mexico; and, having fulfilled this biological purpose, migrate back across the Pacific to the feeding grounds off Kamchatka and the western Bering Sea.

There is no system of lines or barriers that can be erected to provide a sensible system of ownership over these resources by Mexico and California. The problem of conservation of these resources is simply not tractable to this sort of management system. Yet both countries quarrel over extensions of fishery jurisdiction as between themselves, with their neighbors, and with nations whose long-range fishermen come into the area. They are not fully utilizing these resources, but they seem not to want others to do so. The problem posed by the resources of Mexico and California is just one example; others could easily be found in other parts of the world.

There are four quite severe problems involved in the control of the harvesting of marine resources:

1. At some stage in its development, each fishery must restrict its operation so as not to harvest a given resource beyond the point of maximum sustainable yield.

2. The profits derived from such conservation must be divided among the fisheries harvesting the resource since each is one of its owners.

3. Ownership of a given resource in a particular area does not necessarily result in effective control of that resource since it itself is not a stable factor, in that the fish population in that area may move from it for obvious biological reasons.

4. Because various fish populations migrate in different patterns and respond in different ways to the pressure of fishing within the area, each individual population constitutes its own problem.

The mechanism for settling any conflict arising over the use of marine resources in response to the need to conserve those resources is provided in the 1958 Convention on Fishing and the Conservation of the Living Resources of the Sea. Its successful implementation depends on co-operation among those owners and users that are involved, since only the sovereign governs his own fishermen on the high seas.

97

There is no way to attend to the division of the profits of such conservation among the nations except by agreement on that among the sovereign users. This has not been tractable to general settlement yet, as has the conservation problem, because there are no universal criteria upon which the nations can agree. So far this has been tractable only to case by case negotiation among the sovereign owners. Examples are provided by the North Pacific fur seals (among Russia, Japan, Canada, and the United States), and the Fraser River sockeye and pink salmon (between Canada and the United States). In the one case the owners of the breeding ground do all the managing and harvesting of the resource and divide the skins to others on the basis of proportions established in a treaty. In the other case the responsibility for managing the resource and its harvest is in the hands of a joint commission, and the allowable harvest is split evenly between the two countries under treaty.

There is no general solution in sight for the third sort of problem because there is no practical way to split up the ownership of the resources and provide for conservation and rational management.

VI. *Effects on the Law of the Sea*

Freedom of the seas is essential to the social and economic welfare of man, and the world has now become so full of people and so closely knit together that there is no nation unaffected by this. If sea trade were to be interrupted in any considerable manner for any considerable length of time (as was commonly the case up until the seventeenth century), the whole human population would necessarily shrink back to considerably reduced levels either from the wars which would result, or from the famines that would result until the population came into balance with the new circumstances.

Public order on the ocean has never been kept except through military power, and it has been sea power in the hands of one or a few powers that has preserved the freedom of the seas over the past two hundred years, thus permitting the human population to come to its present stage of development. This military power must be able to reach into all corners to keep down the piracy that always pops up with its removal.

These facts are so plainly evident to all that the nations agree that the high seas must be free to the passage of all, that the air space above must also be similarly free to transit, that the territorial sea must be narrow, and that even within it there must be rights of innocent passage for all. Only the inland waters are subtracted from that part of the ocean which cannot be freely navigated.

It is a major concern that the nations have not been able to agree upon a breadth of the territorial sea because this continues to be a source of friction among them. The United States as a principal power preserving world peace feels this keenly as did England before her. To preserve world peace it is highly desirable, if not necessary, to keep the territorial sea to a minimum breadth of near three miles so that presently international straits will remain that way, as well as for related military reasons. Thus the United States, in the worst way, wishes to preserve the three mile territorial sea or as close thereto as possible.

It was unable to get agreement by a necessary majority to a three or six mile territorial sea at either the 1958 or the 1960 Conference on the Law of the Sea. It fears that without such agreement there will be a continual erosion away from that standard toward the twelve mile territorial sea, which would render its military tasks more difficult and trend toward reducing the freedom of the sea.

It was unable to get an agreement at the 1958 conference because it was unable to dissociate the problem of the territorial breadth from the problem of the jurisdiction by the coastal state over fisheries in the adjacent high seas. It sought and obtained a second world conference in 1960 to consider only these two remaining points: the breadth of the territorial sea and the jurisdiction by the coastal state over fisheries lying in the adjacent high seas. It had made up its mind by this time that the military issues involved in the narrow territorial sea were so overriding to it that as necessary it would sacrifice its fishing interests in seeking a solution to the territorial problem.

It did not realize then, and it does not realize now, that those problems are inseparable diplomatically and cannot be solved separately. The United States stands so strongly among its allies and other countries that its allies assumed that in a military showdown the United States would find a successful solution to the military aspects of the freedom of the seas. In the interval, they needed to eat and strengthen their economies, and they did not feel that they depend upon the United States to attend to these functions for them to their satisfaction, and they did not wish to be dependent in such a manner. Accordingly they wished to have maximum access to the resources of the sea, and they voted in such a manner as to protect this right.

The effect of this was that the United States tried every form of compromise, diplomatic pressure and persuasion at the 1960 Law of the Sea Conference and was still not able to quite get a two-thirds majority for any proposal. It did succeed, however, in doing two things which have continued to work toward eroding its desired position on the breadth of the territorial sea.

It moved, for compromise purposes, to a six mile territorial sea position hoping to influence required votes by this means. It did not get enough. In fact it is questionable if it got many. Upon the failure of the conference it reverted to a three mile policy, and it has since defended this militarily (Matsu Island and the Gulf of Tonkin). But the temporary move away from the three mile position (drawing United Kingdom, Canada and others with it) forever weakened that concept.

Secondly, and more importantly, it permitted (also for compromise purposes) the breadth of the territorial sea and the limits of fishery jurisdiction concepts to be separated in its policy. It hoped by this compromise to get rid of the fishery problems so that it could concentrate on solving the breadth of the territorial sea problem. It failed to do this but by casting loose the fishery limits problem from its firm anchor to the territorial sea problem it lost its ability to control the outward surging of the fishery limits.

Thus in the ensuing years there has been a continuous drift among the nations toward a twelve mile limit for fisheries. Now there is strong consideration in the United States Congress, and passivity in the executive department, for the United States also to adopt a twelve mile limit for fisheries. Again there is the wishful thinking that if the United States did this it could get agreement on a twelve mile limit for fisheries among the nations, stabilize that drifting front, and thus stabilize at the same time the narrow territorial sea front.

The delusion in this strategy is fully illustrated by the testimony received by the appropriate committees of the Congress this year on these bills. The proponents of the twelve mile fishery limits freely admit that it will not solve the problems with which they are concerned. Those problems are discriminating against foreign fishermen now fishing adjacent to our territorial sea in competition with our own fishermen. They freely admit that the twelve mile fishery limit is "only a step in the right direction" and will have little or no beneficial effect on their problems.

They represent clearly and concisely the position of the inshore, small-boat, relatively inefficient fisherman all over the world who wants his competitive situation relieved not by becoming more efficient himself, but by doing away with more efficient fishermen. To think that a twelve mile fishery limit will stabilize this internal political and external diplomatic front is day-dreaming. A 200 mile limit will not, in the long run, satisfy this urging nor would it solve the conservation problems. Once the fishing limit boundary is separated from the territorial sea boundary, there is no good place for it to stop for reasons noted above. Since the real fishing problems cannot be solved by an artificial, generally applicable boundary anywhere in the sea, what this strategy has done is not contribute to the settlement of the territorial sea breadth problem, but has instead delayed and prevented its solution while opening new sources of conflict among the nations.

There is no easy and simple way out of these law of the sea conflicts. While the United States for the past twenty years has thought of these conflicts principally in terms of their military consequences, it is reasonable to predict that as fishing effort upon the ocean continues its rapid surge forward, to take care of the world need and desire for animal protein, the quarrels among nations over these fishery limit problems will become the important half of the over-all remaining problem in the law of the sea. In my view the United States would be well advised to work more energetically toward the solution of the fishery problems.

As noted above, the key part of the fishery problems is the scientific aspect. The rate of growth, the rate of annual increment to the population, and the rates of mortality must be assessed and continuously kept track of in order to know when an overfishing problem is going to result and what to do about it when it does. Much other biological and physical oceanographic research must be done to back up these studies and to interpret them. This needs to be done for every fish population where an overfishing problem is expected. The results of such studies on one fish population do not carry over to another. This is hard, slugging, difficult and costly science and there is no other way to attend to the conservation aspect of the fishery conflicts.

As long as a fishery is exploiting a fish population at less than the level permitting the maximum sustainable productivity from it, it is contrary to world public policy for restrictions to be placed on the fishery. To do so would be to restrict the amount of food or other product from that resource which it is naturally capable of producing.

When the fishing effort has increased beyond the point of maximum sustainable yield, the fishery can ordinarily be permitted to expand with-

101

out serious damage to the resource. The reason for this is that ordinarily the fishermen go broke before the fish do. The exceptions are few and restricted to high unit value resources that are easy to catch and not very numerous, such as mammals. This is only wasteful economically and is no worse than the food waste that premature regulations bring by restricting fishing effort and letting the resource die unused by man.

The sensible thing to do, and what the nations agreed to do in the 1958 Convention on Fishing and the Conservation of the Law of the Sea, is to permit fishing to be free up to the point of maximum sustainable productivity in each fishery situation and then regulate fishing effort jointly so that it remains at that point indefinitely for that resource, while the excess fishing effort is diverted to building up a fishery on another under-utilized resource.

At this point there are two things to do: (a) to establish quotas for the fishery applicable to everyone and let the fishery go to those who are the most efficient; or (b) to divide the quota that can be taken by all fishermen by some agreed formula between the different nations involved.

But there will be a quota to divide up only when the population is husbanded by regulations which will keep it at the point of maximum sustainable yield. The nations have so far been very chary of providing the funds with which to support the research at sea upon which all of this depends.

So far as I can see, there is no practical way to divide the fishery jurisdiction over the world ocean among the nations. There is no way to extend fishery limits out a little way, or even quite a ways, into the high seas and thus solve these fishery use and management problems. I see no way available at present to settle these matters by general agreement any further than attending to the conservation part of the problem through the mechanism provided by the 1958 Convention on Fishery and the Conservation of the Living Resources of the High Seas. Beyond that point each problem (dividing up the profits from the conservation) will have to be worked out diplomatically among the nations at issue individually on its own merits.

One can reasonably expect to see these problems exacerbated as fishing effort continues to develop on a world-wide basis. For this reason the apparatus with which to attend to such problems in the United Nations organization and its specialized agencies, as well as in the sovereign governments themselves, will need to be strengthened continuously.

There is a general reluctance in government, both the national and international level, to face up realistically to these rapidly accumulating problems and, particularly, to the cost of dealing with them.

The great tizzy about the twelve mile fishery limit presently in our Congress, which all hands recognize as an inconsequential and unrealistic approach to these problems, is a good example. Instead of meeting the real problem head on, we choose to do something that is politically palatable back home and sweep the real problems under the rug.

Another example is provided by a recent recommendation made by an advisory group to the United Nations that title to the ocean and its resources should be vested in the United Nations so that it could charge fees for using the ocean, thus support itself, and thus provide for the husbanding of its resources. How this would contribute to the solution of any of the real problems involved in enhancing the rational use of the enormous resources of the world ocean quite escapes me. It would add to the cost per ton of harvest, when what is needed to enhance the harvest is lowering the cost per ton of production so that the product can be got to those who need it, at a price they can pay. It would put sovereigns under the regulation of the United Nations, because only sovereigns (not individual citizens) have rights under the law of the sea to use the ocean. It would put a policing job for 70 per cent of the world's surface on the United Nations, when two or three minor policing jobs on land are what is now breaking the organization.

VII. *Conclusions*

1. The harvest of the living resources of the sea has about doubled in the last ten years. It presently takes about 5 per cent of the maximum sustainable yield of such resources which the ocean is capable of producing. The need and desire for animal protein in the world is enormous and increasing. It is likely that the harvest of such resources from the ocean will increase steadily for a long time to come to fill this need.

2. The maintenance of public order on the ocean has been rendered difficult throughout modern history by conflicts over fishing rights in the ocean. Such conflicts have increased in frequency as fishing effort has increased, and this is likely to continue.

3. Such conflicts have been made minimal with respect to land resources by dividing into segments those owned by some group of

sovereign people. This solution has been introduced to ocean problems recently as they concern the non-migratory resources of the sea bed. It is difficult, however, to see how this solution can be practically applied to the living resources of the ocean because of the exceedingly migratory nature of so many of the important ones.

4. From the standpoint of living resource productivity in the ocean, there is no convenient breaking point which can be used to demarcate the offshore from the distant water areas and resources. The migration areas of the different principal resources overlap badly. The very centers of primary productivity do not conform to any regular areal pattern.

5. Overfishing must be eliminated from world public policy. This cannot be arranged with any particular resource unless the whole area in which the resource can be caught is covered by the regulatory measures. Most resources supporting major fisheries can be caught at greater distance than three to twelve miles from land and many of them at greater than 200 miles from land. Most of them that are really strictly coastal occur off the coasts of at least two countries, and often off several. Accordingly, nearly all conservation activities concerning major fisheries must be conducted under international auspices.

6. A suitable framework for attending to all such conservation problems has been provided by the 1958 Convention on Fishing and the Conservation of the Living Resources of the High Seas. The nations are still chary of contributing the funds to support the research required to implement this convention or to require their nationals to abide by the regulations that such a treatment of the conservation problems gives rise to.

7. Internal political pressures often incline a nation to seek to extend its jurisdiction out to sea beyond its territorial limits in order to hamper foreign fishermen in their operations and thus favor local fishermen. This tends toward favoring inefficiency, toward underutilizing resources, and to causing conflicts among nations because other nations do not wish to give up freedom of fishing on the high seas. Such conflicts thrive in an atmosphere of lack of scientific facts about the fish and the effect of the fishery on the population, they smother and often die when illuminated in the full glare of adequate and public scientific fact.

8. No easy or cheap way is apparent out of these problems nor would it be expected that there should be. Conflicts concerning ownership of

land resources have been the subject of costly and intensive activity for a good many thousands of years. The ocean covers more than 70 per cent of the earth's surface, yet miniscule amounts of money are being spent by the nations in scientific inquiry concerning the ocean and its resources.

9. Our experience in dealing with living marine resources is limited to only a few cases. Those we know about indicate a remarkable diversity in the life habits, migratory ranges, reactions to fishing pressure, and other vital parameters of various fish populations. Until recently, fisheries have largely restricted themselves to harvesting those resources that are highly prized as food, and these have been those available in the northern temperate area. The vast resources of the lower latitudes and those of the Southern Hemisphere have only recently been tapped, and we have gained as yet only very little experience with them.

10. It is recommended, finally, (a) that no drastic change be made in the existing regime of the high seas as it affects husbandry of living resources until such time as we have acquired a far more comprehensive knowledge concerning the ocean and its resources and such a change is definitely proved desirable; (b) that nations increase their support of, and co-operation in, the conservation of the resources of the high seas as prescribed by the 1958 convention by expanding research directed toward increasing our knowledge of the ocean and its resources; and (c) that the nations of the world strengthen not only their own agencies devoted to such matters, but also the international commissions on fishery and the FAO Fishery Department, so as to assure that administrative and scientific machinery will be available both to prevent conflicts and to bring about the resolution of those that have already occurred.

Chapter Seven:

THE DISTRIBUTION OF THE SEA'S
WEALTH IN FISHERIES[*]

The fundamental purpose of this seminar is to discuss the distribution of the sea's wealth. We are examining, as is appropriate for every nation, the gains and losses to be obtained from alternative formulations of the law of the sea. Each nation, of course, desires to maximize its own net gain. But, since the resources of the sea are scarce, and since they are shared by the world community, one nation's gain may mean another nation's loss. This is exemplified by the extension of a nation's limits of exclusive rights.

The reaching of decisions among nations will be based upon the trade-offs of gains and losses. It is essential, therefore, that the terms of the trade-offs be understood as fully as possible. It is to be hoped that the analysis of gains and losses will be comprehensive and foresighted, and not the reflection of immediate problems and narrow goals.

It is impossible in a single paper, or for a single observer, to discuss fully all of the complex elements that will make up the trade-offs underlying the distribution of the sea's wealth. One can but suggest some of the dimensions of the problem and propose certain views that might be considered in future discussions. In my case, I am limiting my remarks to fishery resources, and to the economic implications and consequences of various alternatives for wealth distribution. To a certain extent, some of the things said about fisheries also apply to mineral resources—the chief difference between the two being that the former are mobile and the latter are fixed in place, and therefore easier to describe and place within boundaries.

In both cases, however, one conclusion is inescapable; and that is that there is a great need for more research, study, and discussion. And basic to this need is the requirement for increasing the number of highly qualified persons with an interest and a competence in the economic and political aspects of the sea's wealth.

In this paper, I am assuming that all the world seeks international arrangements that will meet three objectives: scientific management, economic efficiency, and acceptability. Arrangements to be viable over the long run must conform to the characteristics of the resource, particularly to the characteristic of mobility. The objective of economic efficiency has been given short shrift in past arrangements. It should receive special emphasis, not only because of its neglect in the past but also because future arrangements will inevitably have to deal directly with the problems of economic costs and returns. The third objective— acceptability—is obvious, but in considering this goal, it is necessary to face not only the short term interplay of forces but also the changing conditions over the long run and how these may affect a nation's views of its gains and losses.

There are some questions about the meaning of the wealth of the seas and about the different interpretations of ownership. These are multifaceted questions for which there are no clear answers. But discussion is important because different interpretations of ownership and of wealth have considerably different implications for the three goals of scientific management, economic efficiency, and acceptability. In this discussion, I shall postulate certain interpretations that may seem somewhat radical, but the reason for these postulates will become evident in the discussion that follows.

Turning from these questions, which essentially deal with the *distribution* of the sea's wealth, I shall then discuss some of the questions about the *production* of the sea's wealth. Under current conditions, and guided by the current conservation regulations, the sea's wealth is dissipated; because open access to the resource leads to the applications of redundant amounts of capital and labor. This is the basis of a long-waged argument between biologists and economists, the former choosing the goal of maximum physical output and the latter the goal of maximum net economic revenue. It should be stated, however, that both the biologists and the economists, as a result of the decade of discussion, have retracted from their extreme positions. Their goals are not in direct conflict and the problem is not so much one of choice of ends as it is the choice of means. The conclusion of the argument is critical; and that is that, somehow or other, it will be necessary to limit the num-

107

ber of fishermen that can participate in the fishery. Such limitations can only be achieved by further restricting the "freedom of the seas"; by excluding the excessive amounts of capital and labor. Such exclusions and restrictions place the spotlight very directly on questions about the meaning of the "freedom of the seas" and about the distribution of the sea's wealth.

And, finally, having discussed the question of the distribution of wealth and the question of the production of wealth, I shall turn to three alternative arrangements for international fisheries and sketch out some of the implications of these for a rational and acceptable fisheries regime. The first alternative would be by a direct license limitation scheme that would permit the participants to gain the economic rent that is produced. The second would prevent excessive entry by removing the economic rent from the fishery, by the use of yield taxes or perhaps, by an appropriate license fee. The third alternative would be by appropriating the resource itself, either by unilateral extension of exclusive rights, or by some form of international agency. In each case, some, though by no means all, of the advantages and disadvantages will be raised. And, if there is any validity to my conclusions about the desirability and inevitability of entry restrictions, then it is these advantages and disadvantages that should receive the greatest amount of study and discussion.

I. *Who Gets What?*

As mentioned above, the essence of this seminar lies in the distribution of the sea's wealth. This is quite clearly the case if we are discussing the further extension of exclusive fishing limits. It is certainly the case if we are discussing restrictions on entry, which will give exclusive rights to some and not to others. It is even the case for most, if not all, conservation regulations; for these inevitably work to the benefit of some and to the detriment of others.[1]

But note that in the three instances mentioned, different items of wealth are being distributed to different sets of nations. The question can be simply stated: "Who gets what?" But the answer, or alternative answers, are far from clear. For the moment, I will try to discuss these questions without reference to the criteria of economic efficiency or acceptability, although inevitably these criteria must be included in the negotiations for future fisheries arrangements.

What are the characteristics of ownership of international fisheries? Who has ownership rights, what do these rights include, and how can ownership rights be evaluated and priced in economic terms? To begin with the most general aspect, there is question as to whether the fishery resources of the high seas belong to no one or, conversely, are the common property of the world community. If the first interpretation is accepted without qualification, then the resources are up for grabs. Any nation feeling capable of it could assert unilateral authority over a high seas fishery far distant from its shores, or would have no compunction in depleting or completely extinguishing a fishery resource. In certain instances, some nations appear to have adopted this interpretation.

Conversely, the resources might be considered to be the property of the world community as a whole. This appears to be the general trend in interpretation. At least, some feeling for world ownership may be serving to restrain unilateral appropriation of fisheries. The basis for this feeling may be mixed. It may, in part, be an unwillingness to incur unpopularity. It may be fear of retaliation. It may be that a nation finds world ownership advantageous to its own interests. Or, indeed, it may be from some sense of equity. But whatever the motivations, the evidence is that world fisheries are coming to be considered as belonging to the world community, at least this is implied in the conservation agreements that impose an obligation upon nations to "conserve" fishery resources.

If, then, the resources are the common property of the world community, how can each nation define its share of this property? This cannot be discussed without discussions of the rights that are attached to ownership. Are these rights simply a generalized right of access, with every nation having an opportunity to participate in the direct exploitation of the fishery? Or is there an exclusive aspect to the right of access? Is it a right to share the resource? Or a right to dispose of the resource? And how can the right, whatever it is, be measured in economic terms?

It is this last question that the economist finds most interesting, since value depends upon scarcity and upon exclusion. If a resource is bottomless and no one can exclude anyone else from sharing the resource, there is no market place for the resource and no price that can be directly attached to it. Sunshine is obviously important to everyone, but it cannot be bought and sold except under certain conditions where scarcity and exclusion become involved. For example, construction of a high rise building may exclude a neighbor's garden from sunshine thereby destroying his crops and creating a cost that is measurable.

Similarly, a generalized right of access to fisheries has no value unless scarcity and exclusion become attached to the right. Under these conditions, wealth, such as it is, is distributed on the basis of nations' abilities and willingness to exploit fisheries. Those that do not exploit, do not share in the wealth. They do, however, keep the option for exploiting sometime in the future, and cannot be excluded from exercising this option. As pointed out later, this generalized right of access, preserving the freedom to exploit a fishery, is accompanied by severe impediments to the goal of economic efficiency.

In some cases, rights of access have acquired scarcity and a semblance of exclusion, or at least, sufficient exclusion so that the rights have been bought and sold. The Japanese and the Canadians have sold their rights to catch fur seals.[2] The United Kingdom and the Netherlands (or individual firms therein) have sold their rights to take whales in the Antarctic.[3] And the adoption of the doctrine of abstention in 1952 involved the sale of rights by the Japanese to fish for salmon in the eastern North Pacific.[4] To be sure, other words and terms have been used in describing these cases, but essentially, they involve the giving up of a fishing right in return for something of value. The value may be explicitly stated in monetary terms; it may be in terms of physical quantities; or it may be a non-quantifiable reward completely unrelated to the fishery resources. But whatever the terms of trade, the right of access in these instances has been valued and has become an item of wealth.

The difference between the generalized rights mentioned above and the specific, saleable rights is that the latter rest on an historic right of access to the resource. That is, the selling nations have made use of their freedom of opportunity to exploit a fishery and thereby have established a right that has a recognized value. Other nations that have not exercised their rights presumably have no marketable stake in the resource. The basis for the value is the presumption that other nations will *not* take up their option to participate and that they are, in fact, excluded from exploiting the resource. If the exclusion is not maintained, then the value of the right diminishes. If, for example, Peru chose to exercise its right

110

of access to fur seals, the shares to the four parties of the treaty would be decreased. The parties may choose to buy out Peru by bringing it into the convention, but if other nations follow Peru's lead, exclusion becomes ineffective and the right of access devalued.

Where historic rights are maintained and become effective forces for exclusion, the wealth of the fisheries is distributed not only to those nations that are exploiting the resource, but also to those nations that *have* exploited the resource. As pointed out later, this concept of historic rights, because of its exclusive properties, may facilitate improvements in economic efficiency, but it raises difficult questions about acceptability.

Another concept of ownership rights is postulated as follows: that world ownership of the resource carries the right of exclusion, and that the rights of individual nations are to shares in the resource rather than to exploitative access to the resource. This may appear to be a radical postulate. It gives the world community (which is not recognized as an individual entity, except perhaps by other planets) an explicit property right—the right to exclude its constituents, or part of its constituents, from participating in the exploitation of the resource. It also gives the individual nations a right to share in the resource itself, which is a more general right than that of the opportunity to exploit. Under this concept, a nation's share in the resource may be expressed as the nation's share in the wealth that is produced, just as each nation has a share in the information produced by weather satellites.

This step from a right of access to a right in the resource is admittedly a major one, although there are precedents and there are analogous situations that indicate its merits. To paraphrase another student of ocean resources, I suggest that we have available a better analogy, in the laws of grazing lands, evolved in the western United States, than we can find in any facet of the law of the sea. Up until the first quarter of this century, western grazing lands were treated as common property resources, a treatment that was initially established because it was felt that the grazing lands were inexhaustible. However, as demand increased, the common use of the resource led to depletion, congestion, and conflict (the same consequences that are occurring on the high seas. The range wars provided dramatic evidence of the attempts of individuals to appropriate the resource for their exclusive use (reflected in unilateral attempts of nations to appropriate fishery resources). Peace on the range was achieved only by an uneasy collusion (reflected on the seas by multilateral and exclusive agreements).

111

By the turn of the century it was clear that open access to the resource would destroy it, and President Theodore Roosevelt, among others, called for the exercise of exclusive rights by the federal government and the leasing of these rights to the individual users. In essence, the public lost the freedom of opportunity to exploit the resource but gained a share in the wealth that is produced.

In summary, I have attempted to indicate some of the different interpretations of ownership of the sea's fisheries and the implications of these for distribution of wealth. Where generalized rights of access pertain, the distribution of wealth is on the basis of willingness and ability to exploit the resource. Under historic rights that exclude new entrants, the wealth goes to those who exploit, or who have exploited, the fisheries. But if ownership is interpreted as a right to share in the resource, then the wealth would be distributed to all nations. Obviously, there are difficulties with each of these interpretations—difficulties with respect to the goal of economic efficiency and to the goal of acceptability. The importance for considering these alternative views is set forth in the following remarks, beginning with a discussion of the necessity for restricting open access to international fisheries.

II. *The Question of Rationalization*

Turning to the objectives for fishery management, I mentioned the argument between biologists and economists; the former advocating the maximization of the sustainable yield from the fishery, and the latter advocating the maximization of the net economic revenue. The economic argument points out that the common property characteristics of a fishery result in uncontrolled access, and, therefore, lead to the attraction of greater amounts of capital and labor than are economically justified.[5] Where a resource is unowned, or owned in common, no one can prevent others from participating in the exploitation of the resource. The economic rent of the industry is a profit that is shared by all participants rather than one that can be appropriated by a single managing agency. And since it is shareable, more and more producers will enter the industry until all the rent is dissipated. At this point, the industry will be operating where total costs and revenues are equal rather than where marginal costs and revenues are equal. No businessman, if he had control of the resource, would select this point of operation. He would, instead, invest only as much capital and labor as would produce the maximum net revenue. But since there is common ownership of a fishery, and therefore no control on the amount of capital and labor, the inevitable result is gross economic waste.

Three recent studies indicate the magnitude of this waste. A study of the Sacramento River salmon fishery has shown that $3.3 million worth of annual catch could be taken with $300,000 worth of effort under rational management.[6] For the Puget Sound fishery, it has been estimated that half of the current amount of effort would be sufficient to take the permissible catch, at an annual savings of between $2 and $4 million per year.[7] And for the Georges Bank haddock fishery, it has been estimated that "the point of maximum profit would be at a level 50 per cent or less of the recent average [amount of effort]." [8] The prevention of this waste can only be achieved by simulating the conditions under private enterprise; that is, by suitable rationing of exploitation rights to reduce the number of producers.

The biologists have a different view of waste. To them a resource is being wasted if it is producing less than the maximum physical yield that can be sustained over time. In order to prevent this waste, they seek controls on the amount of catch, rather than on the amount of effort. The economists reject this objective for several reasons.

First, a physical objective (a certain number of pounds of fish) is not a meaningful guide for an economic industry. No farmer seeks to produce the *maximum* amount of corn that can be grown on an acre of ground, because the increased costs of production are greater than the increased revenues.

A second reason for rejecting the maximum sustainable yield as a desirable objective is that it offers no guidance for the management of two fisheries that may be ecologically related. If two species in demand compete for the same food source, the yields from both cannot be maximized simultaneously.

A third and more important reason lies in the methods of control that are generally sought to achieve a maximum sustainable yield. Most of these methods tend to increase the costs of the industry—for example, by prohibiting the use of technologically efficient gear. This is the reason for the prohibition of salmon traps in the Pacific Northwest, and for the law that oysters in Maryland can only be dredged by sail boats. It should be pointed out, however, that such stringent methods are

113

frequently chosen not so much to prevent depletion as to preserve the fishery for the present participants. In essence, therefore, they are a system for distributing the wealth of the seas.

But the differences of opinion over the objectives for rational fishery management may be becoming academic. The participants in the developed fisheries are becoming more and more aware of the declines in catch per unit of effort. The stocks of fish, such as those on the Grand Banks, are limited in supply. But as the demand for these fish increases, the fisheries attract more effort, so that the available supply is shared by more producers. Therefore, each fisherman's share of the total catch becomes reduced. None of the conservation regulations can prevent this from occurring.

In the future, in the absence of entry restrictions, the waste will inevitably become more severe and more extensive. The demand for fish products is growing at the rate of about six per cent per year. Technology is advancing and reducing the costs of harvesting as well as increasing the ability to take fish. These two pressures will attract greater amounts of effort. Even if technological innovation is prohibited, the presently developed fisheries will become more severely depleted and those fisheries that are less developed at present will begin to feel the costs of declining catches per unit of effort. With technological innovation and no control on the number of users, whole stocks of fish might be wiped out in a single season. This would be especially true if some of the advanced techniques, described in popular literature, become feasible. Or if, for example, it becomes feasible to increase the fertility of a high seas area, what entrepreneur will undertake the capital investment if he has no exclusive rights to the fruits of that investment?

The necessity for restricting entry into a fishery is becoming more widely recognized. The Report of the Third Meeting of the Northeast Atlantic Fisheries Commission[9] pointed out that a 50 per cent reduction in effort would lead to a 10 per cent increase in the total catch of Arctic cod. It then emphasized one of the difficulties of regional, rather than international, approaches to effort reduction. If its sister commission on the other side of the Atlantic (ICNAF) initiated entry reduction schemes, some of the excluded effort would enter the Northeast Atlantic area, and create further depletion and economic waste.

In summary, it is clearly both inevitable and desirable that means be found to reduce open access to fishery resources and to prevent the application of excessive and redundant amounts of capital and labor. This is the first criterion for future regimes for marine fisheries, and it is one that has significant implications for the distribution of the sea's wealth.

III.   *Other Criteria for Fisheries Management*

In addition to the necessity for preventing economic waste, other criteria will have to be considered in the formulation of international fishery regimes. I shall mention a few of these briefly, in order to indicate the complexity of the tasks and the need for additional research.

First, no matter what objective for fisheries management is chosen, management must be technically possible. The prime distinction between minerals of the sea floor and the fisheries of sea waters is that the former are fixed in place and the latter are mobile. The freely swimming fish pay no respect to national boundaries or other artificial divisions of the oceans. Some fish, such as salmon and tuna, may cover several thousand miles during their brief life span, and may appear in the territorial waters of various nations. Other species may be homebodies, but even in these cases, their environment may be influenced by actions far from their habitats. In all cases, it is necessary to define a viable management unit. For those fish that roam great distances, it may be the stock itself. In other cases, a regional approach, covering several interrelated species may be most desirable. It is clear that there will be great difficulties involved in defining management units, particularly if the fish enters the territorial waters of an unco-operative coastal state.

Another criterion is that the regime be sufficiently flexible to deal with changes in the patterns of demand. Currently, there are only a relatively few species of fish that are sought by fishermen. Vast quantities of so-called underutilized species exist in the oceans simply because the market for these species is not sufficient to warrant investment in catching them. It is a common plea of commercial fishermen that every effort be undertaken to increase the demand for these "underutilized" species. If, as is probable, these "underutilized" species are closely related ecologically to species currently in demand, some decisions will have to be made on the relative economic values of the different species, in order to determine how much of each species to produce.

Not only will flexibility with respect to species be required, but also flexibility with respect to the amount and kind of effort. This is particularly important with respect to technological innovations. On the one hand, techniques that reduce the cost per unit of effort will make it economically feasible to *increase* the amount of effort. On the other hand, techniques that reduce the cost per unit of catch, will call for *reductions* in the amount of effort. Such reductions may have to be severe if some of the anticipated technologies become practical. If, for example, it becomes possible to attract fish in great quantities (by lights, electric fields, herding techniques), competition between two or more vessels would lead to obvious wastes. It would be as if there were no control over entry into the radio spectrum. Two units using the same frequency in the same area would result either in impossible congestion or a race to build the biggest tower with the greatest output. Just as radio frequencies are allocated, it is clear that new fishery technologies will require allocation among fishing units.

Other criteria besides the ones mentioned will suggest themselves. The regime should be enforceable. It should not stifle growth. It should encourage the development of scientific knowledge. But in addition to these, and of far greater importance, the regime should be acceptable. Since a prime requisite is the exclusion of excess producers, the question becomes one of determining who shall be excluded and who shall be permitted to participate. And this leads directly to the question of the distribution of the sea's wealth.

IV. *Alternative Methods for Controlling Entry*

I have attempted to demonstrate the inevitability and the desirability for controlling entry to marine fisheries. The difficulty lies not in the determination of the goal, but in its implementation. Three techniques will be discussed: that of direct license limitation; that of the appropriation of economic rent; and that of the appropriation of the resource. Each of these techniques calls for a greater degree of authority than now exists on the sea, but this is inevitable no matter what shape the future regime will take. Each technique also will undoubtedly be accompanied by transitional hardship, as participants find themselves excluded from the fishery. There are, however, ways in which these hardships can be ameliorated.[10]

License limitation.—One possible method is by the direct limitation of the amount of effort. The most effective way would be by granting licenses only to that number of producers that would yield the greatest net revenue to the industry. In this case, as in the case of the New York taxicabs,[11] the economic rent would accrue to the holders of the licenses.

116

There are many difficulties with such a scheme. First, since the fishermen come from different nations with different wage/price structures, conclusions as to the potential net economic revenue and the appropriate amount of effort are likely to vary. In many cases, however, the variations may not be great, but even if they are, it may still be possible to arrive at a compromise that leaves each of the participating nations better off than they were before. This implies, of course, that some system for rationing the licenses among the participating nations has been worked out.

A second difficulty lies in describing the unit of effort that is to be licensed. If it is a single vessel, then the temptation would be to build bigger and faster vessels in order to get as great a share of the catch as possible. This could lead to a race in technological innovation that would be economically inefficient. It could also lead to depletion of the resource and heavier costs for future harvesting. These effects might be overcome by licensing a vessel of a certain size and catching power, but this would then prevent technological innovation from taking place. There could be periodic revision of the standard vessel in order to permit new techniques to be applied, but if these increase catching power, then the number of licenses would again have to be reduced.

Any system that permits the economic rent to accrue to the license holder is certain to encounter difficulties because of the temptation to break the intention of the regulation.[12] But an even greater difficulty would lie in the acceptability of such a scheme. If the licenses are granted only to those nations with historic rights in the resource, then the non-participating nations would either be excluded or have to buy a license from a retiring licensee. This would mean that a nation would have to purchase what is now a free right of access, and it would mean that the wealth of the seas would lie, essentially, in the hands of those with historic rights. It is unlikely that this proposal would receive wide acceptance.

If, in order to overcome this, free right of access is to be maintained, then the exercise of this right would mean either the granting of additional licenses (and the breakdown of the scheme) or the loss of licenses on the part of the participating nations; a loss they would be unwilling to accept.

The Appropriation of Economic Rent.—A second and less direct method for controlling entry would be by the appropriation of the economic rent produced by the industry. A license fee, determined by auction or other means, would add to the costs of effort and discourage the excess producers from participating in the fishery. The same result could be achieved by an appropriate tax on the yield. Those who remain in the industry would be no worse off than before. Society, in the long run, would be better off by having achieved a more rational allocation of capital and labor and by the acquisition of a rent that was formerly dissipated.

But some of the same difficulties of the license limitation scheme would attend this proposal. There would be difficulties in determining an appropriate license fee or tax, in describing the unit of effort, and in allowing for a rational rate of technological innovation. Also, the right of access would no longer be free.

But the essential difference between this proposal and the license limitation method is that the wealth of the seas would be appropriated by a single agency rather than by the participants. This raises the question as to how to distribute the wealth. Some, of course, would have to be devoted to administering the arrangement and managing the resource, but there is likely to be considerable surplus above this. The formula for distribution would have to be worked out by all nations. It might be distributed on the basis of length of coastline, size of population, area, or perhaps on the basis of need. Or it might be turned over to an international agency to be used for scientific research, aid to underdeveloped countries, or for some other purpose that would meet commonly accepted goals. Such a distribution might make many nations more willing to accept the loss of free access to the resource.

The Appropriation of the Resource.—The third method for limiting entry is by the appropriation of property rights to the resource itself. If a single managing agent has full control of the resource and of all access to it, then the common property characteristics are removed. In this case, the problems of economic efficiency, technological innovation, flexibility of management, and similar problems, would be no more difficult than those of an ordinary farmer or businessman. The manager, or owner, would invest only as much capital and labor as would produce the maximum net revenue.

He would buy his inputs in the cheapest market and sell his products in the dearest market. He would have little difficulty in choosing how much of each species to produce, since the market would be his guide.

His investment in new equipment could be amortized over an appropriate number of years. In short, his ownership of the resource would eliminate almost all of the difficulties that presently exist in the exploitation of marine fisheries.

It is important to point out that this case calls for the appropriation and use of exclusive rights by a single managing agency. Nothing is gained, for example, by an agency's acquiring these rights and then granting open access to those producing units under its jurisdiction. The case of the Pacific salmon and the doctrine of abstention is illustrative of the failure to use exclusive rights for the purpose of increasing economic efficiency.

The appropriation of the resource removes most of the consequences of common ownership, but it is, in essence, an appropriation of the sea's wealth and raises, therefore, the question of acceptability. There are two ways in which appropriation can take place. First, it could be achieved by the unilateral extension of a coastal state's fishing rights. Or second, it might be achieved by granting exclusive rights to an international agency or authority. Examples of the former would be the extension of rights to cover the continental shelf, or the unilateral assertion of the doctrine of abstention. Obviously many nations would, and do, oppose such attempts, and it is unlikely that this approach would be successful. But even with this approach, there will be no gain in wealth unless the appropriating nation rationalizes its own effort.

Appropriation by an international authority would also meet considerable opposition. The authority might choose to exploit the resources directly, by buying its own vessels and marketing its products. Or, instead, it might lease its rights to a single nation. But in either case, open access to the resource would be very definitely precluded. The advantages of this system, however, should not be lightly discarded. It would permit a rational and economically efficient fishery to develop. It would ease the course of technological innovation. But of more significance, the individual nations may be willing to give up their rights of access for a right to share in the economic rent that would be produced. This would be in keeping with the view that the sea's wealth is the property of the world community to be shared by all the nations.

Earlier in this paper, I set forth different interpretations of ownership of world fisheries. It was suggested that the world community as a whole has a degree of ownership of the resources lying outside the exclusive rights of coastal states. It was postulated that this degree of

119

property rights might be extended to include the right of exclusion. The rationale for this step lies in the necessity for preventing excessive entry into world fisheries. For individual nations, three different interpretations of rights of ownership were advanced—a generalized right of access; an historic right of access that permits exclusion; and a right to share in the resource. When the first interpretation is maintained, and there are no restrictions on access, the wealth of the sea will be dissipated, to the loss of both the world community and the individual nations. Under the second interpretation, economic rent could be produced, but this would be appropriated by a few nations to the exclusion of others. The third interpretation ties in with the postulate about the expansion of world ownership rights. This would permit the rational production of wealth and grant each nation a share of this wealth. In essence, individual nations would be trading their right of access for a share in the economic rent.

Just as nature abhors a vacuum, society abhors a common property, and all pressures are for filling in the vacancy. This vacancy can be filled by the assertion of historic rights, by the unilateral extension of coastal states' rights, or by the world community's assumption of exclusive rights. The world may select any of these alternatives or a combination of them. One can only hope that the selection will be based on rational objectives; on clear foresight; and that it will be made with a sense of equity and generosity.

* I am indebted to Robert C. Lind, Jay Polach, and other colleagues at Resources for the Future for their critical comments on an earlier version of this paper.

1. See Shigeru Oda, "Recent Problems of International High Sea Fisheries: Allocation of Fishery Resources," *Philippine International Law Journal,* Vol. I, No. 4 (1962). He states that "the most difficult task in the conservation of marine resources is . . . the allocation of limited resources among the States, each of which naturally wants to maximize its own share." He further points out that "free competition . . . does not satisfy nations with less advanced technologies and economies nor States which so substantially pre-empt the fisheries concerned that fishing by any newcomer will necessarily decrease their own catch."

2. Under the Fur Seal Treaty, the harvest of fur seals in the North Pacific is left entirely in the hands of the U.S. and the U.S.S.R., while the Japanese and the Canadians have agreed to forego catching fur seals in exchange for a portion of the harvest.

3. The U.K. and the Netherlands sold their whaling fleets to Japan, but Japan was primarily interested in the shares of the whale quota that accompanied the fleets.

4. The signing of the Peace Treaty with Japan was, in part, conditional upon Japan's acceptance of certain restrictions on its fishing effort. See Shigeru Oda, *International Control of Sea Resources* (Leyden [Netherlands]: A. W. Sythoff, 1962). pp. 65 ff.

5. The first modern exposition of the theory of economic waste in fisheries was advanced by H. Scott Gordon, "The Economic Theory of a Common Property Resource: The Fishery," *Journal of Political Economy,* LXII (1954), 124–42. See also: Anthony Scott, "The Fishery: The Objectives of Sole Ownership," *Journal of Political Economy,* LXIII (1955), 116–24; James Crutchfield and Arnold Zellner, "Economic Aspects of the Pacific Halibut Fishery," *Fishery Industrial Research,* Vol. I, No. 1 (Washington: U.S. Government Printing Office, 1963); Francis T. Christy, Jr., "Efficiency in the Use of Marine Resources," California Museum of Science and Industry, *California and the World Ocean,* 1964; Robert Hamlisch (ed.), *The Economic Effects of Fishery Regulation,* FAO Fisheries Report No. 5 (Rome: FAO, 1962), Fle/R5; Ralph Turvey and Jack Wiseman (eds.), *The Economics of Fisheries* (Rome: FAO, 1957); and Francis T. Christy, Jr., and Anthony Scott, *The Common Wealth in Ocean Fisheries* (Baltimore: Johns Hopkins Press, 1965).

6. Donald H. Fry, Jr., "Potential Profits in the California Salmon Fishery," *California Fish and Game,* XLVIII, No. 4 (October, 1962), 256–67.

7. William F. Royce, *et al., Salmon Gear Limitation in Northern Washington Waters,* Contribution No. 145 (Seattle: University of Washington, College of Fisheries, 1963).

8. Edward J. Lynch, Richard M. Doherty, George P. Draheim, *The Groundfish Industries of New England,* Circular 121 (Washington: U.S. Fish and Wildlife Service, 1961).

9. Office of the Northeast Atlantic Fisheries Commission, *Report of the 3rd Meeting* (London, 1965).

10. An excellent discussion of limitation systems is presented in Anthony Scott, "The Economics of Regulating Fisheries," *The Economic Effects of Fishery Regulation, op. cit.* n. 5 above. A specific proposal for the State of Washington is by William F. Royce, *et al., Salmon Gear Limitations in Northern Washington Waters.* Fisheries Publications, New Series, Vol. 2, No. 1 (Seattle: University of Washington, 1963). See also Christy and Scott, *op. cit.* n. 5 above, Chapters 12 and 13.

11. There are about 12,000 medallions granting permission to operate a taxi in New York City. The current market price for a medallion is between $25,000 and $30,000. The capitalized value of the aggregate of this rent is about $300,000,000.

12. For an excellent statement of these difficulties, see Hiroshi Kasahara, "Japanese Fisheries and Fishery Regulations," California Museum of Science and Industry, *California and the World Oceans,* 1964.

Discussion of Chapman and Christy

1. There is a critical need for social science research (particularly in economics) on the problems associated with the development and use of ocean resources. The wealth in the seas is primarily a function of the economic forces of supply and demand, and these must be fully understood and anticipated if we are to arrive at a rational and orderly regime for the seas. Arrangements, to be viable, must recognize and accommodate the diverse developmental interests.

2. Debate centered around the different goals of (a) maximizing the sustainable yield, and (b) maximizing the net economic revenue. It was pointed out that under conditions of open access to the resource, labor and capital would continue to be applied until the industry's total costs were equal to its total revenues. This is true because any shareable profit produced by the industry will simply attract more producers, thereby diminishing the share available to each. Under these conditions, the profit that would be produced if the resource were under single ownership is wasted, going to neither the producers nor society. As demand for the product increases, the increased revenues will attract more inputs of labor and capital. Eventually, this will tend to deplete the resource. When this happens, the same (or greater) amounts of total revenue can be produced by far fewer units of capital and labor and far less cost.

3. The economists argue that the goal of maximum net economic revenue is preferable to that of maximum sustainable yield, but if society chooses the latter, then the economists would urge that it be done at the least cost. Most conservation regulations seeking to achieve the maximum sustainable yield, serve to increase the costs of the industry. In the case of the halibut fisheries of the North Pacific, regulations are based on a total quota that can be taken in any one

season. When that quota is reached, all fishing must stop until the next season. Under these conditions, the fishermen work as fast as they can to get as great a share of the quota as possible before the total is reached. This results in a very short season, leading to higher costs of processing and distribution and to uneconomic uses of capital and labor during the rest of what used to be a nine-month season. This is a form of management that produces economic waste.

4. One of the problems of the goal of economic efficiency is the difficulty of defining it. Countries competing for the same resource may have very different costs of labor and capital, as well as different prices for the end product. As a result, they may have quite different views as to that amount of effort which will produce the greatest net economic revenue. Most fishing countries now agree on the biological concept of a maximum sustainable yield. This concept, based on natural laws, can be scientifically determined and can be agreed upon easily by all participants. There is question as to whether nations could define, and agree to, a goal based on economic costs and returns. Even though the maximum economic yield may not be definable, it may be possible to demonstrate that each nation can gain from a system that controls the amount of effort. Research on this is vitally important.

5. In a management system either with a goal of maximum sustainable yield or maximum economic efficiency there is the problem of eventually limiting entry. This may not be too serious a problem if only a few countries having the necessary technological capacity are involved (as in the 1911 Fur Seal Treaty, which, to the economist, is an extremely rational one in that maximum sustainable yield is produced at the lowest cost). But demand for fisheries products throughout the world is increasing, more countries are getting into the fisheries, and technological innovations are developing rapidly. By analogy with the fisheries the oil and gas industries through mutual agreements throughout the world regulate production and thereby cut down on economic waste.

6. If one is going to operate an ocean fishery successfully, he must control the stock, which is not a matter of miles, or distance from shore. In some fisheries, such as the anchovy, there is wide variation from

123

year to year in the stock, depending on the survival of the young of a particular species. This survival rate may be found to be dependent largely on the temperatures of the water (or, in the case of the anchovy, of the upwelling conditions during the time of spawning and early growth of the organism). You cannot posssibly find out where you want to stop a fishery or reduce the effort without a close understanding of the biology of the organism you are dealing with, the environment in which it is living, and the effects of one upon the other. And before any fisheries management scheme is adopted at the international level, there must be agreement within the national government as to a desirable ocean management program.

Wilbert M. Chapman, Francis T. Christy, Jr.,
Richard Baxter, Edward W. Allen,
and Giulio Pontecorvo

Chapter Eight:

A SYMPOSIUM ON NATIONAL INTERESTS
IN COASTAL WATERS

CHAPMAN:

To persons not acquainted with the national interests of the United States in the world as a whole, or not concerned therewith, the national interest in our coastal waters is to establish boundaries as far out into the ocean as we can get away with and establish exclusive jurisdiction over everything therein to the United States.

The trouble with this parochial view is that whatever the United States can do in this respect it has to agree that other countries can do the same thing. The reaction we got from the blunder of issuing the Truman Proclamation on Fisheries in September, 1945, is that other countries will claim more than any new claim the United States makes, deliberately interpret the new claim the United States makes in their favor, and use our new claim, their new claim, and their misinterpretation of our new claim, as substantiation for any action they wish to take over and above what the United States wants to do. The parochial view noted in the first paragraph above pushed us into this invidious position in 1945, and we should guard carefully against repeating that mistake.

The over-all, world-wide, national interests of the United States in coastal waters is best served by a national policy containing *all* of these elements:

1. Internal waters demarcated in accordance with the terms of the 1958 Convention on the Territorial Sea and Contiguous Zone.

2. A territorial sea three marine miles in breadth demarcated in accordance with the 1958 Convention on the Territorial Sea and

Contiguous Zone, and as set out in the "Outer Continental Shelf Act of 1954" as adjudicated by the United States Supreme Court.

3. All fisheries, both inside and outside the territorial sea, in which we have an interest managed in accordance with the provisions of the 1958 Convention on Fishing and the Conservation of the Living Resources of the High Seas.

4. No fishery jurisdiction outside the three mile limit beyond that authorized in the 1958 Convention on Fishing and the Conservation of the Living Resources of the High Seas.

5. Sole jurisdiction over the resources (as defined in the 1958 Convention on the Continental Shelf) of the adjacent continental shelf (as defined in the 1958 Convention on the Continental Shelf).

6. Jurisdiction over the resources of the adjacent continental shelf divided as among the government of the states and the Union in accordance with the provisions of the "Submerged Lands Act of 1953" and the "Outer Continental Lands Act of 1953," as adjudicated by the United States Supreme Court.

7. The regime of the High Seas managed in accordance with the provisions of the 1958 Convention on the High Seas.

8. The administration of ocean affairs in the United States government organized along the lines of the Muskie Bill, S. 2251.

9. Adequate support funds from the United States Budget to implement the research and other activities called for by the recommendations above.

10. Adequate attention at the White House level to a National Ocean Strategy, a National Ocean Program with which to implement it, and a National Ocean Budget with which to fund the Program.

CHRISTY:

There are two major problems facing the rational and orderly exploitation of international fisheries. The first is the problem of production, and the second, the problem of distribution of the wealth. These problems are discussed in some detail in my paper and need not be repeated here. Instead, I shall discuss four of the different possible systems that might evolve for the distribution of the sea's wealth in fisheries. These are the continuation of the present system of open access; a distribution on the basis of "historic rights"; unilateral appropriation by coastal states; and some form of international control on behalf of the world community.

Under the *open access* system, presently maintained, the wealth is distributed on the basis of a nation's willingness and ability to invest in exploitation. No nation is excluded, and every nation may, if it wishes, exercise its option to participate in a fishery.

The chief difficulty with this system is that the wealth of the seas is wasted. The open access to the fishery leads to much greater applications of capital and labor than is economically justified, and total costs rise while total revenues are relatively fixed. In addition, this system will necessitate much more stringent conservation regulations in order to prevent depletion. Such regulations will either prohibit technological innovation or impose other, severe, costs on harvesting. The losses will be borne both by the world community and by the fishery industries. It is clear that this system of unrestrained access cannot be maintained.

The three other systems permit controls on the number of fishermen. But since some exclusion is required, these systems face, head-on, the problem of wealth distribution.

One of these systems is to divide the fisheries on the basis of "historic rights." Under this system, where a fishery has been developed and is being exploited wastefully, the participants would agree among themselves to controls on the amount of effort. They could, as in the North Pacific Fur Seal Treaty, leave exploitation in the hands of a single producer and then share the profits. Or they might agree to proportionate reductions in effort so that the relative amount of effort of each nation would remain the same as it was before the agreement. An additional alternative would be to reach agreement on a quota for the total catch and then divide the quota among themselves, permitting each nation to determine its own level of effort. This has been done for the Antarctic whales.

A system based on historic rights would distribute the wealth among those nations that have already made a significant investment in the fishery, and its success would depend upon the ability to exclude other nations. Historic rights are of obvious importance in reaching agreements on fisheries, but there are questions as to whether or not such a distribution scheme would be equitable or acceptable over the long run, and as to the effect on the rate of exploitation. There would, of course, have to be some definition of an historic right, based on the amount, duration, and continuity of investment. But whatever the definition, there would be an incentive for nations to invest in the exploitation of a new fishery, not only on the basis of immediate rewards, but also in order to acquire a right to the resource. That is, by not exercising its option to participate in a developing fishery, a nation might find itself forever excluded when entry controls become necessary. This could well precipitate an uneconomic race to exploit new fisheries; establish historic rights; and acquire as large a share as possible of the future wealth of the seas.

Looking at this system on the basis of current trends in national fishing effort, it is clear that this would lead to distribution in favor of the Soviet Union and the Japanese. The extension of these nations' distant water vessels to all corners of the sea would give them strong claims to the resources, if the principle of historic rights should become the guide for distribution. This might, in fact, be one of the motivations behind the rapid growth in the fishing effort of the Soviet Union and other East European countries. Unless the United States were to radically change its fishing industries, it might forever lose access to those vast fisheries in which it has little or no present investment—saury, hake in many areas, most whales, the fisheries of the Indian Ocean, the South Atlantic, Antarctic, and elsewhere. Most other nations of the world would also find themselves excluded from many of the world's fisheries. Permanent distribution on the basis of historic rights is not likely, therefore, to be widely acceptable.

A third system for distribution, and one that would also receive considerable opposition, is that of *unilateral appropriation* of resources by the coastal states. Some claims along these lines have already been asserted. Chile, Ecuador, and Peru have claimed exclusive rights out to 200 miles from their shores. Under the doctrine of abstention, the United States and Canada have claimed exclusive rights out to the middle of the Pacific Ocean to salmon that spawn in their streams. A twelve mile limit of exclusive fishing rights has no biological or economic rationale. Its political rationale is based only on the fact that a large number of nations have asserted claims out to that limit. In view of growing demands and increasing competition for scarce fishery resources, there will be growing pressures (already evident) to emulate or exceed the assertions of the C.E.P. countries. Only a relatively small number of nations would benefit from such a distribution scheme.

Under the fourth system, *internationalization,* the distribution of the sea's wealth in fisheries could follow any of several different patterns. Initially, some of the wealth produced under this system might be used to "buy out" historic rights, i.e., to help those nations with large investments to ameliorate the transitional hardships that would accompany the loss of access to the resource. An international authority could, for example, buy the whaling fleets of the Japanese, Norwegians, and Soviet Union so that they would incur no loss in giving up their rights to take whales in the Antarctic. But as the international authority would produce some income above and beyond these and other management costs, some other formula for distribution would have to be developed. Several different schemes or combination of them could be followed—population, need, length of coastline—or the income could be used for some generally accepted purpose. But whatever the scheme, it would have to be worked out by all nations, and it would have to be demonstrated that this system for distribution is better than the alternatives. The United States might find this system more to its advantage than one based on historic rights, and the Soviet Union might prefer it to a system based on unilateral appropriation by coastal states. And both nations would be likely to prefer it to the continuation of the open access approach.

While it is impossible to foresee the eventual course that will be followed, it is important to anticipate and understand the alternatives. Decisions based on immediate advantages and disadvantages may be very costly over the long run.

BAXTER:

The current dispute between New Zealand and Japan concerning the fisheries zone established by New Zealand is not a tale of high drama; there is no fisheries "war" in progress. The whole affair has been lacking in color and excitement for several reasons: The first is that although there is a substantial amount at stake economically, these fisheries do not bulk large in terms of the total economies of the two countries. Secondly, with all respect to New Zealand, it has not the physical means of waging a fully effective war against the Japanese fishermen. And finally, outright conflict has not arisen because both countries have simply been altogether polite about their differences.

Up until September of 1965, New Zealand had the normal three-mile limit for its territorial sea. There were some cases of fishing within this area by Japanese fishing vessels, but all of these incursions were taken care of in the diplomatic manner I mentioned a moment ago. The Japanese government would be asked to do something about these fishing vessels, and, so far as I have been able to ascertain, the government of Japan responded by seeing to it that offending vessels left the territorial waters of New Zealand.

The fisheries that are now the source of controversy between the two countries take place not only within the three-mile limit of the territorial sea of New Zealand but also within a newly-established outer zone of nine miles and in the high seas contiguous thereto. The fish are bottom-dwelling fish, the names of which I shall not venture to lay before you. The wet fish which were landed in a recent year were worth New Zealand £1,900,000, and more than half of these came from outside the three mile limit.

On September 10, 1965, New Zealand enacted the Territorial Sea and Fishing Zone Act 1965.[1] The act laid out a New Zealand territorial sea following the sinuosities of the coast and three miles in breadth, with twenty-four mile closing lines across bays [2]—all quite orthodox in terms of the Geneva Convention on the Territorial Sea and the Contiguous Zone of 1958.[3] The more important aspect of the legislation is that it created outside the three mile territorial sea an exclusive fisheries zone of nine miles,[4] which entered into effect on January 1, 1966. There was not, as other countries had provided in connection with the establishment of new fisheries zones, any phase-out period for foreign fisheries. Neither New Zealand nor Japan is a party to the Geneva Convention on the Territorial Sea and the Contiguous Zone of 1958.

At the time of the adoption of the new legislation, there was concern in New Zealand about how that country's coastline of about 4,000 miles could be policed. Assigned to this task New Zealand had only seven vessels, actually nothing more than motor launches, and the government was making energetic plans to bring in a mine-sweeper to supplement this armada. The government pointed out in their defense that aircraft were also available for policing. Members of Parliament representing

130

fishermen were, I think, justifiably concerned about what could be done to keep Japanese, Russian, and other fishermen out of the newly-established zone. Questions were also raised about what sanctions could be employed against the intruders. One, I suppose, would be the seizure of the gear of such vessels, but not being any more of an expert on the criminal law of New Zealand than I am on the fisheries law of that country, I cannot say whether this would be an appropriate and effective sanction in terms of the law and needs of that country.

The enactment of the new legislation led to talks—again on a very polite level—with Japan. And at the end of last year (1965), Japan declared that it was prepared to take this matter to the International Court of Justice, a proposal which heartened international lawyers because the Court was about to run out of business. Both countries have accepted [5] the optional clause [6] concerning the compulsory jurisdiction of the Court, but what remains is the framing of the specific question to be put to the Court. There has not yet been any clash, any specific factual dispute, that could be the basis for proceedings before that tribunal. Japan has now prepared a draft of the question or questions to be passed upon by the court and has submitted its text to the government of New Zealand. Mr. Holyoake, the Prime Minister, mindful of the fact that the Japanese government had taken several months to work out the text and convey it to New Zealand, very artfully said, "This is an important issue and I need hardly say that from the legal viewpoint the draft will be receiving in the next few months the same amount of careful examination and scrutiny on the New Zealand side as has been accorded to it by the Japanese Government in devising its terms."

There have been protests since January of this year from the fishermen of New Zealand that nothing has been done about incursions of Japanese vessels. It would seem that they may be less concerned about the Japanese vessels themselves than about the Russian fishing boats that have a way of following in their wake. There has apparently been a desire on the part of both the government of New Zealand and the Japanese government to avoid any showdown or incidents. New Zealand is in the position of having to balance conflicting interests in connection with its legal case. That country may well be worried that a clash between a New Zealand patrol vessel and Japanese fishermen might lead the court to order interim measures of protection.[7] If matters did suddenly come to a head, the specific factual context in which the clash might arise would not necessarily afford the best possible footing for putting the case of New Zealand before the court. On the other hand, I suppose that if no action is taken against intruding Japanese vessels, failure to protest or to take action might be considered to constitute acquiescence in the fishing by Japan and lead the Court to hold that Japan had acquired a right to fish—or had maintained its right to fish— within the nine mile fisheries zone.[8] Providentially for New Zealand, Japanese fishermen have for the most part been keeping out of the new zone, although, as I have mentioned, there have been a few incursions.

How and when the case will be put before the International Court of Justice depend on agreement upon the question to be submitted to the Court. The case of New Zealand will probably be grounded on the proposition that it is not prohibited by any rule of international law from establishing such an exclusive fisheries zone off its shores and that there is solid precedent for establishing such exclusive fisheries zones adjacent to the territorial sea. It will look to precedents set by the United Kingdom, by Canada, and by numerous other countries. On the other hand, Japan may be expected to maintain that any zone extending beyond the three mile limit is unlawful, particularly in respect of the relationships between two countries that are not parties to the Geneva Convention on the Territorial Sea and the Contiguous Zone; that New Zealand had arrogated to itself a portion of the high seas by its wholly unilateral measures; that there were no international consultations regarding the new fisheries zone; that Japanese fishermen had already been fishing in the area and had acquired rights there; and that, while Japan cannot acquiesce in the fisheries zone, it nevertheless would be willing to negotiate about terms on which both New Zealand and Japanese fishermen might be able to exploit these fisheries.

1. 1965, No. 11, 5 International Legal Materials 1 (1966).

2. Secs. 5 and 6.

3. Done at Geneva, 29 April 1958, arts. 1, 6, 7, pars. 4 and 5, 15 U.S.T. 1606, T.I.A.S. No. 5639, 2 United Nations Conference on the Law of the Sea, Official Records 132 (A/CONF.13/38) (1958).

4. Sec. 8.

5. Japanese Declaration of 15 September 1958 and New Zealand Declaration of 1 April 1940, [1964–1965] I.C.J.Y.B. 53 and 57.

6. Stat. Int'l. Ct. Just., art 36, par. 2.

7. Under article 41 of the Statute of the Court.

8. On the basis of the Fisheries Case (United Kingdom v. Norway), [1951] I.C.J. Rep. 116.

ALLEN:

Various elements of the United States fishing industry are united as to certain practical aspects which affect their approach to government and law and are divergent as to other aspects.

All unite in desiring competency in the fishery divisions of federal and state governmental agencies. This was demonstrated recently in the unanimous support for upgrading the fishery division of the Department of State. Also, they all avidly support oceanographic research. But they are divergent as to ocean fishery protection.

Although no fishery people openly disclaim their attachment to the cause of conservation, some emphasize the necessity for its being applied right now to coastal fisheries, whereas others contend that the potential of ocean fisheries is so great as to negate necessity for high seas limitations. Those who oppose restrictions on ocean fishery exploitation point out that almost any kind of fish can be made into flour to meet the protein needs of billions of people; hence, that the beautiful phrase "freedom of the seas" must be kept pure, sacred and absolute, whereas the first group, while not disparaging the value of fish flour, suggest that, in this country at least, people prefer to know that they are eating salmon, tuna, shrimp, pampano, or cod, rather than risk a diet of spoon-fed conger eel and rat fish powder; hence that practical protection of coastal fisheries is more important than some theory.

These two divergent approaches to the law of the sea met at Geneva with the result that the fishery convention adopted there in 1958 was a compromise; hence its complexity. Although the fisheries convention purported to endorse freedom of the seas, both it and the Continental Shelf Convention in fact contain provisions demonstrating that such freedom is neither absolute nor sacrosanct, thereby leaving the principle open for rational application. This fisheries convention was the last of the four Geneva conventions to secure enough ratifications to bring it into operation. The United States attached a reservation to its ratification, and the convention need not be considered to be the last word on the subject.

Hugo Grotius, champion of freedom of the seas, was no theoretical dreamer, but a great advocate. The English translation of the title to his thesis is "The Freedom of the Seas or the Right which Belongs to the Dutch to Take Part in the East Indian Trade," that is, freedom of the Dutch to course the Indian Ocean and to break into the Portuguese monopoly of the highly profitable East Indies spice trade. Though not specifically mentioning the herring fishery off the British Coast, he made his appeal sufficiently broad so as to justify this Dutch monopoly.

Factually there is as much reason in the twentieth century as in the seventeenth to avoid curtailing trade and communication between nations, and a territorial sea width of not more than three miles is highly desirable as to navigation. But with mechanical power, refrigeration, floating canneries, radar, sonar, power blocks, and nylon nets, today's ocean fishing has an efficiency beyond imagination in the Hugo Grotius days when fishing was done from row or sail boats and it was believed that ocean fisheries were inexhaustible.

The American Bar Association in 1964 passed a resolution urging our government to seek international agreement giving wholly separate consideration to freedom of the seas for navigation, and to the distinct problem of conservation of ocean fisheries.

International law should be kept abreast of the times. If protection of coastal fisheries is essential to their preservation, this should not be hampered by the popularity of an attractive phrase.

PONTECORVO:

Virtually unnoticed among the substantive issues confronting the conference is one technical problem that, in my opinion, is really a major obstacle to further analytical progress: the question of communication. Given a conference attended by marine biologists, physical oceanographers, lawyers, social scientists, and intelligent laymen, how can these people talk to each other? At first glance this may seem a trivial question, but I feel strongly that this is not the case and offer as an illustration some subjective bits of evidence.

Several years ago at a similar conference in Ottawa I suggested in a paper that one of the essential economic aspects of the North Atlantic lobster fishery was that it was an inefficient albeit workable unemployment insurance scheme. This casual remark did not awaken any of the economists quietly sleeping in front of me, but administrators, representatives of several governments, and other defenders of the faith reacted with fury greater than that which would have been elicited by a savage attack on marriage. The essence of their argument was that since the fishery in question provided "employment" it could not be "unemployment insurance."

With this illustration in mind, let us look at the meaning of a deceptively simple word: "overfishing." To the biologists, the concept involves first of all the determination of a physical yield function. For a biologist to say that a given species has been overfished implies that fishing effort has pushed yield somewhere to the right of the hump in the yield function. In these circumstances a reduction in fishing effort would actually increase the physical yield. Note that overfishing does not imply elimination of the stock; it is simply the imposition of a particular mortality rate on the population. If the industry changes the rate of mortality by reducing the fishing effort, the population will grow more rapidly and, therefore, the yield will actually increase. We must note that overfishing is a particular condition applicable to a given population which has a given yield function. We might also note that in economic terms this illustration is an example of partial equilibrium analysis. By this the economist means that the yield and the conditions necessary for that yield, for only one species, out of many in the ocean, is considered.

We have discussed overfishing as a condition of a particular population, but the yield potential for an area of the ocean for all species has not been mentioned. The concept of general overfishing of wide areas of the ocean is so much more complex that thus far it has defied meaningful analysis.

To the conservationist, overfishing is a moral proposition, and it is evil. The destruction of the salmon in Alaska represents a waste (in 1960 the catch was less than one-third of 1936). To the conservationist the reduction in the salmon stocks is identical to the destruction of any valuable national asset. For this reason the conservationist is furious at the biologist who refuses to assert that historically overfishing took place in Alaska—in the absence of knowledge of yield functions.

To the economists, neither view makes much sense. The question posed by overfishing is just another problem in capital theory and not a very interesting or unique one at that. Within the framework of analysis of the yield from any asset, i.e., a stock of fish, the determinants of the rate of utilization are the matrix of prices and costs (originally derived from tastes—note this because international differences in tastes imply different economic equilibrium) that defines the level of output that will maximize the net economic yield from the resource.

Fortunately for the conservationists' blood pressure this particularly physical quality is usually, but not always, less than the biologists' maximum physical yield. For example: there is some evidence that the decision in the early 1930's to "save" or conserve the halibut stocks of the northeastern Pacific was non-economic, i.e., the nation as a whole would have been better off if the then remaining stock of halibut had been overfished or fished out for as long as it paid to do so. If this position is correct, probably today we are poorer not richer as a result of this conservation move to "prevent overfishing"—the halibut offer no comment on the debate.

Faced with these apparent contradictions and this semantic confusion, those responsible for the law of the sea may select an alternative policy at random but they do so at their peril. There are, as indicated above, both questions of scientific fact and interdisciplinary ignorance and confusion in policy alternatives. In Burke's words we need more sophisticated objectives. In the words of an economist we need objectives that fulfil the necessary conditions for long run stability and maximization.

> In more recent times, these objectives have been criticized as being too limited, as over-emphasizing the biological condition of the resource to the exclusion of other considerations; and recommendations are increasingly offered that more sophisticated objectives must be conceived so that the entire social context of fishery exploitation can be taken into account in regulating access to the resources.[1]

For most cases of resource use, the relevant physical quantity of yield that maximizes human material welfare is the one that maximizes the net economic yield, not the maximum physical yield. Therefore, I offer as a basic theorem the proposition that any international legal agreement based solely on physical yield is doomed to economic and probably biological failure.

What is the remedy? This lies in conferences that force the adversaries to face the difficulties in interdisciplinary semantics and in theoretical papers that eliminate apparent contradictions.

---

1. William T. Burke, *Ocean Sciences, Technology, and the Future International Law of the Sea* ("Pamphlet Series of the Social Science Program of the Mershon Center for Education in National Security," No. 2 [Columbus: Ohio State University Press, 1966]), p. 76.

Discussion:

The panel addressed itself primarily to the problem of the distribution of the living resources of the sea beyond territorial limits. National control of fisheries out to twelve miles from the shore seems to have become generally accepted, as a result both of the large number of countries now claiming extraterritorial fisheries zones and of the recent statements by State Department officials at Congressional hearings to the effect that establishment by the United States of a nine-mile extraterritorial fisheries zone would not be contrary to international law. New Zealand's recent adoption of a twelve mile fisheries zone, however, is being protested by the Japanese on the grounds that such an extension of jurisdiction is contrary to the rights of Japan and of all other countries.

Any seaward extension of a coastal state's jurisdiction over fisheries may involve claims by foreign countries to historic rights to those fisheries. Many of the newer countries of the world have no history of fishing off foreign coasts; thus they have no such historic rights, and no particular interest in recognizing this concept as international law. May a coastal state have rights to its own extraterritorial fisheries which place it in a more favored position than foreign newcomers to the area? How long should a country exploit a resource before it acquires historic rights?

Historic rights have economic value only to the extent that they are based upon the presumption of exclusion. Historic rights are implicit in most multilateral fisheries conventions, although such conventions today are generally "open-ended," permitting subsequent entry by other countries into the agreement.

One method of limiting entry into high seas fisheries is licensing. Under this system, licenses would be issued only to the appropriate number of vessels. The appropriate number would be determined by an evaluation of the yields, revenues, and costs, so that the desired amount of catch could be achieved at the least cost. The superfluous vessels would be excluded from the fishery. Such a system, according to economists, would be preferable to the conservation controls that attempt to regulate the amount of catch but permit wasteful applications of capital and labor.

But what organization would manage the licensing, and what would be the criteria for allocating licenses? One authority for handling the

137

licensing program might be the United Nations or one of its specialized agencies, to which revenue might be forthcoming from the licensing fees. But advocates of United Nations control were attacked on a number of grounds, among them the obvious disinclination of powers such as the United States and the Soviet Union to vest control of their high seas fisheries in a political organization such as the UN. Equally important was the question of criteria for issuing licenses. Should it be on the basis of bids, of ability to exploit the fisheries, of national or regional quotas, of historic rights, or of some other scheme? And how would the fisheries be policed in order to insure compliance? Might not better results be obtained from the normal give and take of interested parties?

Again the need was stressed for greater biological and economic study of the living resources of the sea. National control of fisheries more than a few miles from shore should not be designed primarily to protect inefficient producers; nor should it result in extensive stocks being underutilized, when there is actually foreign effort ready to harvest the fish. The Geneva Convention on Fishing and Conservation of the Living Resources of the High Seas has just come into existence; it is based on the principle of demonstrable biological need. Is this convention already becoming outdated through new economic rationale, new fisheries techniques, and new demands for national jurisdiction over high seas fisheries?

K. O. Emery

Chapter Nine:

GEOLOGICAL ASPECTS OF SEA-FLOOR SOVEREIGNTY[*]

I. *Abstract*

The present seaward limit of national sovereignty is defined as the edge of the continental shelf or the depth to which the sea floor can be exploited. Exploitation appears to be a poor criterion in these days of rapidly expanding marine technology. All reasonable geological boundaries of the sea floor (shoreline, shelf edge, base of continental slope, toe of continental rise, axes of trenches, deepest parts of abyssal plains, and the mid-ocean rift) are described according to their origin and value as seaward limits of national sovereignty for mining purposes. All contain uncertainties or deficiencies stemming from present inadequate knowledge of bathymetry, ambiguity of definition, or unreasonable relationship to areas of possible mineral resources. Perhaps the best seaward boundary for coastal nations is the 1,000 meter depth contour (of the main ocean basins) with some form of international jurisdiction applied to the deeper areas of ocean floor. Straight-line boundaries are suitable only for lateral separation of adjacent claims.

II. *Introduction*

A century ago little need was evident for extending political boundaries seaward and precisely defining seawardmost limits of sovereignty for other than coastal defense. During the past two decades, however, many nations have so greatly increased their military and economic capabilities at sea that their areas of interest and potential sovereignty of the sea floor have begun to overlap.

The sea floor, Antarctica, and the moon have in common the fact that no serious consideration was given to their political subdivision a few years ago, but present or future potential exploitation of these hitherto inaccessible areas can now lead even to military action to determine sovereignty. Naval action on the gunboat level made headlines during the past decade when Iceland, Israel, Korea, Lebanon, Peru, and probably other countries attempted to regulate deep-sea fishing off their coasts. Legal action has been more common, particularly in connection with attempts of community, state, and federal agencies in the United States to increase their "rightful" portions of tax revenues derived from sea-floor production of mineral resources by private industry. Overlapping political demands have a habit of developing wherever new sources of revenue are found, whether the competing political units are on the same side of the disputed sea floor (as for the United States) or on opposite sides (as in the Persian Gulf and the North Sea).

Before we consider the possible geological control of political boundaries on the sea floor, let us review the control that geology has exerted upon political boundaries on land. Difficulty in finding up-to-date maps of international boundaries illustrates the fact that military or political power is continually shifting the boundaries. Even casual inspection of any good world map shows two main kinds of international boundaries: irregular (following rivers or mountain crests), and straight lines (arbitrary boundaries). The sixteen-inch National Geographic Society's globe of 1962, supplemented by the *Times Atlas of the World* (Bartholomew, 1955–59) was chosen as the basis for a quantitative analysis. The lengths of the several kinds of boundaries between all nations of the world and between the states or provinces of the United States, Canada, and Australia were measured on the globe. For comparison, the lengths of ocean shorelines were also measured. The precision of the measurements was limited by the scale of the globe (1 inch = 800 km.), which required that all irregularities smaller than about 100 km. be ignored.

TABLE 4

KINDS OF INTERNATIONAL AND INTERSTATE
POLITICAL BOUNDARIES ON LAND

KIND	INTERNATIONAL: THE WORLD		INTERSTATE: UNITED STATES, CANADA, AND AUSTRALIA	
	Km.	Per Cent	Km.	Per Cent
Irregular	157,000	32.0	17,000	13.4
Straight	26,000	5.3	36,000	28.7
Shoreline	307,000	62.7	73,000	57.9

The resulting Table 4 shows that international boundaries are dominantly irregular (rivers and mountain crests) and that state or province boundaries are dominantly straight lines. Irregular geological boundaries mostly separate peoples of different languages or dialects, and straight surveyor's boundaries separate peoples having the same languages. The irregular geological boundaries evidently serve as lines of defense for limited military power. Most straight-line boundaries appear to have been established in areas having little contemporary value, and many were drafted thousands of kilometers from the ground sites. Many statistical relationships could be explored, but the fact is evident that international boundaries on land are chiefly geological ones. Perhaps the seawardmost boundaries of national sovereignty that eventually are recognized will also be geological ones, but almost certainly the lateral boundaries (between adjoining territories claimed by different nations) will be straight or broadly curved lines drafted ashore. The straight lines are to be expected because detailed topographic knowledge is lagging far behind claims, and also because few of the potential topographic boundaries constitute obstacles to the movement of ships. Probably more disputes will arise from these straight-line political and military lateral boundaries than from most of the seaward boundaries of sovereignty that are the main subject of the following discussion.

III. *Shoreline*

Shorelines of both marine and non-marine bodies of water are convenient boundaries for many purposes because they separate areas having greatly different properties with respect to habitation, engineering needs, and resources. However, shorelines are rarely international political boundaries because the precise line is not easily defended. Large interior bodies of water are usually divided along medial lines so that bounding nations or states are sovereign over the parts that adjoin their land areas (Dead Sea, Lake Superior, and Lake Tanganyika). International boundaries in oceans and their adjoining seas and gulfs have generally been taken as three miles from the nearest shoreline, presumably the area that could be dominated by shore guns or, as put by Mouton, the "hypothetical range of an imaginary gun" [1] in the late eighteenth century, or simply a unit of one league. As the guns improved, one would suppose that the boundaries would have marched seaward; instead, little change occurred until recently when a great demand for fish and mineral

141

resources coincided with the development of intercontinental ballistic missiles and of world-encircling satellites.

Even though the designation of shorelines as international boundaries is impractical, their use as local property boundaries warrants a brief discussion of their permanency. Changes of the position of the shoreline come about from worldwide changes of sea level, local changes of land level, and local imbalance of erosion and deposition. The major trend of sea level during the past 19,000 years has been one of rise owing to

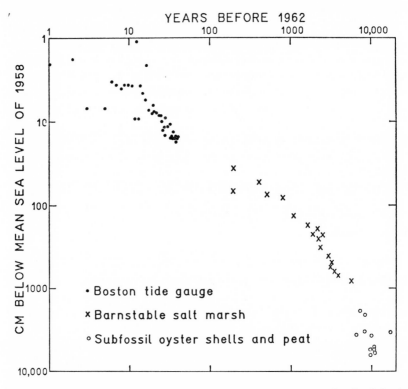

Fig. 4.—Positions of mean sea level during the past 19,000 years for the Atlantic Coast of the United States and Canada. The tide-gauge records are for Boston (Association d'Océanographie Physique, 1940, 1950, 1953, 1958, 1959; and J. R. Rossiter, personal communications, 1962); the salt-marsh peat is from Barnstable marsh (Redfield and Rubin, 1962); and the oyster shells and peat are from the continental shelf (Emery, Wigley, and Rubin, 1965; and Mecof, Clarke, and Erskine, 1965; and Merrill, Emery, and Rubin, 1965).

142

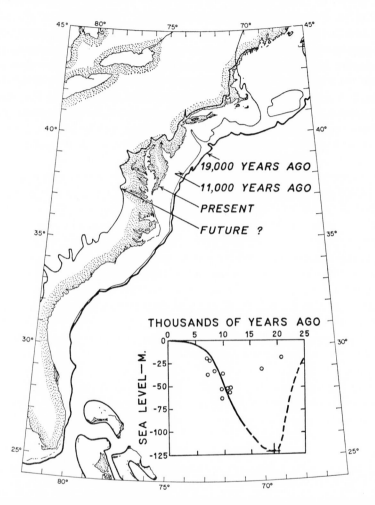

Fig. 5.—Positions of the shoreline along the Atlantic Coast of the United States during the past, present, and future. Positions are based on present bathymetry guided by the sea-level data supplied in Fig. 4, and are supplemented by information on the raised shorelines of Canada (Farrand and Gajda, 1962; and Borns, 1965). The insert diagram shows the changing position of past level derived from radiocarbon ages of shallow-water shells and peat deposits.

the return of water formerly in the ocean, but temporarily stored as glacial ice on land. Four major glacial ages occurred during the past one to three million years known as the Pleistocene Epoch. Growth and melting of the ice sheets was irregular, so that minor variations of sea level were superimposed upon the major trends. One of the lowest sea levels occurred about 19,000 years ago when the level was about 120 meters [2] below the present one (Figures 4 and 5). Virtually the entire continental shelf was then exposed, as indicated by world-wide submerged terraces, shorelines, and relict sediments and by local discoveries of submerged forests, peat deposits, subfossil intertidal oysters, and elephant teeth. Early man probably roamed almost the entire width of the continental shelf off the Atlantic coast of the United States as early as 12,000 years ago, but the slow advance of the rising sea gradually forced him from the shelf. If all of the remaining glacial ice were to melt, sea level would rise another sixty meters, returning the shore to approximately its preglacial position and drowning most of the major cities and densely inhabited regions of the world.

Direct evidence of rising sea level during the past 12,000 years is revealed by radiocarbon dating of submerged oyster beds and peat deposits, during the past 5,000 years by radiocarbon dating of submerged salt-marsh deposits, and during the past few decades by tide-gauge records (Figure 4). Differences in rates of rise recorded at particular localities reflect complications caused by local geological processes among which are faster uplift of a local land area than rise of sea level (such as due to rebound of the land after the melting of an ice load). Elsewhere a rapid subsidence of the land caused by compaction of deltaic or marsh sediments accentuates the advance of the sea. An example is the flooding of Saint Mark's Square and of many public and private buildings in Venice during high tides of recent years. An outstanding example produced by man's activities is the more than 7.5-meter subsidence of the land surface near the shore of Long Beach, California, evidently the result of the withdrawal of large quantities of petroleum from beneath the same area.[3]

Another kind of modification of the shoreline is due to local erosion of beaches and cliffs, particularly of cliffs composed of loose sediment. Many examples throughout the world come to mind, from the remains of undermined trees (Hawaii), ancient towns (Israel), Indian or Eskimo graves (Alaska), property lines (England), and lighthouses (Cape Cod, Massachusetts). Local excess deposition of sediments at

144

the mouths of rivers has converted once prosperous seaports into abandoned inland ruins (Ostia, Ephesis, and Tarsus among others in the Mediterranean Sea). Prograding of valuable beach property in southern California has resulted in many lawsuits to determine whether the accretion was due to natural processes (when the accretion belongs to the owner of the adjacent upland property) or artificial (when it belongs to the state). Other lawsuits have resulted from extensive erosion downwave from groins that were built to retain sand that normally moves continuously downwave. A basis for future additional suits may be the trapping of sand by dams across streams, thus preventing the free movement of sand to replenish beaches of the shore zone (a current example is the Aswan High Dam of Egypt, which probably will cut off most of the supply of beach sand to Israel).

The determination of the extent of natural and artificial movement of the shoreline is commonly tied to an estimation of an "original" position of the shoreline—or the position at a given time during the past. For this reason, old charts are in great demand for legal purposes. Most old charts, however, are unsatisfactory due to their lack of precision and to subsequent destruction of the landmarks that were used in the original surveys. Doubtlessly, as man continues to crowd into shore areas and as both natural and artificial changes of the shoreline increase, the legal demand for past precise surveys will increase greatly.

IV. *Seaward Edge of Continental Shelf*

The next natural boundary seaward of the shoreline is the edge of the continental shelf, commonly known as the shelf edge or shelfbreak. The International Committee on Nomenclature of the Sea Floor [4] proposed the following definitions:

> *Continental shelf, shelf edge* and *borderland.* The zone around the continent, extending from the low-water line to the depth at which there is a marked increase of slope to greater depth. Where this increase occurs the term shelf edge is appropriate. Conventionally, the edge is taken at 100 fathoms (or 200 meters) but instances are known where the increase of slope occurs at more than 200 or less than 65 fathoms. When the zone below the low-water line is highly irregular and includes depths well in excess of those typical of continental shelves, the term continental borderland is appropriate.

The same definition was used by Guilcher, *et al.,*[5] in their description of the continental shelf for UNESCO that presumably was considered when

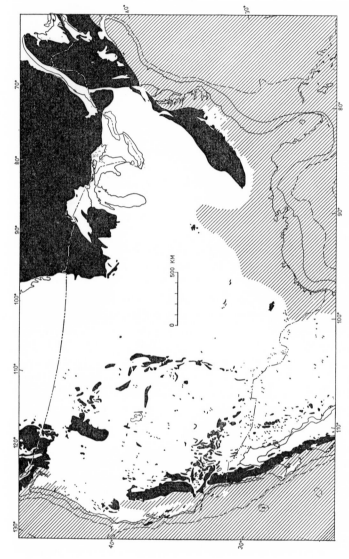

Fig. 6.—Simplified geological map of the United States and adjoining parts of Mexico and Canada and adjacent sea floors. Pleistocene and recent cover is ignored. Solid black is used to indicate areas of exposed intrusive igneous and associated metaphoric rocks; cross-hatching, to indicate areas of marine Tertiary sedimentary strata. Land data are derived from Goddard (1965); sea-floor data, from many sources.

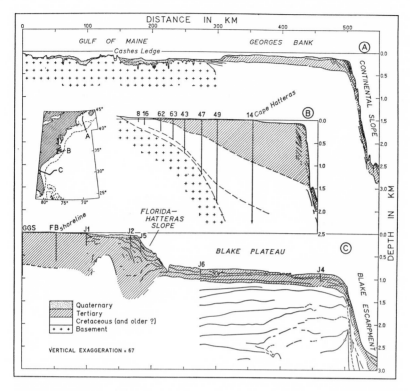

FIG. 7.—Selected geological profiles across the continental margin off the Atlantic Coast of the United States. Compiled from continuous seismic reflection profiles, dredgings, test wells on the sea floor, and oil wells on land. As described by Emery (in press).

the Convention on the Law of the Sea was adopted by the United Nations Conference at Geneva during April, 1958. The present United States Board of Geographic Names (1964) likewise defined the shelf edge as "The line along which there is a marked increase of slope at the outer margin of a *continental* (or *island*) *shelf*."

While sovereignty for mining purposes is related to the full width of the continental shelf, many nations claim the overlying waters for additional purposes. Many have separate claims on belts having differen' widths for their territorial seas, customs, fishing, neutrality, and sani tary regulations, as shown by a tabulation that was prepared in 1960

147

for the Second Geneva Conference on the Law of the Sea.[6] Several of the claims reach 200 miles from shore, especially for fishing rights.

Continental shelves are characterized by structure and stratigraphy that are similar to, or are natural continuations of, the structure and stratigraphy of the adjacent land. A general impression of the similarity is given by a highly generalized geological map of the United States and its adjacent sea floors (Figure 6). In cross-section the continuity is even more evident (Figure 7) for areas where investigation has been adequate. These and other studies have shown that the continental shelf is merely a seaward continuation of the continent. Off most mountainous coasts the shelf appears to be largely erosional in origin because it is shallowly underlain by bedrock. Off most flat coasts deposition has been more important, coupled with relative subsidence, so that the shelf is underlain by a thick sequence of sedimentary strata that gently dip seaward.

Economic resources found on land may continue seaward, expand seaward, or be replaced by different resources. Oil and gas are highly valuable examples. Some oil fields in southern California continue seaward (in fact, the Summerland oil field that was discovered on land was followed seaward by offshore drilling during 1896). Some oil fields (such as the Wilmington field) are centered offshore so that only a fringe underlies the land. Other fields on the sea floor are isolated from the land, but some of them are associated with salt domes that pepper both sea floor and land off Louisiana and Texas; others are almost restricted to the sea floor (illustrated by recently found gas fields off England in the North Sea).

Altogether about one-sixth of the annually produced ten billion barrels of oil comes from the sea floor. Within a decade or two the marine production should more than double its share even with a doubled total production. The value of this resource has led to many legal disputes over ownership of confined shelf areas having high production. Some offshore recovery of sulfur and salt occurs off Louisiana and Texas in close association with oil and gas. Additional mineral resources on the continental shelf are sand (for land fill and concrete aggregate), shell (for land fill and cement), and potentially phosphorite (for fertilizer and chemicals).

The great value of mineral resources on the continental shelves led to the Outer Continental Shelf Lands Act by which Congress in 1953 [7] claimed the subsoil and sea bed of the shelf adjacent to the United States as subject to the jurisdiction, control, and disposition of the United States, but it does not affect the international rights of navigation and fishing. Jurisdiction over the inner three miles is left to individual states by the Submerged Lands Act of 1953,[8] but many legal battles have resulted from differences in interpretation of the baseline for measurement as related to bay mouths and offshore islands; still other lawsuits came from confusion about original charter rights to three marine leagues (rather than to three geographical miles) off Texas and other states that border the Gulf of Mexico.[9] Rights for all coastal nations extending beyond those claimed by the United States in 1953 were approved by the 1958 United Nations Conference on the Law of the Sea[10] and ratified by the last of the required twenty-two nations on June 10, 1964.

Legal battles are certain to develop from any definition of the outer limit of the continental shelf, because this limit is an imprecise one. The steepening of declivity at the shelf edge occurs in a distance of less than 1 to more than 10 km., and locally two or more separate zones of steepening are present. Differentiation by depth alone is impractical, because the shelf edge ranges from 20 to 550 meters and averages 133 meters deep.[11] Adding to the difficulty is the fact that important economic resources lie on the sea floor at greater depth: within the continental borderland off southern California (between the true continental shelf and the true continental slope), on the continental slope in many areas of the world, and perhaps even on the deep-sea floor.

V. Base of Continental Slope

The next seaward geological boundary beyond the shelf-break is the base of the continental slope. The continental slope is approximately the true limit of the continents, or the general boundary between the light rocks of the continents and the denser rocks of the sea floor. Because of the density contrast and the thick section of light rocks that underlie the continents, this boundary is probably the most important geological one of the Earth. Unfortunately, little is known (but much is speculated) about its origin and the fundamental cause of the separation of continents and ocean basins.

One general line of speculation has an original continent[12] split apart during Early Mesozoic time (about 135 million years ago), so that the rift is now reflected in the approximately matching outlines of the western margins of Europe and Africa with the eastern margins of North

149

America and South America. Analogies are represented by the similar close matches between opposite coasts of the Red Sea [13] and of the Gulf of California,[14] both of which opened during the Tertiary Period (during the past sixty-three million years). This splitting and moving apart of continental masses is referred to as continental drift, a concept developed by Wegener [15] and others during the early twentieth century, largely abandoned two decades ago, and recently resurrected by evidence provided by paleomagnetic studies.[16] Several objections remain, including the origin and the present position of the original outer boundaries of the precontinent, the origin of the precontinent itself, and the fact that the present opening of the oceans appears to be restricted to a mid-ocean rift, as described by Heezen,[17] rather than to the continental-slope boundary between continents and ocean basins. Other complications in the meaning of the continental slope result from the fact that the oldest rocks of the continents generally crop out near their centers, with progressively younger rocks usually occurring toward their perimeters. In fact, recent geophysical evidence [18] indicates that the continental slope off eastern United States prograded seaward 7 to 35km. by deposition of sediments during the past sixty-three million years.

As shown by Heezen, Tharp, and Ewing,[19] the continental slope is bounded on its seaward side by the continental rise, a vast apron of debris from the continent and of calcareous skeletal material from near the sea surface. The apron shape reflects the landward source of most of the sediment (brought by turbidity currents and suspended sediment) and its movement and redeposition by bottom currents that appear to flow parallel to the contours.[20]

The boundary between the continental slope and the continental rise is not everywhere clearly marked, owing to inadequate soundings and to the fact that sediments of the continental rise overlap the continental slope [21] and can eventually bury it.[22] For convenience in identification, Heezen and his associates take a steepness of 1:40 as the boundary between slope and rise. The boundary is unrelated to depth, for it ranges from less than 1,000 to more than 4,000 meters. A proposal once was made to extend the territorial limits of the United States to the 1,000 fathom contour. The intent presumably was to avoid the imprecision of the shelf-break and to include some of the economic resources seaward of the shelf-break. In a geological sense a 1,000 fathom seaward limit for the maritime nations is about as unreasonable as a 6,000 foot landward boundary for them, but the precision and legal advantage of a

150

1,000 fathom, or better a 1,000 meter, limit may be so great as to eclipse geological considerations.

The continental shelves and slopes of the world have an area of about 55.4 million km².[23] This area is more than one-third the 149.8 million km² of the subaerial parts of the continents. If added to the sovereign territory of adjacent nations it would expand some of them by a factor of more than ten while adding nothing to the areas of such inland nations as Bolivia, Czechoslovakia, and Mongolia. This is obviously an unfair distribution of new territory, depending only upon the chance that determined the positions and shapes of existing nations. It also fails to include potentially important mineral resources that are located still farther seaward.

VI. *Deep-Sea Boundaries*

Several geological boundaries occur beyond the base of the continental slope (Figure 8). Some are worthy of consideration as seaward limits of national sovereignty of the sea floor. One is the toe of the continental rise, where it adjoins an abyssal plain. Heezen and his associates have found that this junction is approximately indicated by a change from steeper than to gentler than 1:1,000. The continental rise is wide where the supply of sediment from the continent is large, narrow where the supply is small (low rainfall, small drainage area, nearshore sediment traps), and it is absent where the continental slope is bordered by a deep-sea trench (Figure 9). The main advantage of including the continental rise under the sovereignty of bordering nations is the potential value of petroleum in the upper part of the rise. Source beds are organic-rich sediments that slowly accumulate on the continental slope in a depth zone of oxygen-deficient water; later some of these sediments slide away down the slope, accounting for a hummocky topography near the tops of some continental rises. Intermittent deposition of sand layers by turbidity currents may provide adequate reservoir beds.[24] The volumes of the continental rises are enormous (the largest sedimentary deposits of the Earth) and the quantities of oil and gas may well be commensurate. The main obstacle to the investigation and exploitation of these possible oil and gas resources is the great depth of water above them (1,500 to 4,500 meters); in contrast, few oil wells now produce from beneath water depths of more than 150 meters.

151

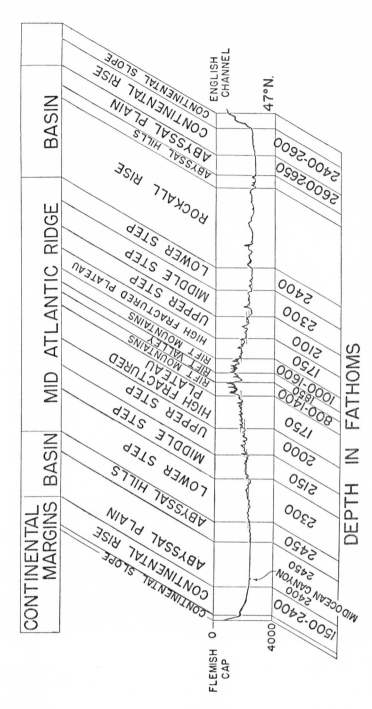

FIG. 8.—Physiographic provinces of the North Atlantic Ocean shown in profile. Similar provinces probably occur in all oceans that have a median ridge and rift valley. Vertical exaggeration is 40:1. From Heezen, Tharp, and Ewing, Fig. 42 (1959).

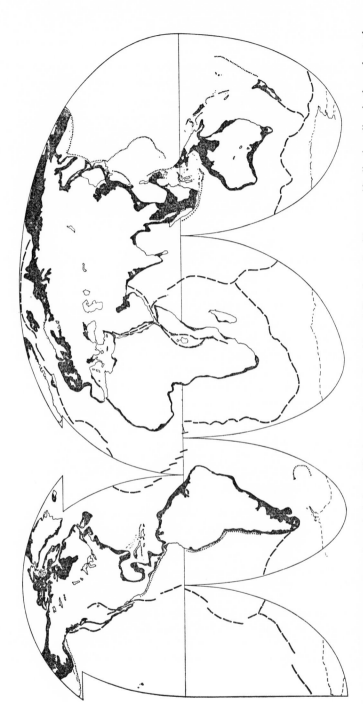

Fig. 9.—Distribution of continental shelves (black areas), trenches (dotted lines), and mid-ocean rift (broken lines) throughout the earth. The mid-ocean rift (redrawn from Heezen, 1962) contains many offsets by large strike-slip faults.

A geological boundary nearer the middle of the ocean is provided by the line of greatest depth (other than in trenches), that is located along the seaward sides of the abyssal plains (Figure 8). Another boundary that seemingly would provide an all-ocean sovereignty is the mid-ocean rift [25] that stretches 75,000 km. through the world ocean (Figure 9). However, the rift is not present off all coasts; locally it forks, and where well known, it consists of discontinuous units separated by offsets produced by strike-slip faults. One might suggest as a substitute a medial line through all oceans as the ultimate boundary. Although such a line was drawn by Menard,[26] its position is not unequivocal, mostly because of uncertainties and differences of opinion about how to select shore points and how to strike arcs from them.

Subdivision of the deep sea will be required if all areas of manganese-oxide nodules are to be included under national sovereignties, for the nodules are widespread on abyssal plains and on seamounts throughout the oceans.[27] However, the writer wishes to point out that subdivision of the deep sea floor is unlikely to be necessary for the purposes of manganese mining alone because of the low concentrations of the manganese (relative to silicon) and its associated cobalt, copper, and nickel.[28] The cost of metals extracted from the nodules probably will be greater than the cost of metals from land mines for many years unless heavy special sea-floor subsidies are granted.

VII. *Depth of Exploitation*

The 1958 United Nations Conference at Geneva in its Convention on the Continental Shelf stated as follows:

> For the purpose of these articles, the term "continental shelf" is used as referring (a) to the seabed and subsoil of the submarine areas adjacent to the coast but outside the area of the territorial sea, to a depth of 200 meters or, beyond that limit, to where the depth of the superjacent waters admits of the exploitation of the natural resources of the said areas; (b) to the seabed and subsoil of similar submarine areas adjacent to the coasts of islands.[29]

The key word, *exploitation,* is not defined. Does the recovery of a few manganese nodules as curios constitute exploitation? How many tons of nodules per year per unit area constitutes exploitation? Is profit on a free and open market required, or will large governmental subsidies substitute for profit? Manganese nodules with their content of cobalt, copper, and nickel are the chief deep-sea resources that generally receive mention, but does the recovery of a few million dollars worth of these metals per year warrant assignment of sovereignty to huge areas of the earth? What happens if sovereignty is assigned and a few years later the mining is considered unprofitable?

The convention fails to set any real limits. Accordingly, the half-dozen nations that now are or soon will be competent to drill or otherwise exploit mineral resources of the deep-sea floor are likely to have different interpretations of what is thine and what is mine. For example, if mining of manganese nodules should prove profitable, the United States theoretically could mine the Blake Plateau off Florida (where the nodules are abundant) and continue mining down the continental slope and across the continental rise and abyssal plains, up on the Mid-Atlantic Ridge and down into the next abyssal plain, continental rise, and continental slope. England could do the same from the European side to North America. The territories of interest can widely overlap. What then is the role of distant offshore islands (such as the Azores) as centers for radial claims? Fortunately, this confused state of affairs is not likely to develop from international greed for manganese nodules, because technical aspects of the extraction of their metals may render them worthless. Moreover, the restriction of potential deep-sea oil fields to the tops of the continental rises should largely eliminate conflicting claims; so may the high costs of exploitation. Nevertheless, the development of new methods of sea-floor mining and of milling and the discovery of presently unforeseen mineral resources may translate fantasy into reality in a few decades. Pressure of conflicting claims for mining of the sea floor may parallel those for fishing rights that already extend far beyond some shelf-breaks and beyond the continental slopes as well.

VIII. *Results of Sea-Floor Claims upon Research*

One might suppose that the need for knowledge about the sea floor that is required for proper basing of territorial claims would increase the pursuit of that knowledge. In fact, however, no obvious increase of data has resulted from territorial claims. The small countries have neither the money nor scientific talent for effective work. The efforts of large countries have been increasing for many years, but for military and

155

scientific reasons rather than for gaining knowledge to better define political boundaries. Sufficient reason exists for believing that the present conflict of demands for sea-floor sovereignty tends to reduce research.

The present Convention on the Continental Shelf (Article 5, Par. 8)[30] says:

> The consent of the coastal State shall be obtained in respect of any research concerning the continental shelf and undertaken there. Nevertheless, the coastal State shall not normally withhold its consent if the request is submitted by a qualified institution with a view to purely scientific research into the physical or biological characteristics of the continental shelf, subject to the proviso that the coastal State shall have the right, if it so desires, to participate or to be represented in the research, and that in any event the results shall be published.

One can readily imagine that permission may often be refused or so delayed that the effort required to gain permission will exceed the effort needed for actual sampling; then, of course, the marine scientist turns his attention to more fruitful work. In one instance the writer had to abandon an effort to learn about the topography of part of the Mediterranean shelf because permission to enter claimed territorial waters was delayed by suspicion about possible military motives. Probably more common are delays caused by inertia and lack of interest on the part of government officials.

IX. *Conclusions*

At present the assignment of geological limits to sea-floor sovereignty seems unlikely because of inadequate precision of these limits and because some of the geological limits do not include all of a potential mineral resource or do not exclude conflicting claims. Straight-line boundaries are likely to cut across mineral deposits. Any kind of contiguous sovereignty greatly favors nations that span a great length of coast for unrelated reasons. Depth of exploitation heavily favors nations that are highly industrialized or that are willing to subsidize offshore mining. We gain nothing by delay in better defining of sovereign limits through hope that the problem will "go away," because the problem is bound to increase as the half dozen active nations continue to develop their capability for undersea investigation and exploitation. Recent evidence is the development of deep offshore drilling, continuous seismic profiling, deep-diving research submarines, and long-period accommodation to man to the undersea environment.

156

A suggestion about seaward boundaries can be made from the viewpoint of mineral resources and certainty in identification. All presently exploited sea-floor resources and many potential ones would be encompassed by bordering nations if the seaward limit of sovereignty were put at the 1,000 meter contour of the deep-sea floor (exclusive of relatively small closed basins off southern California, in the West Indies, and in the East Indies, for example). Mineral resources at greater depth may be developed eventually, or perhaps be given up as hopeless. While the various nations are developing their capability for exploitation (and learning more about the sea floor), the sea-floor regions deeper than 1,000 meters might well be left to the control of the United Nations or to some other more effective international group. Tax revenues, if any, could serve to defray costs of administration, with excess revenues being distributed to land-bound nations that otherwise might not share in the possible future wealth of sea-floor resources.

* Contribution No. 1824 of the Woods Hole Oceanographic Institution. After making the first draft of this article, the author profited from discussions with several active marine geologists, especially B. C. Heezen and H. W. Menard. The final draft incorporates some of their suggestions. It is the author's hope that this published version will serve as the basis for further investigation, especially on the part of those whose greatest competence is in the field of international law.

1. M. W. Mouton, *The Continental Shelf* (The Hague: Martinus Nijhoff, 1952), pp. 192–200.

2. W. L. Donn, W. R. Farrand, and M. Ewing, "Pleistocene Ice Volumes and Sea-Level Lowering," *Jour. Geology*, LXX (1962), 206–14.

3. K. O. Emery, *The Sea off Southern California: A Modern Habitat of Petroleum* (New York: John Wiley & Sons, Inc., 1960), p. 318.

4. J. D. H. Wiseman, and C. D. Ovey, "Definitions of Features on the Deep-Sea Floor," *Deep Sea Research*, I (1953), 11–16.

5. André Guilcher, Ph. H. Kuenen, F. P. Shepard, and V. P. Zenkovitch, "Scientific Considerations Relating to the Continental Shelf," UNESCO, Conference on the Law of the Sea, 13/2, 1957 (mimeo.).

6. A. L. Shalowitz, *Shore and Sea Boundaries, with Special Reference to the Interpretation and Use of Coast and Geodetic Survey Data* (Publication of the U.S. Coast and Geodetic Survey, No. 10–1) (Washington, 1962), pp. 398–419.

7. Public Law 212, 83d Cong., 1st Sess., 67, Stat. 462.

8. Public Law 31, 83d Cong., 1st Sess. 67, Stat. 29.

9. Shalowitz, *op. cit.*, pp. 136–44.

10. *Ibid.*, pp. 371–88.

11. F. P. Shepard, *Submarine Geology* (2d ed.; New York: Harper & Row, 1963), p. 257.

12. Gondawanaland, Pangara, etc.

13. D. H. Swartz and D. D. Arden, Jr., "Geologic History of the Red Sea Area," *Bull. Amer. Assoc. Petroleum Geologists,* XLIV (1960), 1621–37.

14. Warren Hamilton, "Origin of the Gulf of California," *Bull. Geol. Soc. of America,* LXXII (1961), 1307–18.

15. A. Wegener, *Die Entstehung der Kontinente und Ozeane,* (Braunschweig: Vieweg, 1922).

16. S. K. Runcorn. "Palaeomagnetic Evidence for Continental Drift and its Geophysical Cause," *Continental Drift,* ed. S. K. Runcorn (New York: Academic Press, 1962), pp. 1–40.

17. B. C. Heezen, "The Deep-Sea Floor," *Continental Drift,* ed. S. K. Runcorn (New York: Academic Press, 1962), pp. 235–88.

18. Elazar Uchupi and K. O. Emery, "Structure of the Continental Margin off the Atlantic Coast of the United States," *Bull. Amer. Assoc. Petroleum Geologists,* in press.

19. B. C. Heezen, Marie Tharp, and Maurice Ewing, "The Floors of the Oceans," Vol. I, *The North Atlantic,* Geol. Soc. of America, Spec. Paper 65, 1959.

20. B. C. Heezen, C. D. Hollister, and W. F. Ruddiman, "Shaping of the Continental Rise by Deep Geostrophic Contour Currents," *Science,* CLII (1966), 502–8.

21. Hartley Hoskins, "Seismic Reflection Observations on the Atlantic Continental Shelf, Slope and Rise Southeast of New England," *Jour. Geology,* in press. Also, Uchupi and Emery, *op. cit.,* in press.

22. R. S. Dietz, "Geomorphic Evolution of Continental Terrace (Continental Shelf and Slope)," *Bull. Amer. Assoc. Petroleum Geologists,* XXXVI (1952), 1802–19.

23. H. W. Menard and S. M. Smith, "Hypsometry of Ocean Basin Provinces, *Jour. Geophys. Research,* LXXI (1966), 4305–25.

24. K. O. Emery, "Oceanographic Factors in Accumulation of Petroleum," Sixth World Petroleum Congress, Frankfurt, Germany, Sec. I, Paper 42 (1963), PD2, pp. 483–91.

25. B. C. Heezen, *op. cit.*

26. H. W. Menard, "Development of Median Elevations in Ocean Basins," *Bull. Geol. Soc. America,* LXIX (1958), 1179–86.

27. H. W. Menard, *Marine Geology of the Pacific* (New York: McGraw-Hill, 1964). Also, J. L. Mero, *The Mineral Resources of the Sea* (New York: Elsevier Publ. Co., 1965).

28. K. O. Emery, "Geological Methods for Locating Mineral Deposits on the Ocean Floor," Marine Technology Society, *Trans.* Joint Conf. and Exhibit, 27–29 June, 1965, Washington, D.C., pp. 24–43.

29. A. L. Shalowitz, *op. cit.,* pp. 376–77.

30. *Ibid.,* p. 377.

Additional References

Association d'Oceanographie Physique, 1940, 1950, 1953, 1958, 1959, "Monthly and Annual Mean Heights of Sea Level." Liverpool Observatory and Tidal Institute, Birkenhead, England, Publ. Science Nos. 5, 10, 12, 19, and 20.

BARTHOLOMEW, JOHN (ed.). 1955–59, *The Times Atlas of the World,* Mid-Century Edition. Cambridge, England: Houghton-Mifflin Co., Vols. I–V.

BORNS, H. W., JR. "The Paleo-Indians' Geography of Nova Scotia," *Int'l Assoc. for Quaternary Research,* VII Int'l Congress (1965) Boulder, Colorado, Abstracts, p. 41.

EMERY, K. O. "The Atlantic Continental Margin of the United States during the Past 70 Million Years," *Proc. Geol. Assoc. Canada,* in press.

———; WIGLEY, R. L.; and RUBIN, MEYER. "A Submerged Peat Deposit off the Atlantic Coast of the United States," *Limn. and Oceanog.,* Vol. X, supplement (1965), pp. R97–R102.

FARRAND, W. R., and GAJDA, R. T. "Isobases on the Wisconsin Marine Limit in Canada," *Geog. Bull.* No. 17 (1962), 5–22.

GODDARD, E. N. (chairman). *Geologic Map of North America,* scale 1:5,000,000, 2 sheets, U.S. Geol. Sur. (1965).

MEDCOF, J. C.; CLARKE, A. H., JR.; and ERSKINE, J. S. "Ancient Canadian East-Coast Oyster and Quahaug Shells," *Jour. Fish. Res. Bd. Canada,* XXII (1965), 631–34.

MERRILL, A. S.; EMERY, K. O.; and RUBIN, MEYER. "Ancient Oyster Shells on the Atlantic Continental Shelf," *Science,* CXLVII (1965), 398–400.

REDFIELD, A. C.; and RUBIN, MEYER. "The Age of Salt Marsh Peat and Its Relation to Recent Changes in Sea Level at Barnstable, Massachusetts," *Proc. Natl. Acad. Sciences.* XLVIII (1962), 1728–35.

United States Board of Geographic Names, 1964, "Undersea Terms and Definitions," revised after GEBCO meeting of May, 1964. U.S. Dept. of Interior, 4 pp: mimeo.).

Chapter Ten:

I am not certain that my remarks are particularly pertinent to the legal boundaries in the oceans and on the continental shelf. That is a subject about which I have a distinguished ignorance and so advised the organizing committee. However, I do have some knowledge, which may be of value, about mining in the sea. I am not going to review again the statistics on how many tons of bromine there are in a cubic some-thing-or-other of sea water or how many square miles of manganese nodules pave the floor of the ocean. I have no knowledge of such matters. Rather I represent a group of practical mining people now engaged in undersea mining around the world for a number of different minerals and in a number of ways. As a matter of fact, after hearing the session at the Marine Technology Society the other day, we made the calculation that if only people who were *experienced* in the ocean talked at such meetings and they only talked about things they had actually done, instead of about what they propose to do, it would cut a three day meeting down to about an hour and fifteen minutes. There is a lot of rather wild speculation about undersea mining, but there is some actually going on in the world.

Let me explain briefly about our company and how we got into this business, and that will set the stage for what I have in mind later. Ocean Science and Engineering, Inc., was started just over four years ago, and it spawned a series of subsidiary companies, mostly in ocean mining. It was formed by six men brought together by a project not connected with mining, but by coincidence three of us were mining engineers, and so it was natural that our interest should turn toward undersea operations of that kind. Mainly we are design engineers. We design ships, buoys, control systems, winches, all sorts of hardware that goes into the ocean. The devices we build work, we stand behind them, and so we know quite a lot about what is possible to do, how one deals with dynamic stresses in a seaway, how to anchor heavy ships under difficult conditions, and so on.

One of our earliest major contracts had to do with the surveying of a major part of the coast of south and southwest Africa. We got this job because we managed to present a proposal to the management of the DeBeers Corporation at precisely the right moment, with exactly the right words in it. We offered to evaluate a series of undersea mining concessions, and eventually we did an extensive geophysical survey of about 600 miles of the coast between Walves Bay on the north and the Oliphants River to the south. I believe that we know that piece of the African coast as well as any 600 miles of the United States coast is known. We were trying to find diamonds. If one finds a diamond—which is a very small object indeed—he must go back and be able to find the one next to it. So the survey work was done with great precision. We found a great many diamonds. We prospected in great detail four of the five undersea diamond concessions, and on one of these we mapped at least ten million carats of diamonds spread among thirty separate areas. We cannot really define these areas as ore bodies yet because, by definition, ore is a mineral which can be mined at a profit. No profit has yet been obtained by mining these diamonds, but in my opinion a proper management and engineering organization would succeed in making very substantial profits out of the operation.

As a result of our experience in Africa, our company and the DeBeers group joined forces to set up a new company to do ocean mining around the world. It is known as Ocean Mining A.G., of Zug, Switzerland. This company is about half owned by us and half by DeBeers; our operations are financed in various ways from various sources. Ocean Mining's offices are in Washington, D.C., but we are mainly operating in the outside world with capital whose origin is unknown. This is most important in some parts of the world which are not particularly friendly either to South Africa or to England itself.

Ocean Mining began by making a rather extensive paper study of where one might look for ore deposits. We did, I suppose, the obvious thing. We examined the geologic situations offshore, around the world, opposite places where successful mining had been done onshore. We looked for such things as steep stream gradients, which would move these minerals into the sea, and for places where there is substantial

161

oceanic motion—both wave motion which would create a natural processing mechanism, and current motion which would sweep away the gangue material which is not wanted. We sought grooved and chinked rocks in which the heavy materials would remain more or less indefinitely as though on a riffle bed. As a result of studies of this nature we determined there were about fifty places that looked like they were possible ore targets. We assigned priorities to these and dispatched teams into the field to examine them in the order of priority to see how they looked. We were concerned with many subjects besides geology and oceanography. We investigated the legal aspects including how one can own underseas concessions in various parts of the world (in some countries the rules are rather sticky—although generally they compare favorably with the United States laws).

Our first experience with direct prospecting at sea was in Alaska where last summer we worked on our own claims up there for about three months under rather miserable conditions. Our company holds about 55,000 acres of undersea land off the coast of Alaska, largely in Norton Sound between the towns of Nome and Bluff, but also some areas around some of the islands and some near Goodnews Bay. Ocean Mining A.G. spent some $150,000 to send a small ship up there to run several hundred miles of sonic traverse, to determine the thickness of the undersea gravels and sands and to determine where the stream beds were buried. We had along a small sampling device which we named the Mickey Mouse—it was too small to really tell us much about the sub-bottom conditions, but it gave a rough qualitative indication of whether or not there was gold present. In some seventy-five holes that we drilled up there, we found gold in every one. This indicated we were in the right part of the world, but none of these assayed high enough to get us really excited. However, although we are not going to be in Alaska this summer, perhaps we shall go back next summer and look a little more. In this business, as I suppose in most other areas of oceanography, persistence is the greatest virtue. One must keep looking in spite of discouragements.

From Alaska we then proceeded to New Zealand, which was our next target; there we made a rather extensive geological reconnaisance on shore, by air, and by small boat. For reasons which I will not go into here, we decided against the area for the present; we simply lowered its priority on the list and moved to Tasmania. At this moment our

162

company (I should say our group of companies because there are six or seven companies involved in our group at the moment) hold about 10,000 square miles of undersea property off Tasmania and off Australia. Some of this is off the east coast of Tasmania at Oyster Bay; some is on the northern coast of Tasmania; some is around King and Flanders islands; and there are some areas that extend well out from shore.

All of the Bass Strait area, that is, the area between Tasmania and Australia proper, is shallow water—rarely over a couple of hundred feet deep—and the geological possibilities look rather good for tin and heavy minerals (rutile, zircon, ilmenite) and so on. We are now involved in the early stages of prospecting and have completed about 2,000 linear miles of sonic surveying. These data are used to make detailed maps of the bedrock topography and the surface topography; from these we get at the thing we are most interested in—the relationship between the thickness of the sediment and the sub-bottom structure. We have also picked up rather substantial areas along the coast of Australia proper— in Queensland, in New South Wales, and in western Australia.

In order to get the money to operate this Tasmanian concession (10,000 square miles was obviously going to take a lot of money—we estimated the cost of a prospecting venture down there as $800,000), we put together a joint venture called the Tasmanian Offshore Exploration Company, which includes several major worldwide companies. We also have people in the Philippines, in Thailand, and in Malaya, and several other countries, which I shall not name, working on undersea mining problems. We are just completing a new drilling rig for taking samples in a new way beneath the sea floor. The ship on which it is mounted sails from our Long Beach offices for Australia the end of this week. This rig is known as the Horton Mining Sampler, and we have great hopes that it will take clean efficient samples beneath rough water.

But discovering the extent of the mineral deposit even when you know its quantity and grade, and can make a reasonable estimate of the future markets in it, is only a part of the problem. That is to say, a detailed chart of the deposit is only half the job. In order to determine whether or not one can make it into a successful mine, one must know exactly what to do with it. That is, what sort and capacity of dredge would be used? How deep must it work? How thick are the gravels, and how rough is the bedrock? How much material would be processed each

163

day (or to what level does one process aboard)? What is to be done with the tailings? What kind of people are required? What support ships? Shifts? Salaries? etc. We are in the process now of designing several dredging systems to fit various properties. Mining is a marginal business in the sense that it is not something you can do with an all-purpose tool. Design studies begin with a specific ore body of known extent and grade for which you can calculate the markets over some period into the future; then you determine property life and set an amortization rate for the machinery which hopefully is written off to zero on the day that the mine is worked out.

We are in the process of making such studies for several properties now, and in each case the equipment will be rather different. There will soon be new kinds of dredges that scoop up material from the sea floor, treat it in a plant on board, get rid of the tailings, and send the concentrates ashore. However, each mine in each country has a lot of local complexities—for instance, where does one keep the crew? Is it worthwhile to keep them on the beach and trade them back and forth every day, or maintain them at sea for twenty days at a time and send them back at the end of that time, and so on? Religions cause food problems and holiday problems.

I should perhaps note that in our search for undersea minerals, we began at the top of the scale with diamonds, and then we descended through platinum and gold, tungsten, tin, and we are getting down to the lower levels now. I think we may never get down to manganese nodules.

We have had a series of legal problems connected with these various operations; there are complexities to setting up companies in parts of the world where the natives are not used to our system. Even in a country like South Africa—which, at least to the casual observer, is similar to the United States (it is disappointingly like home)—American methods of operation are so different that an American is clearly an outsider even though he looks the same and speaks the same language. There are many currency problems that one encounters—foreign exchange control problems, such as: How does one move money out of a country after it has been made?

How does one determine how much comes out and how much stays there. In Mexico, for example, outsiders are not allowed to own sea-coast property or, presumably, offshore property. In Thailand and the Philippines, American companies are favored. The point is that each country has special laws and customs which one must learn. Few countries, including the United States, have clear offshore mining laws.

I would like to mention other kinds of problems, including the ethical problems with which one could become involved. Please understand, there is more to running a mining company than simply worrying about where the ore is. Sometimes I think that finding the minerals is the very least part of our problem: the other parts of management are much more difficult.

In the course of these examinations and explorations we have had a series of problems with local laws and with political pressures and with ethics. Of these, the legal problems seem to me to be simplest because although these laws may be unfair, or badly written (perhaps they are not even written at all), or archaic, or difficult to observe, they at least offer a set of guidelines and are sort of an indication of what the local people would like done. We have been able to get along without any serious legal problems that could not be straightened out by the lawyers we retain around the world.

Politicians are somewhat more difficult because it is hard to identify their objectives. But, once it is discovered what their objectives are, they are relatively easy to deal with. However, I have felt that my own most difficult problems were those of business ethics. Often the question is: what compromises can be made of one's own standards in return for the concessions one hopes to obtain from the local people? I have set down a series of sample problems: Should one tell the Minister of Mines of some unspecified country who owns his Swiss company? Sometimes the Minister of Mines rather specifically does not want to know. He wants somebody to come in and develop his country; he does not particularly want to deal with any of a dozen companies which he has on a blacklist. If he does not ask, should he be informed of exactly whom he is dealing with?

Should one *ever* pay squeeze or graft to a politician, a government official, or a bureaucrat? If one does not, an official may take one's application for prospecting permits and summarily reject them or quietly bury them. And I have personally been propositioned by the representative of a West African country in the United Nations lounge; he wanted a substantial sum to pass our concession request on to the proper minister and help it. Finally the attorney with me said, "Well, sir,

165

instead of this direct appropriation, do you suppose that if we were to donate to your country a traveling medical unit with your president's name painted on the outside of it, that that would be a suitable substitute?" And he said, "Oh, yes sir, that is exactly what I had in mind all along." Well, we decided against it, but no bribe means no concession in several countries.

Should one buy currency on the black market when his competitors are doing it? In Vietnam today piasters sell for about eighty to the dollar on the official trading rate at the bank, and one is required by law to deposit the money in the bank. The official military rate is 120 piasters to the dollar: at the back door of the military exchange there is a sort of unofficial military rate of 135 piasters per dollar; and on the open black market, which is any place outside the doors of a fenced-in military establishment, piasters sold recently for about 170 to the dollar. What does one do? In Vietnam there really is not the competition in the same sense as in other parts of the world, but it is a perfectly good example. While I was in Indonesia, the black market rate escalated by a factor of five in two days. You are a darn fool if you don't and perhaps unethical if you do.

Should one give the customs inspector a case of liquor to encourage him to process an incoming shipment a week earlier? He couldn't care less whether the parts needed to make machinery operate are on time. He will get to it in his own good time; as a matter of fact if he thinks there is an possibility of collecting a "tip" he will be even slower about it because he knows it will be offered eventually.

Should a chartered boat be insured for more than it is worth with Lloyds? In a recent experience, we chartered a vessel in Thailand, and when it was inspected by the local ship surveyor he valued it at $35,000, which was very generous. But the owner said if it is not $50,000, the boat cannot be had! We are covered by Lloyds, with whom we have a very good relationship, so we simply reported the whole story to our broker at Lloyds. He said, "Don't worry about it. Put it in at $50,000." I do not know why Lloyds was willing to do that; it surprised me. But what does one do? We could not be in the position of attempting to cheat our good friends at Lloyds. Luckily, we did not have to, but we needed the boat in the worst way.

Most basic is the question: Should standards of ethics be different in South America or the Orient than they are at home? We have had many discussions about this, and we have never reached any final conclusion. I honestly do not know what is right. All of these problems that I have mentioned have arisen in the last year (plus a lot more which are even stickier which I decided I would not mention).

[EDITOR'S NOTE: The following is a verbatim transcript of the questions and answers following Mr. Bascom's paper. These are included because of their technical value as a supplement to the paper.]

QUESTION: I would like to ask Mr. Bascom how these concessions are obtained to these mines. Do the mines go from the shores to the continental shelf or is there a more precise definition?

BASCOM: In every country it is a bit different. For example, Southwest Africa operates as a state of South Africa. In the southwest the concession lines go out to the "edge" of the continental shelf, which happens to be poorly defined because there the shelf slopes gradually off into about 6,000 feet of water. In South Africa, under the same federal government, concessions go to the three-mile limit. The somewhat more difficult problem is where the shore line is because the shore line changes every day and there are very valuable diamond concessions that run up to what is described as the shoreline. Legal discussions of the true meaning of a word like "foreshore" have consumed many days of debate down there. In one area this finally was decided when DeBeers simply bought both sides.

QUESTION: When you are permitted to go to the "continental shelf," I wonder if you've run into the question of the extremely ambiguous definition given in the 1958 Convention of "200 meters or beyond, depending on technological conditions"?

BASCOM: Well, up until now, technological conditions have not brought us to that brink. Most of the deposits with which we have been concerned are in as close to shore as you can get. The reason is, I think, fundamental. You are not likely to have substantial ore deposits of an alluvial nature on the outer shelf. I have really been discussing placer deposits

167

all this time, perhaps I should have said so earlier. These placer deposits are mainly submerged beaches which are like windrows, parallel to the shore, created by lower stands of the sea at various times in the geologic past. The lowest stand that I remember anybody mentioning is on the order of a couple of hundred feet below present sea level. Most of our operations have been between about 150 feet of water and in as close to shore as we can get. Our problem has been that the ships are just barely outside the breakers all the time and they have some rather hair-raising experiences. Perhaps you have read about the seven vessels that have been lost off the coast of southwest Africa in the course of the diamond exploration down there.

Every country is quite different. In the Bass Strait area the shelf extends for several hundred miles in each direction. It is a submerged piece of flat land and the edge of the shelf is distant and more or less immaterial. In other places of the world the situation is more difficult. In Alaska, for example, our claims are granted by the state of Alaska and they extend to the three mile limit; beyond that is federal land which may very well be auriferous, but they are not willing to discuss it with you. There are no ground rules, and they won't talk about it. We send them letters, and they write back and say, write us again next year.

QUESTION: You mentioned that 150 feet is your maximum depth. How much of this prospecting is done by bringing up samples and how much is done by scuba diving or hard hat diving?

BASCOM: I said I would talk about gear and I didn't ever get to it. By the way, there is no immediate technological limit on the kind of equipment that we use. Off the coast of Africa we were using a vessel named the "Rockeater," which we designed and built to operate with a whole series of specialized equipment. When you finance a ship you go to the bank and the first thing the bank says to you is, "When the present contract blows up then what will you do with the ship?" And so we had to be able to say, "We'll put it to work in the oil business." Now, in order to be used as an oil prospecting vessel the drill has to have a reach of at least 6,000 feet, even for very modest oil prospecting operations. So this ship that we were using in 150 feet of water was at least capable of drilling to 6,000 feet if it had any reason to.

168

The difficulty in sampling is in obtaining samples which the geologists will accept. The problem is to get a sample of the bottom which is clearly representative of it. This is particularly true in the diamond business where the multiplication factors are exceedingly high. That is to say, if you drill a hole and find a diamond you start multiplying the volume of this hole by the volume of the deposit as a whole and the multiplying factor may be as much as a million. So, if you have missed a diamond, or if somebody steals a diamond from you, which happens, it multiplies out to a tremendous error. In our system we rotated a drill bit down, using high pressure jets ahead of it and air-lifting the material to the surface through a pipe. We had endless arguments with the geologists about whether the water from the jets pushed material outside of the bit or whether at times the suction on the inside was so great that it pulled extra material in; whether the hole had caved at the sea floor and how much material sloughed into the hole; and whether the bit really got down to bedrock.

Mostly we did not use divers for sampling although we used them to make studies of the bottom. Once in a while they come back with an exceedingly useful piece of information. There has been a lot of talk about using small submarines and divers and so on. I submit the people who say that have never really seen a mine. We're talking about moving 10,000 cubic yards a day and I can't imagine a diver wanting to get anywhere near the cutting head of such a dredge.

Our Rockeater is a truly remarkable ship; in its first year at sea Rockeater drilled 6,045 holes in the bottom, which must be nearly ten times the previous world's record. It brought the drilled material on deck, processed it for diamonds, and the geologists had the answer in diamonds on the ship within fifteen or twenty minutes. But, Rockeater was a fairly expensive vessel. We had about $1,500,000 in it, which was cheap for such a ship but still a lot of money. So we recently devised a tool called the Horton Mining Sampler which vibrates a six-inch casing into the bottom to take a perfectly clean sample with a virtually undisturbed core.

QUESTION: I suppose that about 90 per cent of the gold and diamonds that you find are in the bottom 10 per cent or so of the overburden? My figures may be a little off but maybe they are of that order.

BASCOM: Yes, sir. That is about right.

QUESTION: That is the most difficult part to tackle, I would assume.

BASCOM: It is.

QUESTION: And particularly the bottom one per cent. The most important part to get is the most difficult.

BASCOM: In the main, what you've said is true. It certainly is true of the heavy minerals, particularly the very heavy minerals like gold and, to some extent, tin and tungsten. Diamonds are a bit different though generally what you say is true. In our sonic work we determined that in some areas there was a very clear "second layer" of sedimentary material above the bedrock there. In our drill records that layer was 100 per cent correlatable with the occurrence of diamonds and in that second layer the diamonds appeared to be more or less distributed through it. This would suggest that there was a concentration throughout that layer in some previous geologic period, and it has now been covered by overburden of some more recent age.

QUESTION: Well, would you say the gold lies mostly on top of the bedrock—the top of the bedrock is quite irregular—and if it is hard rock it would be a very difficult thing to get most of the gold out of the cracks and so forth?

BASCOM: Yes. It is always hard to get the gold from the cracks. In rather protected waters off Phuket, Thailand (where there are tin deposits now being mined at a profit), the sub-bottom material is soft, and the bucket-type dredge simply cuts into it and takes tin, cracks and all.

QUESTION: Aren't the problems of underwater mining such that it is hard for you to be competitive with your competitors in the land-mining business?

BASCOM: We feel no competition at all. Metals are sold on the world market at a specified price. The problem is, do you wish to sell your material at that price. It is unrelated to what anybody else is doing in

170

the world. The prices go up and down as you know. Tin has been high lately, and, of course, a very high price and a restricted supply forces people to find substitutes. The best thing that can happen is for the price of tin to drop to somewhere near where it was a couple of years ago. I think it is quite irrelevent to say that ocean mining must wait until ore deposits have been discovered and mined out on land. It doesn't seem to me to make any difference. Nobody in the metal market knows or cares whether the material came from sea or land.

William T. Burke
Northcutt Ely
Richard Young
Bernard E. Jacob
Bruce A. Harlow
Quincy Wright

Chapter Eleven:

A SYMPOSIUM ON LIMITS AND CONFLICTING USES OF THE CONTINENTAL SHELF

BURKE:

I only want to make two or three non-controversial points. First, about the definition of the shelf, I think we have probably labored that pretty much already, but I did want to emphasize what has already been said, that the convention, despite the literal interpretation that seems to be current among some people, obviously envisages a limit on the shelf. I do not think this can be said too often because it does seem that the information doesn't get around very fast or at least that it isn't heard by some people.

The second point is that with the concern that many people are expressing these days about ocean exploitation and with the extension of boundaries for various purposes, sometimes even for the purpose of claiming national sovereignty, it is possible that we shall overlook an area in which industry plays a role, but it is not in terms directly of production of wealth, and that is the area of scientific research. It is possible that these extensions of boundaries—and this has happened, of course, with respect to certain boundaries in the ocean already—that these extensions will hamper, perhaps very gravely, the conduct of scientific research for gathering knowledge about the ocean on which all of these other activities will ultimately be based. The Continental Shelf Convention in particular has already in certain instances led to interference with what appeared to be purely scientific research. I have heard of three or four incidents of this kind occurring, that is, of outright refusals by the coastal states for research, including research in the water above the shelf. The convention requires the consent of the coastal state for research undertaken in the shelf, apparently attempting to distinguish between that research and the research in the waters above. The paper which I have written, which I am not going to give tomorrow—I shall give something else—has passages about this and about the difficulty of making this supposed distinction (at least I think that is the distinction that is written into the convention.) I believe that this is a matter that is presently of some seriousness and may be of increasing seriousness in the future as scientific activities are expanded. And I think that as a part of the process of expansion, it is the responsibility of government officials especially to see that these unwelcome intrusions on scientific endeavors are minimized. Scientists already have enough of a burden with the activities of the immediate operation without adding diplomatic complications and communications to them as well. I am aware of, but not familiar with, the military implications of this provision on scientific research in the Convention, and I think part of the emphasis that I spoke of ought also to be that the military restrain itself as much as possible in this area so that research by industry or by universities or others may be carried on.

The third and last point I wish to make deals with part of the title here: conflicting uses of the continental shelf. The projections for technological development in the next ten to twenty years call for an extremely high number of varied activities in continental shelf areas. We already do have some problems of conflict immediately, and in the area of the North Sea, about which Dick Young has written, the problems are likely to come upon us rather quickly in view of the intensity and variety of activity in that area of water. It is likely that institutional mechanisms will have to be established on a continuing basis to deal with these problems because the area of the North Sea, large as it is, is still likely to lead to difficulties.

There is the possibility that I think is emerging that states are going to extend controls over the continental shelf outside the Continental Shelf Convention. This has already occurred in one instance: the Netherlands North Sea Installations Act extends Netherlands legislation, any legislation that may be authorized by the Netherlands government, to any installation on the continental shelf no matter what its purpose. Now there may be a number of reasons for placing installations on a shelf, among them scientific, I am thinking particularly of marine geodetic equipment which is serving a legitimate purpose. It is not necessarily used for direct exploration and exploitation, although it could be employed for that. I think that the Netherlands legislation, when adopted by other states, may be used as a precedent for very undesirable interferences by coastal states with legitimate, non-threatening activities that take place on the continental shelf.

173

ELY:

When we speak of the continental shelf, in whatever terms we define it, we are referring to a very substantial piece of real estate. If the definition is restricted to areas of the sea bottom which are submerged to a depth of less than 200 meters, these areas total about 20 per cent of the exposed land masses. The continental shelf adjoining the United States, so measured, amounts to more than 850,000 square miles. This is half again bigger than Alaska, almost equal to the combined area of Texas and Alaska. One writer has commented that when the Convention on the Continental Shelf went into effect in 1964, the jurisdiction of the United States was confirmed over an area about as great as that acquired by the Louisiana Purchase. Another has said that if the sea should drop in elevation only half of 200 meters, an area as big as Alaska would appear in the Bering Sea, and a new continent as large as Australia would surface in the Southwest Pacific.

When the expression "continental shelf" is used, most of us think of a sloping submarine plateau, an extension of the shore and its beaches, bounded on its seaward side by the beginning of a steeper slope to the ocean floor. The question of definition would be one for the geographers and the geologists, not for the lawyers, but for the fact that within the last quarter-century there has been such an acceleration of interest in the minerals of this zone that a whole new chapter of international law has hastily evolved.

As recently as 1939 a distinguished arbitrator in a dispute between an oil company and a sheikhdom of the Arabian peninsula decided that there was no international law at all on the rights and powers of a coastal state over the submerged lands beyond its territorial seas, but that, as a matter of common sense, the coastal state should have some degree of control and jurisdiction. In 1942 the ice was broken by an agreement between Great Britain and Venezuela respecting the Paria Gulf. In 1945 President Truman issued his proclamation that

> . . . the Government of the United States regards the natural resources of the subsoil and sea bed of the continental shelf beneath the high seas but contiguous to the coasts of the United States as appertaining to the United States, subject to its jurisdiction and control.

But, he added:

174

The character as high seas of the waters above the continental shelf and the right to their free and unimpeded navigation are in no way thus affected.

This proclamation extended to the sea the legal principle of multiple use of a resource, with which we are familiar on the public lands and in the navigable streams of this country. Importing a third dimension to this principle, the Truman proclamation established a distinction between the use of the sea bed and the use of the overlying water. It is the distinction between the concept of the use of the sea bed as a potentially valuable mining property which is covered by some very wet and unstable overburden, and the concept of the use of this overburden, a column of fluid valuable for its content and for its ability to support buoyant vehicles, which we call the high seas.

Within a few years thereafter, some two dozen nations had eagerly issued similar proclamations, some of them not so modest in disclaiming jurisdiction over the surface and content of this wet overburden.

In 1958, at Geneva, under United Nations auspices, the nations of the world signed four conventions. One was captioned "The Continental Shelf." It is to be read in connection with another, on the subject of "The Territorial Sea and Contiguous Zone," because this fixes the landward scope of the continental shelf convention. The other two agreements deal with "The High Seas," and "Fishing and Conservation of the Living Resources of the High Seas." All four have since gone into effect. It is significant that the international law thus formalized in the Convention on the Continental Shelf had coalesced in less than twenty years, whereas the other three conventions are concerned with subjects that have involved several hundred years of evolution of the law of the sea.

The Convention on the Continental Shelf, which went into effect in June, 1964, provides that it shall be subject to review and revision five years after that date. Today, therefore, we are about half way into that five years.

The Convention on the Continental Shelf deals in general with the lateral extent of the exclusive jurisdiction of coastal states over the exploitation of the sea bed, and the vertical planes of division of jurisdiction as between adjacent states and as between states which confront each other across a body of water. With respect to the sea bed, the real estate, the coastal state is apparently confirmed in the same exclusive proprietary and sovereign rights, as against a stranger, that it enjoys with respect to its fast land. With respect to the overlying water column, its content and its surface, the community of nations is confirmed in its inclusive right of access to these resources as high seas.

Since I am in the company today of some of the men best qualified, in the whole United States, to discuss the problems of international boundaries and of the conflicting multiple uses of the sea overlying the continental shelf, I shall defer the discussion of those two aspects of these interlocking conventions. Instead, I shall move to the other topic of this discussion, the limits of the continental shelf, and share with you some of my confusion on this subject. I find that I am not alone in this condition.

The problems of limits are primarily on the seaward side. How far, and how deep, does the coastal state's flag march under water?

Article I of the convention says:

> For the purpose of these articles, the term 'continental shelf' is used as referring (a) to the seabed and subsoil of the submarine areas adjacent to the coast but outside the area of the territorial sea, to a depth of 200 metres or, beyond that limit, to where the depth of the superjacent waters admits of the exploitation of the natural resources of the said areas; (b) to the seabed and subsoil of similar submarine areas adjacent to the coasts of islands.

By definition, the coastal state's exclusive jurisdiction over the sea bed does not end at the 200 meter depth. How much farther does it extend?

The continental shelf is defined by Webster in this fashion:

> A submarine plain of variable widths forming a border to nearly every continent. The water above it is comparatively shallow (usually less than 100 fathoms). The rapid descent from it to the ocean depths is known as the continental slope.

Does the coastal state's jurisdiction extend beyond the 200 meter depth line, but stop at the commencement of the continental slope, as the dictionary's definition does? The convention's definition is not in dictionary terms. Read literally, it is a legal fiction, extending right on down the submarine slope or precipice to whatever depths, and out to whatever distance, the exploitation of the sea bed becomes possible. How deep, how far out? I once expressed my puzzlement in this fashion:

176

If some stranger proves, by doing it, that wells can be drilled at very great depth at a distance of hundreds of miles from the nearest coast line, then, if this language means what it says, he has automatically established, ex post facto, the exclusive jurisdiction of some coastal state which was incapable of this technical exploit itself, did not license this exploration, indeed, never heard about it, but now acquires sovereign powers to prohibit it, or police its operation, and collect taxes and royalties and control disposition of production. Perhaps this is a good and necessary result, but it is a curiously casual one. Is the coastal state bound to maintain order in this new outpost of its sovereignty and protect it from other powers? What are the limits, if any, on its ex post facto jurisdiction, if aimed away from any other islands below the horizon?

Moreover, wherever this ambient jurisdiction ends, the sea bed of the high seas begins, and we encounter a new problem: by what regime, if any, are the super-hazardous investments in the sea bed beneath the high seas to be controlled and protected? Since the outer limit of the coastal state's jurisdiction is apparently determined by the status of the art of undersea exploitation, and this art is in its infancy, we are perhaps discussing at this point the boundary between the unknown and the unknowable.

But the pressure is on us for some kind of blueprint. This pressure comes from the foreseeable competition of military necessities, and from the foreseeable requirements of the world's mineral industries.

Four general alternative concepts have been suggested:

1. The solution recently proposed by a Committee on Natural Resources and Development to the White House Conference on International Cooperation was this: Treat the minerals beneath the high seas as the common property of mankind, but recognize that "producers must have exclusive mining rights to areas that are sufficiently large to permit them to operate economically and without fear of congestion or interference. And if rights are to be granted for resources that are the common property of the world community, then decisions on the allocation of these rights or on the methods of acquisition must be made within the framework of international law. A specialized agency of the United Nations would be the most appropriate body for administering the distribution of exclusive mining rights." My comment is that this

administrative solution is a long way off, and will become necessary only after some major discovery is made at great depth, and touches off competition. Right now, there is plenty of room.

2. Assume, until the contrary develops, that all practicable undersea mineral development is sufficiently close to a coastal state that the Convention on the Continental Shelf applies, and that the nearest coastal state therefore should have plenary jurisdiction. This factual assumption will quite probably be correct for a long time, but it begs the question of the control of resources which, by hypothesis, are outside the scope of the convention.

3. Treat the sea bed beneath the high seas as open to appropriation and occupancy by all, free of the licensing authority of any state or international organization, but subject to the qualification that conflicting appropriations must be accommodated either by agreement or by resort to some rather general principles of reasonableness of use, to be evolved case by case, as need arises. This simply postpones the questions of what nation's laws shall govern and what the content of those laws should be.

4. Let the exploratory operation carry the flag of some nation with which it has a "genuine link"—this is the test of recognition of the flag of a vessel under the High Seas Convention. This is what is required as long as the operation is both sea-borne and mobile, and it is arguable that there is no reason to change that status when it establishes permanent contact with the sea bottom. As a practical matter, the explorer thereby appropriates a segment of the sea bed, and the jurisdiction of his flag attaches to the discovery. When the first significant discoveries are made, the flag nations of the sea-borne exploitation mechanisms, if they are in conflict, are likely to arrive at an accommodation, just as Venezuela and Great Britain did in the Gulf of Paria. If they fail at an accommodation by agreement or arbitration, and if enough nations sense an interest of their own in the outcome, then the problems will justify the negotiation of a modification of the convention—perhaps even at the end of the current five-year trial period.

The Convention on the Continental Shelf crystallized international law very rapidly when need arose, and did so precisely to the extent necessary to enable the exploitation of the shelf to go forward to the full extent justified by the state of the art. We can expect similar advances in the law to accompany further advances in the art.

YOUNG:

I share the concern of my colleagues over the problems that arise from technological advance and new competing uses of the sea and from the uncertainties of existing law. These are major issues and require the fullest study. But merely for the sake of variety in the menu of our discussion I propose to take up briefly a different set of problems: those relating to the establishment of boundaries on a continental shelf shared by two or more states. While these matters do not involve great questions of principle, they do present practical problems which are both difficult and of immediate concern to exploitation programs now under way.

As you know, Article 6 of the Shelf Convention provides that in the case of states whose coasts are opposite one another, the boundary on the shelf between them shall—in the absence of agreement or unless another line is justified by special circumstances—be a median line. A median line is defined as a line equidistant at all points from the nearest points on the baselines from which the territorial sea of each state is measured. In the case of adjacent states on the same coast, the boundary shall be—again in the absence of agreement or special circumstances—a line equidistant throughout from the nearest points on the respective baselines.

I have no quarrel with this general principle of equidistance as a fair method of determining a boundary. The trouble comes in its application to specific situations where the general language of the convention fails to provide a clear or adequate answer. This is the more regrettable because Article 6 gives the appearance of furnishing an automatic solution on which one could rely when the states concerned could not agree. In my experience, this expectation has often proved illusory. Let me illustrate by suggesting two or three types of such difficulties.

179

One type of difficulty, which arises from the wording of Article 6 itself, relates to the baselines from which the boundary is to be measured. Suppose states A and B are opposite each other and both are parties to the Shelf Convention, but that only B is a party to the Territorial Sea Convention. A measures its territorial sea from baselines further seaward than those specified in the Territorial Sea Convention. Under a literal interpretation of Article 6, the shelf boundary between A and B is the line equidistant between the baselines, even though A thereby acquires substantially more shelf area than B, whose baselines have been restrained by the convention rules. A similar displacement of the line will occur in cases where the states concerned are adjacent to one another rather than opposite.

A second class of difficulties arises from geographical facts rather than legal attitudes and is exemplified by the problem of islands. What role is to be assigned to islands in determining the equidistant boundary line? In narrow seas, this can make a great deal of difference. The Shelf Convention is silent on this point, except to affirm in Article 1—rather unhelpfully in the present context—that islands also possess appurtenant shelf areas. Article 6 speaks only of baselines, not "mainland" or "island" baselines. If state A possesses islands three-quarters of the way across the sea toward state B, does this mean that state A gets seven-eighths of the shelf between itself and B? If B possesses other islands close to A, does the shelf boundary zig-zag accordingly? In narrow seas, I can assure you that some rather peculiar lines can be projected which cannot be called contrary to the language of the Shelf Convention. You can imagine for yourselves a wide selection of other variations on this island theme.

Still a third group of problems, non-legal in nature but still a practical obstacle to determination of a line, relates to the charts or maps used in establishing the baselines and constructing the boundary. Sometimes no accurate large-scale charts exist; sometimes they are grossly in error; sometimes the official charts of state A differ substantially from those of state B. I know of at least one case in which the charts of the two countries were based on wholly different datums, with noticeable discrepancies resulting. The convention rules do not resolve this kind of dilemma.

Lastly, the convention fails to define the "special circumstances" in which it recognizes that a boundary other than the line of equidistance may be justified. The omission is quite understandable, but it leaves the

180

way open for raising all kinds of allegations regarding "special circumstances" in order to prevent the application of the equidistance rule.

I fully appreciate that all these obstacles can be readily removed, as the convention provides, by agreement among the states concerned. The progress that has been made in the North Sea demonstrates this. Such an agreement need not even be an agreement directly on the line; it can be an agreement to submit the matter to some form of impartial third-party determination. (The convention, of course, contains no requirement for such submission.) But those who may become involved in these boundary problems should be aware that the convention rules do not furnish guaranteed and automatically applicable solutions, even in cases where the parties are bound by them in principle. The convention is only a point of departure for negotiation.

JACOB:

I shall dwell a moment, I think, on the Convention on the Continental Shelf and the problem which the dual criteria raises. The particular problem, I think, is that it provides a ground for an indefinitely extensible claim into the ocean for mineral exploitation purposes. I do not think that a determined proponent of this reading of the convention will be embarrassed either by its language or by such legislative history as is available. I am not either especially comforted by the words "adjacent to the coast" which Mr. Stone mentioned this morning. That phrase seems only to indicate the people who are to play in this game and not the prize they are to win. So neither the language of the convention nor its legislative history will embarrass a coastal nation, say in Africa or South America which sees in deriving a rent from deep ocean exploitation a kind of handy kit for turning itself into a new Saudi Arabia or Iraq or Iran.

I do not suppose that even this kind of delight in the wonderful new resources that one might have will fail to affect even the United States. Certainly we got into the whole continental shelf game by claims made by the United States. Nevertheless, I think we have to begin to examine each kind of deep ocean exploitation and such exploitation in a projected

181

aggregate as we come to know it, as problems that have to be considered without reference to the convention; for, first, the convention may not be accepted as applying, and, second, even if it is, it may not prove workable. Now, that means that the status of deep ocean exploitation is uncertain. Will that uncertainty retard deep ocean exploitation? Perhaps. Certainly Oliver Stone was right in saying that he would expect that people who are interested in making the considerable investment in such exploitation will demand an assurance of exclusive right to development. However, I shall point out that petroleum exploitation on dry land has developed despite a considerable number of situations that could only be characterized as a "license to catch," that is, the right of all superjacent owners to exploit at will a given pool. The petroleum industry has generally worked out this problem by the most diverse and indirect means, and yet it has not been noticeably retarded in its development. And I think the same thing applies to deep ocean mineral exploitation. It is to some extent, as we heard, going on, and apparently it will increase greatly, leaving us lawyers in the embarrassing wreckage of the Convention on the Continental Shelf to work out the problems as or just before or—most likely of all—after they arise.

HARLOW:

One may wonder why the Navy is interested in the legal meaning and extent of the continental shelf regime. It is primarily because it may not be long before some U.S. citizen or corporation asks for protection in these areas of the high seas. The Navy will certainly play an important role in affording the protection that may be legally and properly granted. The Navy has, therefore, given considerable in-house thought to this problem, but my remarks do *not* represent an official or final Navy position on this matter. Now as mentioned previously, Article 1 defines the continental shelf as an area adjacent to the coast to a depth of 200 meters or beyond that limit to the extent that the depth of the water permits exploitation of the natural resources. This is a double-barreled definition—depth of 200 meters or depth of exploitability. The United States Department of the Interior has already leased land for resource extraction on the outer portion of the continental shelf to a depth of 250 meters which, in a conceptual sense, is beginning down the slope toward the deep ocean floor. Therefore, the question is upon us today of how far out a coastal nation may claim exclusive sovereign rights over natural resources pursuant to this open-ended provision.

Although the continental shelf concept has existed since 1958, usage and judicial decisions are not available to establish a customary or agreed limitations on the maximum scope of this legal concept. Several qualified observers have maintained that under this open-end provision a nation may legally claim exclusive rights to ocean resources any distance from its coast or down to any depth, perhaps to the mid-ocean areas, so long as that nation has the capability of exploiting those resources. One delegate to the 1958 Geneva Convention expressed concern that the Continental Shelf Convention could be so construed and would thereby permit the big powers to claim vast ocean areas conceivably up to another nation's continental shelf.

The legal status of the areas within the territorial seas affords little difficulty because the coastal nation has full sovereignty over the super-jacent water as well as the sea bed and subsoil. But beyond the territorial seas are the high seas, so to speak beyond the borders of any single state. What then is the legal rationale underlying the exclusive right of resource development which is granted to a coastal state by the Continental Shelf Convention in an area which is admittedly beyond its borders and which retains its superjacent character as high seas. An understanding of the legal rationale and basis of this convention is essential in making a judgment concerning the logical and proper limits of its application.

It is submitted that the basis in law for these extraterritorial rights accorded to coastal states by the convention can be summarized as follows: first, the existence in a geological sense of the continental shelf. In other words, superior rights accrue to a coastal state simply because there is a distinctive geological area which can be distinguished from the deep oceans in general. This is evident not only in the legislative history of the convention but also by the repeated use of the geological term "continental shelf" in the convention itself. Dr. Chapman referred to the records of the Eighth Session of the International Law Commission which had spent a great deal of time on this problem. To a great

extent the final convention did incorporate the thoughts and language as recommended by this law committee. And I think it is significant to note that although they did depart to a certain extent from the geological concept of the continental shelf, thereby changing this concept from a strict geological sense into perhaps a unique legal sense, they nevertheless retained the terminology "continental shelf." Some members of the commission recommended that because of these changes they should refer to these areas as "submarine areas," but in the final analysis the majority of the commission decided to retain the term "continental shelf" because it is in current use and because the term "submarine areas" would *not* give sufficient indication of the nature of the area in question.

The second basis appears to be a superior *natural* right of the adjacent coastal state. This right appears to be based on the fact that the continental shelf is a natural continuation of the above-water land mass that is already within the state's complete domain. The limitation of this natural right is evident when one considers that the convention defines the area in which the coastal state enjoys these superior rights as being "adjacent to its coast," a point which was well emphasized by Mr. Stone, and further when one considers the abrupt slope which signals the falling away of the continental land mass.

In view of this rationale, then, how far into the ocean may a state properly make exclusive claim pursuant to the Continental Shelf Convention? It is submitted that a state may not claim the right of exclusive resource development to any great distance down a continental slope without doing violence to the intention and purpose of this convention. The further down the slope one goes, the less it appertains to the land mass and the geological definition of the shelf, and hence the legal regime of the continental shelf, and the more it appertains to the deep oceans.

WRIGHT:

The present international law of the sea provides for freedom of the high seas for navigation and fisheries with recognition of the need for regulation of fisheries for purposes of conservation; for sovereignty of the maritime belt by the adjacent state subject to the right of innocent passage by vessels of all states; and for exclusive right to exploit the resources of the continental shelf by the adjacent state.

As the use and exploitation of the sea and the sea bed increases with increase in the world's population, the need for more extensive and precise rules of international law on the subject has been recognized, but the different policies and interests of the states has made it difficult to establish such rules. There should be a clear definition of the seaward limits of the maritime belt sufficiently flexible to fit the various conditions of the sea coast as recognized in the Norwegian Fisheries Case.

It is even more important that the limits of the continental shelf be fixed in order to avoid serious international controversy, as the development of technology permits exploitation of the resources of the bed of the sea at great depths. It is unfortunate that the Continental Shelf Convention qualified the 200 meter depth definition by the uncertain concept of technological capability.

Finally, and most important of all, is the establishment of the status of the bed of the sea beyond the continental shelves. Presumably the concept of "freedom of the seas" covers the bed of the sea, as well as the waters above it, but obviously the situations are very different. Exploitation of the bed of the deep sea requires a clear and exclusive right for a period of time by the exploiter to an area far more than does a high sea fishery. The agreements concerning the Antarctic continent, outer space, and celestial bodies point the way to a general agreement on the bed of the high seas.

It seems clear that the principle that states can not acquire title to any portion of the high sea, accepted after a vigorous debate in the seventeenth century, is even more applicable to the bed of the high seas. If the principle of acquisition by discovery and occupation were applied to this vast area, as it was to the American continents after their discovery by Europeans, the world would be faced by rivalries and wars even worse than those of the sixteenth, seventeenth, and eighteenth centuries among the maritime nations.

In the interests of world peace, of efficient exploitation of vast resources, and of equitable opportunity to develop and utilize these resources by all nations and peoples, the bed of the sea and indeed the sea itself should be controlled by a world agency competent to make appropriate regulations and to license rights of exploitation in prescribed areas and for defined periods of time. In giving such licenses, consider-

185

ation should be given to the technological capability of the company or nation applying for a license, and to fair distribution of such opportunities among the nations and people of the earth. The sea and its bed should be considered a heritage of mankind, and as its utilization proceeds, all should share equitably in its benefits.

Discussion

1. Persons interested in exploiting the resources of the continental shelf might wish for precision in the definition of its outer limits, yet the delegates at the 1958 Geneva Conference were purposely imprecise in defining these limits because of their lack of knowledge of the resource potential beyond the 200-meter isobath. Actually, the decision by a government whether to push for a broad or a narrow continental shelf depends in part on what the status of the bed of the high seas will be. The Continental Shelf Convention may be subject to review and revision five years after its coming into effect (i.e., 1969), and greater precision in defining the outer limits may prove to be both desirable and possible at that time.

2. With respect to the U.S. continental shelf, the Department of the Interior has issued leases for exploratory drilling off the west coast in depths exceeding 1,500 feet. So far as the state-federal boundaries on the shelf are concerned, it was noted that the possibility of changes in the configuration of the shoreline may affect such boundaries in the Gulf of Mexico, but not off the coast of California, inasmuch as the Supreme Court recently fixed a permanent baseline in that state from which the outer limits of state control would be measured.

3. Several alternatives were suggested concerning the status of the sea bed beyond the limits of the continental shelf. One was that any development of the minerals of the sea bed or subsoil beyond the shelf might be seen as justifying an extension of the shelf itself, with no limit placed on the depths involved. But would the extension of one country's capabilities (and control) to depths, say, of 600 meters, imply that all

other coastal countries might also lay claim to the sea bed off their own coasts to an equal depth? If actual exploitation becomes the criteria for claims beyond the 200-meter isobath, would this not favor the technically advanced countries to the detriment of other coastal states? Or would it turn out that any country which has exploitable resources on or beneath the sea bed off its coasts might permit exploitation of these resources by one of the technically advanced countries and thus would be able to claim the sea bed, out to and including the site of these resources, as its own?

A second alternative might be that nationals of a particular coastal state might secure possession of the sea bed off that country's coast in the name of the country—as a result of exploitation—but possession would be limited to the immediate site of the resource development, without affecting the status of the rest of the sea bed.

On the other hand, it might be that any country could secure possession to a limited area of the sea bed in any part of the world on the basis of exploitation, the only criteria being that one of its own companies is actually exploiting the sea bed and that there is a "genuine link" between this company and the country making the claim.

Still another possibility would be to rest ownership of the bed of the high sea with the United Nations, or some other international agency, with the power to lease portions of the sea bed to companies which will exploit the resources. Rent from the leases could revert to the international agency.

Finally, it was suggested that the wisest course is to resist any new laws and to wait until situations develop in which some arrangements are necessary for ownership of the sea bed.

4. Questions arose as to the compatability of the doctrine of ownership of the bed of the high seas and the freedom of the high seas themselves. Would the principle of possession, based on discovery and exploitation of the sea bed resources, justify ownership? One opinion expressed was that the mineral resources of the sea bed are so vast that it will be a long time before serious problems of ownership emerge, but this was countered by the statement that from an economist's point of view, even now, there is not so much room in the sea that problems of ownership can be considered as being unimportant.

Bruce A. Harlow

Chapter Twelve:

FREEDOM OF NAVIGATION

I. *Introduction*

Navigation of warships on the high seas is free for all nations in time of peace. The United States Navy has therefore opposed any significant reduction in the world's high seas whether it be by convention or by unilateral state act. For many years it has been and continues to be today the Navy's policy to completely, absolutely, and categorically support: (1) The United States adherence to a territorial sea three miles in breadth; (2) The United States view that it need not recognize foreign territorial sea claims in excess of three miles. I suggest, however, that the time is ripe for a reappraisal of certain aspects of this policy. I should emphasize that I am writing as an individual and that my thoughts do not represent the position of the United States Navy, Department of Defense, or any other agency of the United States government.

Few aspects of the international law of the sea have provoked more controversy or elicited more divergent views and opinions than the question of the breadth of the territorial sea. The practice of states with regard to territorial claims, particularly in recent years, has been in a state of accelerating and—to many people—alarming change.

International law has long recognized that a coastal state may exercise jurisdiction and control within its territorial sea in the same manner that it can exercise sovereignty over its own land territory. In a legal sense, the territorial sea constitutes an integral part of a state's domain, and, as such, is treated accordingly—with one important exception. In time of peace, international law accords the right of innocent passage to ships of other nations through a state's territorial waters. Passage is "innocent" so long as it is not prejudicial to the peace, good order, or security of the coastal state.

One may ask: How does the territorial sea concept affect the mobility of our naval forces in time of peace in view of the fact that the law recognizes the right of "innocent passage"? Several points in this regard should be made clear. First, it is entirely possible that coastal states may unreasonably restrict this right—thus, while the right of innocent passage is clear in theory, it could be highly ambiguous and restrictive in actual practice. Secondly, several states, such as the Soviet Union, argue that warships generally do not possess the right of innocent passage. Thirdly, aircraft, civil or military, do not possess the right of innocent passage— hence, territorial waters can be overflown only with permission of the coastal state. Finally, there are *specific restrictions* limiting the right of innocent passage. For example, in territorial waters a submarine must navigate on the surface and must fly its national flag. Under certain conditions the right of innocent passage may be temporarily suspended in portions of the territorial seas (see Article 16[3] of the Convention on the Territorial Sea and Contiguous Zone). From the foregoing it is apparent that an increase in the breadth of the territorial sea could substantially restrict the mobility and flexibility of our naval, air, and sea forces.

II. *Background*

The territorial sea concept has existed as a cornerstone principle of the law of the sea for many centuries. This concept derived its origin and historic rationale from the fact that coastal states have always deemed it essential to exercise effective jurisdiction and control over a belt of seas adjacent to their sea coast in order to secure, and maintain, the security of their citizens.

The territorial sea concept had its most significant origin in the seventeenth century, developing through a process of state action and interaction, claim and counterclaim. By this process there became established, during this period, a fairly widespread and generally accepted body of customary international law indicating that, except for limited territorial sea claims, the seas were *free* for the reasonable use of all states. Thus the territorial sea concept developed through the gradual

189

establishment of an international consensus as evidenced by widespread custom and practice, and not through any particular international treaty or convention. By the nineteenth century, there was a general consensus among the major maritime powers that a coastal state could legitimately claim as its territorial sea, a three mile belt immediately adjacent to its coast.

Many of the classic legal writers during this formative period, in discussing the vague and often ill-defined national policies with regard to territorial sea claims, often made reference to what is commonly termed today as the "cannon shot rule." This theory, in essence, was that since the territorial sea concept was based on a state's natural right of security and self-preservation, a state could legitimately claim a belt of seas adjacent to its coast out to a distance that its shore batteries could reach. In other words—out to the limit to which that state could effectively exercise this natural right. During much of this period, three miles was the maximum effective range of most shore batteries. Implicit in the cannon shot rationale, however, is that the increased range of shore-based guns or *other* technological changes in weaponry, would permit a state to *legitimately* claim a broader belt of territorial seas. This is historically correct, provided however—and this is an element that is often overlooked—that the security requirements of the state otherwise warrant such a claim. That is, in order to justify a territorial sea claim a state must be able to demonstrate a *need* for the claimed zone in terms of security or self-preservation as well as an *ability* to effectively satisfy that need within the claimed zone.

Placing this historic rationale for a unilateral territorial sea claim, in todays's context, it becomes clear that it is *not* legally sufficient to argue that simply because a state possesses defensive weapons with an effective range greater than three miles, that state may *ipso facto* unilaterally claim a proportionally larger area of high seas as its territorial sea.

The United states made a provisional claim to a three-mile territorial sea in 1793, initially, for the purpose of protecting its neutrality. A letter to the British minister, written by Thomas Jefferson, included the following statement: "Reserving, however, the ultimate extent of this [speaking of the three-mile limit] for future deliberation, the president gives instructions to the officers acting under his authority as restraining them for the present time, to one league or three nautical miles from the seashore." For the 170 years since that time, the United States has consistently adhered to the three mile limit. The Supreme Court has referred to the three mile claim as "the law of the land."

In spite of the once general international acceptance of the three mile territorial sea, this century has seen an increasing number of states claiming territorial seas in excess of three miles. There are at present some fifty-three states which claim territorial seas greater than three miles, while the list of nations claiming three miles stands at approximately thirty-two. Many claims range from six to twelve miles and a few extend well beyond that distance.

Some of the claims in excess of three miles have been longstanding. For example, Sweden claimed four miles in 1779, Norway claimed four miles in 1812, the Soviet Union claimed twelve miles in 1909, Mexico claimed nine miles in 1935. At the present time, one state claims 130 miles and two claim 200 miles.

There have been three unsuccessful attempts to reach international agreement on the breadth of the territorial sea—at The Hague in 1930 and at Geneva in 1958 and again in 1960. The 1960 conference failed by one vote to reach agreement on a six-mile territorial sea with an additional six miles in which a coastal state could regulate fishing.

A majority of the International Law Commission of the United Nations, in 1956, following exhaustive study, concluded that International custom and practice was no longer uniform in regard to territorial sea claims but that international law would not permit a claim in excess of *twelve miles*.

The Commission, however, was unable to decide whether a state possessed the right to unilaterally fix the limit of its territorial sea between three and twelve miles.

At the close of the 1960 Geneva Conference, failing agreement to the contrary, the United States reaffirmed its adherence to the three mile rule and, more importantly, expressed the view that there was no obligation on the part of states adhering to the three mile rule to recognize claims on the part of other states to a greater breadth of territorial sea.

III. *Need for Reappraisal*

Meanwhile, however, the relentless proliferation of jurisdictional claims in excess of three miles has continued. Recognizing that one of the sources of international law is the custom and practice of states, it

191

seems clear that the United States is approaching the point in time, when it will be difficult, if not impossible, to maintain that a state may *not* legitimately claim, in accordance with accepted principles of international law, a territorial sea belt in excess of three miles, up to twelve miles.

It is this growing practice of states which, in my estimation, requires a reappraisal of the territorial sea concept. One compelling reason is that a clear change in international law, which would permit a state to make a unilateral territorial sea claim, from three to twelve miles, would *invalidate* the present United States position that it has no legal obligation to recognize *foreign claims* in excess of three miles. For, if a state may legally make such a territorial claim, other states must recognize it and abide by its terms. As stated in Article 2, of the United Nations Charter:

> All Members shall refrain in their international relations from the threat or use of force against the territorial integrity or political independence of any state.

In the event one were to conclude that international custom and practice does in fact point to an impending compromise of United States policy in this regard, it would be appropriate to search for, and discover, if possible, viable alternatives to this policy. Alternatives which will preserve that which is essential to the Navy and vital to the security of the United States—the world-wide mobility of its forces.

At the same time, there are strong domestic pressures for a reappraisal of our three mile policy. It is well publicized and disturbing to many Americans that the Soviets have intelligence gathering vessels off our coasts. Such vessels also maintain stations off our Guamanian waters. They are, of course, at present, free to navigate passively on the high seas as long as they stay more than three miles from our shores.

Another problem of great political and economic concern is that foreign fishing vessels are exploiting what we have, in the past, considered to be primarily United States fishing grounds. You will recall the furor that was created a few months ago when it was discovered that a Soviet fishing fleet was working the waters off the coast of Oregon. For years Soviet trawlers have been present in large numbers off our Eastern shore.

It is evident, therefore, that the United States policy-makers are presently faced with a dilemma. On one hand, there is impetus to expand our territorial sea claim because of domestic concern for security and fear of oceanic resource depletion in areas adjacent to our shores. And on the other hand, there is a military need to preserve freedom of navigation by maintaining a narrow territorial sea; for if the United States were to unilaterally declare an expanded territorial sea, it could no longer refuse to recognize foreign claims to a like or larger amount. Such action would, furthermore, encourage other states claiming only three miles to increase the breadth of their own territorial seas.

Claims to expanded territorial seas would have a marked effect on the mobility of United States military forces; for the passage of the ships of one nation over the territorial sea of another must be "innocent" —must not, that is, prejudice the peace, good order, or security of the coastal state—and aircraft are granted no right of innocent passage over territorial waters. Consequently, very serious problems of access arise when a ship must pass over narrow straits that lead from one area of the high seas to another when these straits are claimed as territorial waters. Under the present three mile limit, for example, passage of the Strait of Gibraltar is possible over a narrow strip of water belonging to the high seas. If a twelve mile limit—or even an eight mile limit—were imposed, the Strait would become exclusively territorial water. In the same manner, the Straits of Dover now permit passage of the English Channel over a narrow strip of high seas not covered by the three mile limit that would completely disappear if a twelve mile limit were effected. This same expanded limit would lengthen the present route from Saigon to Guam, now following a strip of high seas traversing the Suriagao Strait, by a sufficient number of miles to add one day of sailing to the time now required to reach the Vietnamese port.

And so it is in many parts of the world. By accident of geography, most of the more important narrow passages which link the oceans around the world are high seas with a three mile limit, and territorial waters with a six or twelve mile limit.

We have determined that a six mile limit would result in fifty-two major international straits coming under the sovereignty of coastal states, and that a *twelve mile limit* would likewise affect *116 straits.*

One possible solution to the territorial sea dilemma is to create special zones of limited jurisdiction without increasing the territorial sea claim itself. Such jurisdiction might be for the limited purpose of preventing foreign intelligence activities or fishing. You are, of course, aware of

193

the bills before Congress at present that adopt this concept. In particular, the bill sponsored by Senators Bartlett and Magnuson would create a twelve mile fishing zone without altering our territorial sea claim of three miles. There is legal precedence for making such a distinction in the contiguous zone concept. As stated by a leading writer on international law, "The distinction between a right of sovereignty over a particular area and a right to exercise a preventive or protective jurisdiction over or within an area that is *outside* of the national domain is a real one."

As mentioned in earlier discussions, at the present time, New Zealand and Japan are contemplating referring this particular question to the International Court of Justice in connection with New Zealand's recent unilateral claim to a nine mile exclusive fishing zone, which Japan feels will unduly and illegally interfere with the fishing activities of its nationals on the high seas. Other maritime countries will, of course, watch these developments with great interest.

Such a solution, however, may not provide a complete answer. While it allows states to protect their fishing interests without extending their territorial seas, it does not guarantee that they will not make extensive territorial claims.

Another possible solution that bears analysis is to negotiate, on a multilateral or bilateral basis, for the maintenance of high sea passageways through international straits. This would permit extensions of the territorial seas without unduly jeopardizing the mobility of our naval forces. In this event, it seems clear, however, that international safeguards would necessarily have to be established; as they have been in international waterways such as the Suez and Panama canals or the Dardenelle Straits. Such safeguards would be essential as a substitute or *quid pro quo* the protection afforded coastal states by the present concept of innocent passage.

It is impossible at present for anyone to penetrate the fog of coming events and identify or seize all the essential factors which will determine the final and correct solution to this problem. While the final outcome is not clear, what is clear is that it is essential to launch a searching appraisal of the evolving law of the territorial sea in relation to the requirements of the United States in the international system of tomorrow. Such an appraisal is essential not only to fully protect the security interests of the United States but its economic and political interests as well.

194

Gerard E. Sullivan

Chapter Thirteen:

INTERNATIONAL REGULATION OF COMMUNICATIONS
FOR OCEANOGRAPHIC EQUIPMENT

An almost sudden curiosity—man's reaction to his intellectual neglect of the vast sea regions surrounding him—has led to and characterizes today's accelerated activities in ocean research. The early voyages of the English corvettes, Beagle (1831) and Challenger (1872), and the converted American "man-of-war," Porpoise (1838), cast the traditional mold for data acquisition, i.e., extended scientific cruises, occupying consecutive "oceanographic stations." From the standpoints of efficiency, in terms of time and coverage, and scientific value, in terms of simul- taneous reporting and analysis, the mode of operation has obvious limitations. Recognition of these limitations together with the broadening scientific and geographic scope of these research activities has in turn fostered plans for the use of stationary platforms to acquire and record vital data. Timely and profitable use of these data, however, presents unique problems to the marine scientist, problems that are completely divorced from his usual concerns in the ocean spaces. They are legal, technical, and administrative at the same time. They are the problems of ocean communications.

Probably the first formal recognition of the need for radio com- munications in oceanography—in the United States at least—can be traced to a study conducted by the National Academy of Sciences Committee on Oceanography (NASCO) in 1959. The NASCO study identi- fied two general uses for systems of oceanographic communications: nearly simultaneous data transmission from multiple buoy systems and "command nets" linking individual research units with shore-based laboratories and evaluation facilities.

Undeniably, the two needs are closely related in terms of use, but they pose separate and distinct problems from the standpoint of radio technology and frequency allocation. This discussion will concern itself with the first and most pressing of these needs, long range synoptic reporting of data in the context of international regulation.

The subject of radio communications in oceanography came under international scrutiny when the Intergovernmental Oceanographic Commission (IOC) a co-operative scientific organization operating within the framework of UNESCO, commissioned by Resolution at its First Session, a Working Group on Communications (UNESCO/IOC, Res. I–6). At its first meeting, during August of 1962, this body recommended certain engineering standards for data transmission which would permit a nominal 300-bit capacity message, transmitting a maximum of 100 bits per second, using a 300-cycle maximum bandwidth for messages, and limiting antenna output to 100 watts. Frequency requirements were stated as a minimum of one 3 Kc/s channel in each of the six mobile maritime exclusive frequency bands, assigned for the sole use of oceanographic and meteorological communications. These assignments would be from those band sections reserved for single-side-band work. The six bands in question are:

> 4063 to 4438 Kc/s
> 6200 to 6525 Kc/s
> 8195 to 8815 Kc/s
> 12330 to 13200 Kc/s
> 16460 to 17360 Kc/s
> 22000 to 22720 Kc/s

In addition, a 3.5 Kc/s channel was requested in the 510 to 525 Kc/s band exclusively for Arctic and Antarctic use, since auroral disturbances usually render higher frequencies useless.[1]

Before proceeding further it may be worthwhile to give very brief consideration to the other alternatives which were before the IOC at the time they were formulating their requirements. The following sketch of frequency alternatives is abstracted from a report entitled "Ocean Engineering," prepared under the auspices of the National Security Industrial Association.[2]

I. *VLF and LF Bands (10 kc to 300 kc)*

Although frequencies in these bands have been very effective for reliable long-range communications and electronic navigation, their limitations in antenna efficiency and signal-to-noise ratio, make them less than desirable for oceanographic purposes. High transmitter power is required to correct the noise difficulties and large antennas impose an unmanageable metacentric height in light of stability requirements and buoy size.

II. *MF Band (33 kc to 3 mc)*

Frequencies in this band have been characterized by reliable ground wave propagation over moderate distances (100 to 300 miles), but ionic conditions, particularly during daylight hours, severely limit sky wave propagation. Again antenna size—though smaller than VLF and LF—is not compatible with contemplated platform size.

III. *VHF and UHF Bands (30 mc to 3000 mc)*

For all practical purposes, radio wave propagation in these bands is limited to line of sight with a resultant transmission range of 30 miles or so, at the outside. Longer ranges have been obtained using small antenna configuration and low to moderate power, but these results have been attributed to "radio refractive ducting," a phenomenon which possesses as many disadvantages, as it does advantages.

IV. *Satellites*

Although satellite communications may become the ultimate solution to the oceanographer's dilemma, their use today is not—in the minds of most—economically justifiable. Experimental use in an ancillary operation may be within manageable limits in the near future, but their use for these purposes alone cannot be said to support an independent launching.[3]

So what are the oceanographers left with? To be sure, they are left with the immediate need for a synoptic data reporting system, and the indispensable communication structure to support that system. And today, it surely appears that scientific comprehension of the oceans can best be served by the use of frequencies in the HF band, at least until developments in other areas can provide more effective means of communication and data transfer. From the standpoint of economy, the HF band, with its already existing facilities and well-developed technology, offers the most promising means, for a number of years to come, for collecting oceanographic data from sources spaced over wide areas.[4]

Having delineated the requirements, let us examine the international framework within which they will either be met or rejected.

In essence, the mission of the International Telecommunication Union (ITU) is to preserve order and eliminate chaos in the conduct of global communications. By treaty, ventures into the realm of the radio-frequency spectrum—which must be viewed as a finite resource or commodity, subject to use by everyone—are regulated by the ITU, through the joint actions of its member states. Or in the words of the ITU Convention, which is the Organization's Charter, jurisdiction extends to: "Any transmission, emission or reception of signs, signals, writing, images and sounds of intelligence of any nature by wire, radio, optical or other electromagnetic systems." [5] With regard to these transmissions, the stated purposes of the ITU are the maintenance of international co-operation respecting the rational use of all telecommunications and the development of technology for improving the efficiency of communication services so as to make them available for public use to the maximum extent possible. To achieve these general goals, the Union shall:

a) effect allocation of the radio frequency spectrum and registration of radio frequency assignments in order to avoid harmful interference between radio stations of different countries;

b) coordinate efforts to eliminate harmful interference between radio stations of different countries and to improve the use made of the radio frequency spectrum;[6]

Unlike most of the other Specialized Agencies within the United Nations which came into being following the creation of the UN itself, the ITU traces its history to earlier times and is in fact the oldest of all. Grave concern over the prospects of a telecommunications monopoly headed by the astute English Marconi interests, prompted the delegates of twenty nations to assemble in Paris in May, 1865.

On May 17 of that year, a Convention was signed creating the ITU and bringing uniform regulation to Europe's international telegraph system. Only England—because of the private nature of its telegraph system—was not numbered among the major signatories. Of almost

198

.equal importance was the 1868 Vienna conference establishing a permanent headquarters, and a Secretariat staff in Berne, Switzerland. The International Telegraph Union was then on its way to a permanent posture in the international agency structure.

Remarkable achievements in telegraphy and the birth of radio were on the world scene when the First Radio Conference was convened in Berlin in 1906. The conference drew up the first International Radio Regulations which among other things adopted the SOS distress signal and of even more consequence obligated the ship and coastal radio stations of signatory nations to accept transmitted messages, regardless of the nationality of the message originator, or that of the equipment manufacturer. The introduction of the broadcast method in the 1920's confronted the ITU with one of its most serious and continuing problems—intelligent radio frequency allocation. The first attack on this problem was launched at the Washington Radio Conference of 1927 which allocated frequency bands to all of the different radio services including maritime and broadcasting.[7] In 1947, the organization became a specialized agency of the United Nations by special agreement and its headquarters were transferred to Geneva.[8] By this agreement, ITU structure assumed its present form which includes four permanent subdivisions:

1. The General Secretariat
2. The International Frequency Registration Board (IFRB)
3. International Consultative Committee for Radio (CCIR)
4. International Consultative Committee for Telegraphy and Telephony (CCITT).

A recent ITU achievement pertinent to this discussion is the 1963 World Space Radio Communication Conference in Geneva which allocated 6,000 mcs (approximately 15 per cent of the entire radio frequency spectrum) for outer space work.[9]

Procedurally—or as Professor McDougal termed it when he launched these discussions "constitutively"—the functions of the ITU are carried out by the following organs in the following manner: Members of the union meet in Plenipotentiary Conference at intervals of approximately five years. Since the Plenipotentiary Conference is the supreme authority of the ITU, it is responsible for general policy, reviews the union's work

199

since the last conference and of primary importance—revises the convention if such revisions are considered necessary. It also elects Members of the Union to serve in the Administrative Council as well as the Secretary-General and Deputy Secretary-General.

With respect to the administrative conferences, there are three held by Members of the Union: ordinary, extraordinary, and special or regional conferences. Most important are the ordinary administrative conferences whose major task is to revise the separate radio, telegraph, and telephone regulations, the principal documents which govern the international operation of these basic communication forms. Extraordinary and special conferences are periodically convened to consider unique telecommunication matters, or to revise specific parts of a given set of regulations. It should be further noted that ordinary administrative *radio* conferences elect the members of the all-important International Frequency Registration Board (IFRB). They also review the actions of this board.

The IFRB is composed of eleven independent radio experts, not more than one from the same country. Their main task, which is of a continuing nature, is to decide whether frequencies which countries assign to their radio stations (notice of which assignments have been served to the board) are in accordance with the convention and with the current radio regulations. If the board's finding in a particular case is favorable, the frequency is recorded in the master international frequency register which is kept by the IFRB. It is in this manner then, that a *frequency obtains formal international recognition and protection.* Also germane to oceanographic considerations is the fact that the IFRB works out seasonal high frequency broadcasting schedules, based on environmental data evaluations.

Within this "constitutive" structure then, what recourse is available to the marine scientist in his quest for the technological and regulatory support so vital to his investigations? Article 14, Section 2 of the convention states that the provisions of the convention are completed by the following sets of administrative regulations which shall be binding on all members and associate members; namely, the telegraph, telephone, radio, and additional radio regulations. The radio regulations in turn stipulate that final allocation of frequencies to any service can be made only by an appropriate administrative radio conference. Accordingly, it became incumbent on the proponents of the ocean data service (an international scientific concept) to present most vigorously their needs

200

to their individual national representatives in the ITU in the hope of obtaining sufficient national support and ultimate consideration by the appropriate Administrative Conference.

The focal point within the United States for such "case presenting" is the Interdepartmental Radio Advisory Committee (IRAC) which advises the President through his telecommunication adviser/officer. The IRAC also co-ordinates government use of radio frequencies; the FCC, which is represented on the IRAC, regulates the non-governmental use of frequencies. In this sense then, IRAC may be said to be the "management agent" for the Department of State in developing United States policy and positions, and the general handling of the U.S. activities in international communications. Ultimate policy determinations of course continue as a function of the latter department. This is all before the fact. When these specialized conferences are complete—some lasting as long as seven or eight weeks—joint consultations between the IRAC and FCC produce a "blue book" of frequency use by public and private entities under United States jurisdiction.

In spite of the able and dedicated leadership of several persons in this country—Mr. James Snodgrass of the Scripps Institution of Oceanography just to mention one—progress to date has been slow. To an individual not at all familiar with the problem, it has been almost imperceptible. It is fair to say, however, that the diligent efforts of these people have succeeded in convincing national authorities that a very real and valid need for exclusive oceanographic frequencies exists. In fact by March of last year, accommodations had been reached with United States authorities whereby one 3.5 Kc/s channel in each of the designated bands could be obtained for oceanographic use on an "experimental basis." [10] In turn these national authorities or "administrations" are confronted by exercises of discretion in terms of the proper timing, estimates of support from other nations, and the judicious guarding of general U.S. interests with respect to the entire r-f spectrum. [11]

Leadership has come from other sectors as well as witnessed by the most recent oceanographic effort at the Aeronautical Extraordinary Administrative Radio Conference in Geneva during March and April of 1966. This conference also serves well to illustrate the close relationship between international legal procedures, politics, and diplomacy, as well as the increased possibilities when international organizations are able to co-operate. The delegation from the Federal Republic of

201

Germany to the Fourth Session of the Intergovernmental Oceanographic Commission suggested to the IOC that its delegation to the pending ITU Conference this spring would be willing to give favorable consideration to the following proposal as an *interim* solution to oceanographic difficulties: That one 3.5 Kc/s band from each of six bands already allocated to the Aeronautical Mobile Service be—not reallocated either to this service or to an oceanographic service—but rather, consigned to no one and reserved for considerations of future use in oceanography. Again feelings of optimism which existed in some quarters proved to be unjustified. Nevertheless this same approach (termed "tactically ingenious" by at least one authority) may be taken at a future time of which I will speak shortly.

Other efforts at an interim solution were made including a French proposal for the use of frequencies in the bands allocated to the fixed service in conformity with Article 9 of the Radio Regulations. Considerations were also given to the latitudes expressed in Article 3, Section 3, wherein frequency usage is authorized " . . . on the express condition that harmful interference shall not be caused to services carried on by stations operating in accordance with the provisions of the convention and of these Regulations."

Last month, at the Sixth Meeting of the Bureau and Consultative Council of the IOC, this country's delegation to that meeting was asked if the United States would consider representing the ocean data interests at the Maritime Mobile Conference in 1967. This was done at the behest of the German delegation and with the full approval of the Bureau and Council. Assistance would be provided by the Republic of Germany in the form of a detailed report of its experiences at the Aero Mobile Conference this spring. Should no policy objection be interposed—and I am aware of none as of this date—the German experiences, and possibly their proposal of which I spoke earlier may be combined with an effective argument in favor of the intrinsic relationship between oceanographic and meteorological uses (as perceived in the plan for a World Weather Watch), and the ends sought to be met by the Maritime Mobile service.

Notwithstanding the frustrations encountered in these undertakings, I think it is well to note that communications in oceanography can be considered a microcosm of one of the principal themes with which we are dealing here—namely the equitable disposition of a finite commodity, subject to use by all, and demanding our most conscientious and intelligent efforts within an established legal order.

1. Report of the First Meeting, Working Group on Communications, UNESCO/IOC, Paris, 6–10 August, 1962.

2. Richard D. Terry, of North American Aviation, served as report director and editor.

3. NSIA, "Communications and Navigation," Vol. II, *Ocean Engineering,* Western Periodicals Co., 1966.

4. *Ibid.,* p. 23.

5. *International Telecommunications Convention,* Art. 31 and Annex 3, 12 UST 1761, TIAS 4892, 1959.

6. Art. 4, Sec. 2.

7. 45 Stat. 2760, TS 767, 94 LNTS 97, 1927.

8. 63 Stat. 1399, TIAS 1901, 1947.

9. *Partial Revision of 1959 Radio Regulations,* 15 UST 887, TIAS 5603, 1963.

10. J. M. Snodgrass, "Communications Problems of the Oceanographer," *Signal,* Vol. XX, No. 2, October, 1965.

11. E.g., mention by Snodgrass, *Ibid.,* of ITU Admin. Council Res. 564 asking member administrations for their views on ocean communications for possible consideration at a Maritime Mobile EARC during 1966 or early 1967.

Chapter Fourteen:

LAW AND THE NEW TECHNOLOGIES

I. *Introduction*

A currently favorable theme in international law is that of calling attention to the difficulties experienced or to be expected in adjusting the international decision-making process to changed conditions in the world social process. The recent growth in attention to science and technology in the development of the ocean, and the consequent concern of many for effective exploitation of this environment, has evoked a widespread interest in the law of the sea, past and future. The following discussion examines the interplay of some technological developments in ocean exploration and use with international law. For this purpose inquiry centers upon the continental shelf, scientific research, and fishery operations.

II. *The Continental Shelf*

Easily the most important technological advance affecting ocean law since World War II, excluding military instruments and operations, is the emergence and rapid spread of offshore oil exploration and exploitation.[1] Offshore oil drilling prior to 1945 did occur on a minor scale, but the great expansion in this industry came thereafter and primarily in the past decade. The effects of this achievement upon international law (and upon domestic law) have been extensive and profound and major impacts are still to be experienced. In a relatively few years, indeed with very great speed as these matters go, states accomplished the task, through the media of reciprocally recognized unilateral pronouncement and of explicit multilateral agreement, of allocating the resources of the continental shelf.[2] In addition, by agreement states

sought to provide for the accommodation of mineral resource exploitation with other important activities on the shelf or in that region.
Despite the speed of this adjustment, however, it is instructive to note
that some very important problems were not finally resolved and others,
perhaps *because* of the alacrity of state action, were anticipated in less
than desirable ways.

Thus, although states were able to agree, both tacitly and by explicit
arrangement, that the mineral resources of the shelf were to be disposed
of by the coastal state, such agreement does not extend to specification
of the area to be defined as the continental shelf. The Geneva Convention
formula, incorporating the outright cession of the area within the 100
fathom line and the contingent further incorporation of the area in
which exploitation becomes feasible, is in practical effect a means of
postponing decision regarding the limit upon exclusive exploitation.
Although delegates were aware that technology could expand the area
feasible for exploitation, it was apparently the general belief that the
100 fathom criterion was ample for a substantial period of time. In this
light is it worthwhile to note the preparatory document by Dr. Mouton
which sought to provide the conference with "the latest technical information concerning the possibility of exploiting the mineral resources
of the subsoil." [3] Although not made entirely clear, the conference could
reasonably surmise from this document that definition of the shelf in
terms of 100 fathoms would embrace exploration and exploitation for
the next twenty years, i.e., until 1978.[4] In terms of this projection the
situation in 1966 is in remarkable contrast, for offshore drilling rigs
are now working in water depths of 1000 feet, and, with certain ship
positioning systems, drilling can be, and has been, carried out in 12,000
feet depths.[5] Moreover, exploitation, the actual production of oil or gas,
is reportedly feasible, if not yet economical, at 1,000 foot depths. The
observation that the situation just described prevails within eight years
of the Geneva Conference and only two years after the Shelf Convention
came into force provides ample illustration of the problem of anticipating
the pace of technological and economic change.

Moreover, other impending changes in conditions of access to the
deep ocean floor could portend even greater difficulty arising from the
definition of the shelf in the 1958 Convention. Although evidence of
serious commercial interest is not easy to come by, there is no doubt
of a growing interest in the exploitation of hard minerals on the deep
ocean bed.[6] Here, too, the Geneva conferees were, understandably,

without sure guidance, for in the same preparatory document noted above it was asserted that this form of exploitation need not be taken into account for boundary purposes because either the concentration of minerals was too insubstantial to warrant exploitation, or mining was not commercially feasible when sufficient quantities did exist.[7] Despite this fact, and despite other evidence that the conference did not conceive of the ocean mining problem, many believe that the Shelf Convention prescribes for the division of the sea bed underlying entire oceans.[8]

In considering the provisions of the Shelf Convention aimed at the accommodation of mineral exploration and exploitation with other uses of the ocean, more stringent commentary is warranted. Here, too, as with the boundary problem, the strategy adopted was, at least for navigation, fishing and conservation, that of leaving the problem for subsequent resolution. The prescription of Article 5(1) that there must be no "unjustifiable interference" with these activities is, as others have observed, so general that the details of accommodation in specific contexts must now be worked out on an *ad hoc* basis, with little, if any, authoritative guidance from the convention.[9] Perhaps the uncertainties then felt about future developments and about the many and varied concrete circumstances to arise made this appear to be the only appropriate alternative. But in view of the rapidity with which intensive offshore oil exploration and exploitation are evolving, threatening (and already imposing in certain instances) interference with valuable fishing and shipping operations, more determined effort at general guidance would have been highly desirable.

If uncertainty about the future explains the reluctance to cope with this problem, it is even more difficult than otherwise to understand, much less appreciate, the lack of temerity displayed by the framers of the Shelf Convention in disposing of the problem of scientific research in the shelf region. For in this instance there was no discernible tendency to postpone consideration to the future. This attitude would not matter, of course, if the provisions adopted offered satisfactory protection to research activities in the shelf area, but there appears to be reason to doubt that this was achieved.

In seeming contrast to the qualified protection afforded the other activities on the shelf, the convention provides that there must be no interference with "fundamental oceanographic or other research carried out with the intention of open publication." The stated purpose of this provision was to permit the conduct of research without obstruction by coastal states. At the same time, however, Article 5(8) requires the consent of the coastal state "in respect of any research concerning the shelf and undertaken there," and also declares that this consent shall not normally be withheld "if the request is submitted by a qualified institution with a view to purely scientific research into the physical or biological characteristics of the shelf, subject to the proviso that the coastal state shall have the right if it so desires, to participate or be represented in the research, and that in any event the results shall be published."

To the extent that careful reading of a rather jumbled, and certainly summary, record of debate can be expected to disclose meaningful interpretative data, and surely caution is advisable in reaching conclusions from such examination, these provisions are to be construed harmoniously by confining the consent requirement to research into the shelf as an operation which is wholly distinguishable from research into the waters above. While it may be true, and this judgment is left to those qualified to make it, that this distinction can sometimes be made, it seems also distinctly possible that no such line can easily or conveniently or usefully be drawn on many occasions. This means, to be clear about it, both that research into the waters above may necessarily require research into the shelf below and that the reverse is true.[10] Hence, the requirement of consent might be far more extensive, in this interpretation, than the intended distinction suggests. Furthermore, assuming the two types of research are distinguishable, the convention is far from requiring the coastal consent envisaged. Even if the institution seeking consent is fully "qualified" and pursues "purely scientific research" into the specified characteristics of the shelf, the coastal state need not grant the request. There is little of an imperative nature in the injunction that it should "normally" not withhold the consent. The failure to provide criteria for what is and is not "normal" could, in the absence of continued attempt at clarification, result in repetitive deference to arbitrary unilateral decisions.

Furthermore, it should be evident that this article contains an ample number of vaguely specified conditions that enable, whatever the facts may be, a reasonably imaginative government official to support the contention that the request does not qualify for the "normal" consent. It does not require an enlarged creative capacity to perceive the various themes that can be played about the terms "qualified institution," "purely scientific research," and so forth.

207

To be sure the coastal state is authorized to require agreement to certain protective measures and this, it was hoped, would minimize the possibility that consent would not be forthcoming. But perhaps the realism of these opportunities for protection can be questioned. If the richest nation in the world finds difficulty in producing adequately trained oceanographers, it is at least conceivable that many far less well-endowed states find relatively cold comfort in the opportunity to participate in the scientific research in question. Either persons with the necessary talent are lacking altogether or, if theoretically available, are engaged in work more directly related to the coastal states' own interests. If there is apprehension about the research involved, but still a genuine desire to co-operate, it may be impossible to divert the necessary skilled people to the operations concerned. Finally, the publication requirement might ring a little hollow if the interval between research and publication becomes elongated, as there might be good reason to expect. The problems of data collection, analysis, and dissemination have their own demands and these may require many months and years for processing and publication.

All these horrible imaginings are merely irrelevant if states do not seek to invoke the requirements of the convention to obstruct research. Solid evidence of difficulties in obtaining consent, under conditions in which it might be expected, has not been discovered, but some incidents are known to have occurred in which consent has been refused outright.[11] Given the fluid and uncertain character of relations between states it would seem reasonable to speculate that more than a few such occasions arise or will do so. Apart from the possible refusal of clearance for a particular research undertaking, the additional administrative and diplomatic problems imposed by the procedure for securing consent are undesirable additions to the already ample burdens of scientists.

In any event, since the Shelf Convention is in effect, and since even states not parties to it may claim that consent for shelf research must be obtained,[12] the problem is how to minimize the interference with legitimate research efforts. In view of the critical nature, for many purposes, of research into the ocean environment in shelf regions (which are, it is worth reiteration, not well defined for some legal purposes), and especially considering the interdependency between the "parts" of the ocean, any trend toward excessive coastal intrusion into legitimate scientific research warrants grave concern on the part of all affected, including government officials with responsibility in this field. The pertinent provisions of the convention are phrased in very general terms and questionable applications of them to the detriment of research merit every feasible effort in response to assure reasonable interpretations which do not threaten closure of important areas to scientists. At present levels of research activity, isolated refusals of consent to research may not inflict consequential harm beyond the immediate project, but if, as seems likely, the scientific study of the ocean environment is to intensify further, refusals could become more frequent and more damaging to the general interest in knowledge of the sea.

Focus upon potential difficulties arising from the Continental Shelf Convention should not obscure the need for an equivalent concern about the extension of coastal state controls over shelf installations and activities based on alleged general principles of international law, for it is quite probable that recent developments in this direction could impose undesirable restraints on ocean research and development. The recent developments mentioned consist of the promulgation in December, 1964, of the North Seas Installations Act by the Netherlands. A recent study of this legislation, and the events leading to it, assures us that this enactment is not based upon the Continental Shelf Convention and that

> There is . . . every reason to conclude that the action taken was based upon a *new* rule of international law, which may be summarized as being that a coastal state may exercise jurisdiction over all installations erected on the soil of its continental shelf, no matter for what purpose.[13]

The authors of this study, Drs. van Panhuys and van Emde Boas of the University of Leyden, confidently predict that "there is no likelihood" that "the future practice of states might lead to a rejection of the (alleged) new rule." [14]

If this prediction is borne out it does not seem to take any great prescience to anticipate grave difficulties in gaining access to, and making effective use of, the ocean regions of the continental shelf adjacent to many states. To support this statement it is necessary to describe and to assess the provisions of this legislation and the legal theories underlying it.

The genesis of the Netherlands Act consists of the construction and operation of a radio and television station outside the territorial sea but on the continental shelf adjacent to the Netherlands.[15] The station was designed to, and did, transmit programs into the Netherlands, apparently

209

in violation of Netherlands law which establishes a monopoly over broadcasting in five broadcasting associations, each of which, it is said, "represents an important religious or political faction of the population." [16] Although it was a purpose of the North Sea Installations Act to provide domestic authority for dealing with the radio and television station, the government explicitly sought to accomplish a much broader purpose, namely that of regulating any and all shelf installations no matter who emplaces them and whatever the purpose sought. Since the Shelf Convention is concerned only with installations for resource exploitation, it was felt necessary to base the legislation on supposed principles of general international law. The language of the North Sea Installations Act, including even its title, was chosen so as to avoid reliance upon the Continental Shelf Convention. The act in its entirety appears as follows: [17]

Whereas We have deemed it desirable to make provision for the protection of legal interests in respect of installations on the bed of that part of the North Sea the boundaries of which correspond with those of that portion of the continental shelf which appertains to the Netherlands, until such time as the matter is regulated by international agreement;

So We, having heard the views of the Council of State and with the advice and consent of the States-General, have approved and understood, and do approve and understand, the following:

Section 1. In this Act the term "sea installation" shall mean an installation erected outside territorial waters on the bed of that part of the North Sea the boundaries of which correspond with that portion of the continental shelf which appertains to the Netherlands.

Section 2. The criminal law of the Netherlands shall apply to all such persons as commit any offense on a sea installation.

Section 3. Provision may be made by Order in Council that any provisions of the statutory law of the Netherlands shall apply on and with respect to sea installations.

Section 4. Provision may be made by Order in Council for the extension to sea installations of the jurisdiction of authorities and officials entrusted with the implementation of the provisions referred to in Section 3 above, or with the investigation and prosecution of offenses or with the bringing to trial of those responsible or with the execution of any sentences that may be passed by any court.

Section 5. Provision may be made by Order in Council that the criminal law of the Netherlands and such statutory provisions as are referred to in Section 3 shall not apply to such sea installations as are described in such Order in Council or shall apply to such installations only to a limited extent.

Section 6. If, within three months of the coming into force of an Order in Council, issued in terms of Section 3 or Section 5 above, We have not had a bill laid before the States-General to replace such Order in Council, or if such bill is withdrawn or defeated, We shall without delay repeal such Order in Council.

Section 7. Regulations may be made by Order in Council in respect of installations erected or to be erected outside territorial waters on the bed of that part of the North Sea referred to in Section 1, in the interests of shipping, the fishing industry, the conservation of the living resources of the sea, pure scientific research, the laying and maintenance of submarine cables and pipelines, and the prevention of the pollution of the sea, as well as for the protection of such other interests as are recognized by international law.

Section 8. Any contravention of regulations made under Section 7 shall be punishable by a fine not exceeding ten thousand guilders. Such contravention shall be considered to be an "overtreding" [corresponding to the French *contravention, i.e.,* a minor infringement of the criminal law].

Section 9. This Act may be cited as the "North Sea Installations Act."

Section 10. This Act shall come into force on the first day following the date of its publication in the *Official Gazette.*

Be it ordered that the above be published in the *Official Gazette* and that all government departments, authorities and officials concerned do conscientiously enforce it.

Given at Our Palace of Soestdijk, this third day of December 1964.

JULIANA

The immediate occasion for this legislation, the closure of Radio and TV Noordzee, appears to provide ample basis for some coastal action, and it may turn out that this legislation will have little impact upon legitimate activities offshore the Netherlands. However, the blanket provision for the extension of national law to any installation on the shelf could, both in this case and in others involving governments less concerned for free access to, and use of, the ocean floor than the Netherlands, be employed to inhibit and even prevent efficient use of this area. Certainly there would seem to be little doubt that legislation so broadly conceived and phrased would permit the extension of any provision national decision-makers chose to adopt, without regard to effects upon the use of the area. Nothing in this legislation suggests standards or criteria for determining what laws should extend to offshore installations, and it seems to me rather obvious that officials in some states could, pursuant to identical legislation, harass and perhaps completely frustrate legitimate scientific or other operations in the adjacent shelf region.

211

There appears to be no doubt, of course, that some installations, such as the radio-television operation offshore the Netherlands, can have undesirable impacts within a coastal state and that coastal officials should be competent to prescribe and apply local policies to such installations and activities. However this may be, it does not at all lend support to the far-reaching claim underlying the Dutch legislation that *all* installations are subject to the legislation of the adjacent coastal state. At least it would seem that the coastal state has the heavy burden of demonstrating that because certain installations may have detrimental effects upon the coastal social order it is therefore necessary to assert authority to extend unilateral controls over any and all such activities in the area. The problem of reconciling the interests involved would seem to require more sophisticated and selective treatment than that. Insofar as I am able to judge, the legal justification offered by the Netherlands in support of this legislation falls far short of discharging this burden.

As described by Drs. van Panhuys and van Emde Boas the Netherlands relies on a "legal vacuum theory," the protection of legal interests, and the notion of contiguity.[18] The "legal vacuum" theory assumes that there is no authority over shelf installations and activities thereon unless it is that of the adjacent coastal state. The protection of legal interests also justifies the exercise of jurisdiction on the high seas, the interests being those of the acting state or of the international community. Finally, and supposedly supplementary, the notion of contiguity is invoked to identify the adjacent state as the one to fill the vacuum and protect certain interests. It is upon highly legalistic, and in part unsound, reasoning of this type that the Netherlands now proposes to control all installations on the adjacent shelf. Only the second theory mentioned appears to have any real substance since it is obviously true that protection of certain interests warrants the exercise of "jurisdiction" on the high seas. However the key word here is "certain" since it is not assumed, and certainly need not be, that coastal state interests are always detrimentally affected by offshore installations. The other theories smack of convenience and expediency and in any event neither stretches far enough to provide a firm foundation for the Dutch legislation.

These general comments may be given more precise focus by examining certain more specific potential (or actual) legal problems of research into the ocean. The following remarks are concerned with the employment of fixed oceanographic stations, especially buoys, practices in geological and archeological investigations, and prospective developments in marine geodesy.

III. *Scientific Research*

Actual and anticipated use of ocean buoys, and of other devices under the general heading of fixed oceanographic stations, suggests a great many legal problems only some of which can be mentioned here.[19] Questions of jurisdiction and substantive issues of liability for accidental damage to ships and to the buoys call for study in terms of admiralty law principles which is beyond the scope of this discussion. It suffices to say that this could be a task of very considerable dimensions which merits the creative energies of students of admiralty law.

The major issues for purposes of this discussion involve the areas in which research buoys may be used as a matter of right. In 1962 a joint "preliminary report" to the Inter-governmental Oceanographic Commission from the UNESCO-IMCO Secretariats made the suggestion that "freedom of research" on the high seas should be recognized as explicitly as other rights of use of the high seas, such as navigation and fishing, and that such right of research extended to the use of buoys for scientific purposes.[20] Whether or not the "freedom of research" is expressly regarded as a component of freedom of the seas is not as significant as the fact that in practice scientific investigation is a fully established right in the use of the ocean. So far as can be discovered no state has ever asserted any authority to interfere with or prohibit scientific research, except when such authority purportedly derived from international agreement and then only for a certain type of research. Insofar, therefore, as an area is considered as part of the "high seas," i.e., beyond the territorial sea of any state, there is a right under customary international law to emplace buoys, subject to the reasonable requirements of safety of navigation. Moreover, it is not at all necessary to rely only upon customary international law for support of "freedom of research" as one of the protected aspects of freedom of the seas. Article 2 of the Convention on the High Seas expressly states that there are freedoms other than the four enumerated in the article and

213

it may be recalled that in its comment appended to the corresponding draft article the International Law Commission declared that the freedom to engage in scientific research was one of the freedoms of the seas.[21]

If this were all that was involved, problems would be minimal. Unfortunately, as mentioned above, the Convention on the Continental Shelf not only contains a provision seeking to preserve the superjacent waters as part of the high seas, but also authorizes the coastal state to prohibit, by withholding consent, certain research in the shelf area. Does such authority include the power to prohibit the use of scientific research buoys by any state or group other than the coastal state? In view of the purpose sought by Article 5(8) of the convention the answer seems to me to be that the coastal state would very seldom, if ever, have any such authority. The purpose of Article 5(8) apparently was to prevent the surreptitious exploration of the shelf for commercial purposes under the guise of scientific research for advancing knowledge. Unless buoys can be made to serve as exploration devices in a consequential manner the conclusion should be that the coastal state has no authority over them. More explicitly, coastal authority extends only to research "concerning the continental shelf and undertaken there" and if buoys are used only for other research, as into water characteristics, the coastal state would be without any competence whatsoever.[22] Emplacement of buoys as part of a meteorological network would thus appear to be beyond any control of the coastal state.

The territorial sea is another area within which coastal states might claim control over emplacement of buoys by a foreign state or group. The joint UNESCO-IMCO Report concludes that the coastal state has complete authority over research buoys in the territorial sea. Relying primarily upon Article 1(1) of the Convention on the Territorial Sea, which provides that state sovereignty extends to the territorial sea, the report states:

> From the foregoing basic rules, it would seem that the following tentative conclusions may be suggested as respects the territorial and internal waters.
>
> 1. The coastal state may exercise its sovereign rights in governing the use of oceanographic research buoys.
>
> 2. The coastal state may freely permit or deny permission to employ such devices.
>
> 3. The coastal state may interpose such restrictions, limitations or regulations as it deems fit on the placement, purpose or use of oceanographic buoys, subject to the safety rules discussed herein.

214

4. No one may claim an absolute international right to place oceanographic buoys in the internal or territorial waters of any state without the express or implied permission of the government of that state.[23]

These conclusions, though tentative, deserve serious consideration and constructive criticism. One may assume that on occasion it is desirable or even essential to place buoys within the territorial sea for legitimate scientific purpose, but nothing inherent in the notion of the territorial sea dictates the conclusions reached in the UNESCO-IMCO Report. The reference to "sovereignty" over the territorial sea in Article 1(1) of the Convention, if considered in isolation and without consideration of other factors, certainly does suggest that a very comprehensive coastal control over buoys is contemplated by present international law, but there are other factors to be weighed that might put the matter in a different perspective.

The legal regime of the territorial sea is not weighted completely in deference to the coastal state and, in fact, certain provisions of the Convention on the Territorial Sea seek to accommodate the general community interest in freedom of use of the ocean. Thus the provisions for a right of innocent passage for foreign vessels, according to which these vessels have a right of access to the territorial sea under certain conditions, are an attempt to reconcile the coastal interest in self-protection with the wider community's interest in making efficient use of the sea for transportation. In this instance the "sovereignty" of the coastal state does not mean that the coastal state may "freely" prohibit passage by foreign vessels.

When these basic policies are considered in this new and different context it seems wholly reasonable to seek to make a similar accommodation. The problem here is to evolve an arrangement which preserves in substantial measure the exercise of the freedom to engage in scientific research by means of buoy technology and at the same time permits the coastal state to exercise sufficient authority to protect its legitimate interests. The assumption underlying this approach is that for purposes of research the ocean cannot be fragmented by political boundaries anymore than it can be for making effective use of it for transportation, and that freedom of research ought, therefore, to be accorded protection from unwarranted interference within territorial waters in a fashion similar to that accorded transportation. Because of possible hazards to navigation the coastal state obviously must exercise some regulatory authority, such as specifying reasonable requirements for location,

215

lighting, marking and communications. But this authority need not be conceived or expressed in terms of an absolute discretion to forbid buoy emplacement nor need the regulatory authority be exercised to have that effect in practice.

Under this proposal it would probably be necessary to require notification by the sponsoring agency to the coastal state concerned so that the above problems could be appropriately resolved. Such notification would properly include information on the characteristics of the buoy and associated equipment. Assurance of a right to emplace the buoy might be achieved by requiring reply, specifying reasonable conditions of access, by the coastal state within a specified period.

This problem, if in fact it is one, suggests the more general observation that previous experience in the law of the sea was limited almost entirely to manned vehicles and that considerable care should be taken in drawing upon this experience for use in the context of unmanned objects. What seems to be necessary in this situation, as it always is when new issues emerge, is to place the emphasis upon all of the fundamental policies involved and not upon the details of specific prescriptions.

The surprising scope of the potential legal problems involved in oceanic research may be further illustrated by the employment of "photographic" sonar for archeological research in submarine areas and for geological research for purely scientific purposes.[24] The reason a question, and potential problem, arise is that this device is reported to be useful, and has been used, for oil exploration. A coastal state might, therefore, seek to impose a requirement of consent for operation of this equipment in the shelf area, even if it is employed for archeological or non-commercial geological purposes. Such a condition might be regarded as falling within the scope of coastal authority granted in Article 5(8) of the Shelf Convention which calls for consent to "any research concerning the shelf and undertaken there." In such a determination it seems obviously relevant that photographic sonar is a multipurpose device, one purpose of which relates directly to the "sovereign rights" of the coastal state in exploration for natural resources. On the other hand, despite the breadth of the convention reference to research, it is doubtful that archeological investigation was regarded at the time as one of the critical activities for which consent should be sought. Since the convention contemplates that "purely scientific research into the physical or biological characteristics" of the shelf would normally

216

receive consent, such activity as historical research, which is not even directed at these aspects of the shelf, would probably have been regarded as beyond even the need for a request for consent. Unfortunately, whatever the intent of the framers, the development of devices useful for varying purposes, including one unrelated to the coastal interest in the resources of the shelf and one directly related, suggests a legitimate concern by the coastal state warranting the application of Article 5(8). If, however, proper safeguards can be established to assure the use of the equipment for archeological or non-commercial geological purposes, then refusal to consent for such inquiry appears to be an unreasonable application of Article 5(8). Ample protection of coastal interests could be secured by observance of these safeguards coupled with the presence of coastal representatives.

Another potential problem, in some ways similar to those just discussed, is suggested by recommendations for the establishment of a world-wide marine geodetic system. This network would involve the permanent emplacement of equipment on the ocean floor for locating and identifying bench marks useful for a variety of purposes. A recent report by Mr. George Mourad of Battelle Memorial Institute summarizes the advantages of this system as follows:

> Among the activities that would benefit from an ocean geodetic grid system are spacecraft recovery, ocean engineering, open ocean tide measurement, calibration of inertial and electronic navigational systems, and seismic and magnetic mapping. Surface and underwater highways could be established on the basis of such a system. Surveying of ocean farming and mining areas would also be facilitated. The grid system could also be used as a basis for an ocean meteorological network of weather observing stations.[25]

In general the kinds of legal issues raised by the proposed network could include rights of access to particular areas or submarine regions, the accommodation of the system, or units of it, with other activities that might involve conflicts in use, and the allocation of competence to prescribe and to apply prescriptions regarding liability for damage.[26] The degree to which these issues will emerge as real problems depends, among other things, upon the characteristics of the system in terms of the numbers, size and distribution of the equipment required. For example, if the United States establishes a system only in regions adjacent to the United States, the potential problems may be fewer than if this country sought to create a regional or hemispheric or

217

larger network. Additionally the exact kind of equipment involved would appear to be an important factor. The range in size of individual installations might effect the kind of accommodation necessary with other uses. Relatively small units would probably fit in better with other uses than huge installations. The type of communications system employed could be important for assimilation with other systems. The number of bench marks required, which might vary according to the purposes served, obviously has a bearing on the need for access to particular areas.

Finally, the degree to which a marine geodetic system, emplaced on a global basis, serves widely shared interests would seem very significant in determining the likelihood of legal controversy. The impressive catalogue of beneficial uses, quoted above, suggests that there may be a genuine common interest among most states in provision of the network. But at the same time the interests served most obviously are those with the most sophisticated techniques in ocean development and use, a group of very few states. Moreover, if the major advantage, or consequential gain, accrues to the military, the chances may be greater that particular states would object to emplacement of units in the system in "their" adjacent coastal regions.

IV. *Fishery Operations*

Recent experience with the world fishing industry indicates that technological change not only creates problems but also occasionally provides the favorable climate for resolving them. Since World War II rapid and extensive technological developments in fishing, in all aspects, have had substantial repercussions upon the law of the sea. Improvement in boat design, engines, and gear, and innovations in fishing and processing practices, increasingly permit the industry generally, but more noticeably in a few states, to extend operations throughout the entire world ocean. The impact of this more widespread, as well as intensive, activity and of the more sophisticated fishing techniques employed is reflected in the numerous, now familiar, demands for changes in, and additions to, the structure of international legal prescriptions. Accompanying these demands, and in major part inspired by them, are critical commentaries by observers, including social scientists, lawyers, and fishery policy-makers, also calling for reappraisal and change.

In appraisal of the events of the past twenty years it seems apparent that the course of change is steadily demanding far more sophisticated institutional arrangements than have been envisaged by those responsible for decision. The first demands to reflect the perceived pressure of distant water fleets upon local fishing operations began to impinge upon the international legal process soon after World War II. The most consequential initial response, which as we can now see presaged more far-reaching decisions, came from the most unlikely place, the International Court of Justice in its decision in the Anglo-Norwegian Fisheries Case in 1951. Although the roots of the dispute there involved went back for many years, as early as the first two decades in this century, the significance of this case extends far beyond the issues immediately at stake. For while this decision resolved a relatively localized dispute, it has been generalized in subsequent widespread agreement to extend, at least colorably, to numerous other situations around the world.

Moreover, more importantly, the outcome of that case not only indicated that the legal structure was sufficiently flexible, or could be made to be, to protect local fishing interests against more dynamic foreign competitors in a specific situation, but also helped provide the impetus for further and different methods to protect such interests. For even as the Fisheries case was moving through the litigation process, the impact of changes in fisheries practices began to be evident in a variety of places around the world. In moves which were also destined to provoke changes in the legal structure, if in less drastic ways than demanded, Iceland and the Latin American states began the agitation for enlarged exclusive fishing areas, an agitation that has been pursued unilaterally and multilaterally with mounting intensity in the past fifteen years. Again the legal structure has been affected, the first indications appearing unmistakably in the Geneva conferences of 1958 and 1960, and the change is now rapidly approaching, if it has not already achieved, the status of new principles of international law in the form of acceptance of the exclusive fishing zone of moderate width as part of that law.[27]

Two major conditions are prominent in shaping those decisions. First, military considerations have been most influential in diverting the demand for change from enlargement of the territorial sea to expansion of exclusive fishing areas beyond a more or less, although not completely, static territorial sea.[28] Secondly, and of comparable but not as great influence, the technological changes in the industry which first led to

219

the claims to exclusive fishing areas have opened the way to their recognition. This too became apparent at Geneva in 1960 when in desperate effort to secure agreement the United States and Canada urged their six-plus-six plus modified historic rights proposal. The notable point about this, for present purposes, is that the full impact of the six mile exclusive fishing zone was to be postponed for ten years, hopefully providing time for the industry to adopt its practices in ways that would lessen the impact of the larger exclusive fishing area. Whether or not ten years were required for the transition, and whether there was any great need for a transition period, the belief apparently was that the pace of change in the industry was adequate to compensate for losses supposedly to follow from the exclusionary effects of the new policy. In the five years since, there is some evidence suggesting that improvements in the industry may continue to have pronounced effects upon the willingness of states to accept exclusive fishing zones. The European Fisheries Convention adopted in 1964 provides for a limited transitional arrangement relating to part of the exclusive fishing zone there established, although for most of the zone it seeks to maintain certain "historic rights" seemingly for the life of the convention.[29]

If, however, the fishing industry is, by reason of technological improvements, generally able to withstand the modestly enlarged exclusive fishing zones now being established rather commonly around the world, and thus assists in alleviating the political controversy which attend nation-state differences on this matter, it does not at all follow that further conflict is not to be expected. It is unwise to accept for one moment the notion that all the exotic gear and futuristic practices that are apparently on their way to becoming standard in the fishing industry will cause fishery conflicts to disappear. Indeed it seems more likely that worse problems may have to be confronted than thus far experienced. These problems will probably involve, first, vastly enlarged demands for exclusive fishing areas and, second, conflicting demands for allocating scarce resources beyond exclusive fishing areas.

The reason for anticipating that states will seek even more expanded exclusive fishing zones rests on the assumption that the supposed gain or protection from the present exclusive fishing zones will not be realized or, if some gain is realized, that there will still be the urge to enlarge it by extending the exclusive fishing zone even further out to sea. It seems none too soon to anticipate this possibility despite the recent comment by Christy and Scott that this form of recognizing the supposed "special interest" of coastal states has "very little relevance to the principles by which the high seas might be governed." [30] If the word "might" here is understood as "ought," this is a cogent statement (though in contradiction to later statements) ; but if it is intended to indicate the shape of the future, perhaps doubts can be entertained. The question is, for present purposes, what will be left as "high seas" for fisheries purposes if states continue to expand, and make effective, exclusive fishing limits.

If, one inquires, further expansion were contemplated by particular states, what limit would be adopted? The answer, and it does have relevance in my opinion if one is concerned about economic efficiency in allocation of fishery resources, is that states would look to the fishery resources of the continental shelf. Some states already have made such choices, of course, and we are assured by so eminent a participant and observer as Dr. Wilbert M. Chapman that a proposal of this kind to an international conference would receive the support of the majority of states in attendance.[31] In addition, as is well-known, within the United States there is strong sentiment in some quarters for just this arrangement.[32] It perhaps lends little enchantment to this prospect to recall that the "continental shelf," as defined for purposes of the convention thereon, can extend beyond the geological conception of the shelf.

Even if this projection proves inaccurate, and the current, relatively modest, exclusive fishing areas satisfy coastal states, the increased technological efficiency of the industry coupled with increasing demand for fishery products will probably require the creation, alluded to above, of far more sophisticated arrangements in allocating the yield to be obtained. The point is that if technology facilitates acceptance of limited exclusive fishing areas, so that fleets may operate in the deeper waters more distant from the coast in many parts of the world, it will also place greater pressure on high seas resources and the need will then have to be faced of creating institutional mechanisms, policies, and procedures for determining the level of exploitation efforts and allocating the yield.

V. Conclusion

These brief remarks, and extensions that could be made of them, do no more than emphasize again the need for more conscious, con-

221

tinuing efforts in provision of a legal framework within which effective ocean exploitation can be pursued to the common advantage. Although there is an evident need for establishing international institutions, endowed with adequate authority, policies, and procedures for coping with a rapidly changing situation, it would be a mistake to attempt to place too much confidence in the capacity of the international political system to respond to the new demands. This does not mean that progress in creating new international institutions, and improving those already operative, is beyond achievement, but it does mean that recommendations for improvement should take careful account of the many social, political, economic, and military factors that will very likely shape international decisions in this matter. Perhaps there is no need to state that no such accounting is attempted in this paper.

However, it may be desirable in this connection to make brief appraisal of one recent proposal for a new international institution. The Commission to Study the Organization of Peace in its Seventeenth Report, published in May, 1966, recommends that title to the entire ocean (beyond a twelve mile limit for fish and a specifically defined continental shelf for minerals) "be vested in the international community through its agency, the United Nations." [33] The reasons offered in support of this are: the avoidance of controversy arising from competing claims, the assurance of the "economically effective use" of ocean resources, the prevention of military uses, the avoidance of contamination from various sources, the more equitable allocation of profits from ocean exploitation, and the provision of an independent income for the United Nations. In implementation of this "title" the Commission recommends the establishment of a UN Marine Resources Agency with the following functions and duties:

> It should control and administer international marine resources; hold ownership rights; and grant, lease or use these rights in accordance with the principles of economic efficiency. It should function with the independence and efficiency of the International Bank. However, it should distribute the returns in accordance with directives issued by the United Nations General Assembly. Such an agency would present a viable alternative to the anarchy that now prevails and it would, therefore, be in the legitimate interest of most nations to encourage and support the UN Marine Resources Agency.[34]

With deference to the members of the eminent group sponsoring this proposal, it appears to me to suffer the common malady of attempting to divorce the treatment of a complex problem from the social and political environment which affects it and which accounts for its difficulty. No doubt many will willingly concede the wisdom of the long-range objective of complete internationalization of the better part of the ocean by means of organized management, control, and even operation, but, unfortunately, the bare recommendation of this objective hardly advances the prospect of achieving it. Serious recommendations of this sort would gain far greater influence if accompanied both by acknowledgment of the obstacles which must be surmounted and by suggested strategies by which the campaign can be conducted. Here, as in many areas of international relations, we are far less in need of blueprints for utopia than of immediate guidance in influencing the social, and especially decision, processes which must be affected enroute to the goal. In this specific connection, for example, the commission's report can be searched in vain for acknowledgment of one obstacle that seems perfectly apparent, namely that the proposed UN Marine Resources Agency has very little, if any, chance of birth unless the General Assembly is itself reconstituted so that its decision-making processes, especially those disposing of the new source of wealth to be placed in its control, more faithfully reflect the present distribution of power, wealth, and skill among the members. Elsewhere in its report the Commission acknowledges the need for this revision, but this particular substantive recommendation regarding the ocean apparently is intended to stand by itself.

Other, more specific, factors inhibiting the prospect of establishing an agency with this scope of authority and responsibility can be cited. The report rather casually recommends that military activities in the deep sea and sea bed be prohibited by the General Assembly. This seems to be what is intended by the cryptic reference to prevention of military use as a reason for a General Assembly declaration of "international title" to ocean areas and by another recommendation "that the General Assembly should declare that the deep sea and the sea bed must not be used by nations as an environment in which to install or operate weapons, or for purposes intended to further research on potential weapons or their development." If this idea is understood correctly, and unless the Commission is in possession of some special information unavailable to this writer, it seems difficult to conceive of a proposition more suitably designed to insure the most vigorous and powerful opposi-

223

tion to this method of internationalizing the ocean. The effect of this recommendation appears to be to intertwine, probably to share the same fate, a far-reaching proposal for partial disarmament of the major powers with one for international control and management of the ocean. I am indebted to Professor McDougal for what appears to be an appropriate comment on this: to snap at a gnat it isn't necessary to swallow an elephant. The problems of ocean exploitation are no doubt more faithfully depicted than by characterization as a gnat, but surely there are ways to make progress in their resolution without calling for simultaneous settlement of the gargantuan puzzle of disarmament.

Quite apart from the strategic error in inviting the opposition of the most powerful states of the world, since both the U.S. and the Soviet Union are deeply committed to ocean weapons systems, the suggested prohibition of military activity hardly seems to be a necessary consequence of organized international exploitation of the ocean, and in fact the commission does not make such a bald suggestion. Indeed a close scrutiny of the Commission's Report fails to disclose any unique stated reason for preventing military use of the "deep sea and sea bed." In September, 1966, the supplementary papers, on which the report is based, are to be published, and this may shed light upon this aspect of the report. In the meantime, there are no a priori reasons in evidence which justify singling out the "deep sea and sea bed" as prohibited areas for military activities or for research on "potential weapons or their development." The supposed Antarctic analogy, citing the 1959 agreement that Antarctica shall be used for peaceful purposes only, will not stand even cursory examination. It is one thing to prohibit military activities in an area of the most minimal strategic significance; it is far different to contemplate such an agreement regarding the ocean, an area which has been, and is extremely likely to continue to be, of the highest concern to national defense.

One final comment concerns the frequent references in the Report to the desiderata of economic efficiency in exploitation of ocean resources. The assumption is made that the proposed Marine Resources Agency is the institutional modality by which this goal can be attained. Perhaps in the long run this is so, but the minimal effort now devoted to inquiry into economic criteria for the exploitation of fishery resources suggests that present prospects for successful international administration of the high seas fisheries of the entire ocean are dim to say the least. Although unified management schemes are desirable, a more productive approach would probably entail less comprehensive management efforts, aimed at regional groupings rather than a universal system.

1. Details of this development are chronicled in other papers of this symposium.

2. This subject is examined in numerous writings. See, e.g., McDougal and Burke, The Public Order of the Oceans, 630–729 (1962) ; Oda, International Control of Sea Resources, 147 ff (1963) ; Garcia-Amador, The Exploitation and Conservation of the Resources of the Sea, 86–133 (2d ed., 1959).

3. Mouton, *Recent Developments in the Technology of Exploiting the Mineral Resources of the Continental Shelf*, A/CONF.13/25/p. 5 (3 January 1958).

4. "By projecting the present rate of advance of offshore drilling technology into the future, it appears likely that oil exploitation in 200 metres of water may *occur* in twenty years." *Id.* at 18.

5. See, generally, *International Offshore Report*, World Oil, May, 1965, pp. 110–23.

6. Mero, The Mineral Resources of the Sea, *passim* (1965) ; Crawford and Padan, *The Bureau of Mines' Expanding Role in Undersea Mining*, Mining Engineering, March, 1965, p. 67; Pehrson, *Mining Industry's Role in Development of Underseas Mining*, 1966 Transactions, Marine Technology Society 182 (1966) ; Hibbard, *The Government's Program for Encouraging the Development of a Marine Mining Industry, id.* at 197; Bennett, *Legal Climate for Underseas Mining, id.* at 204; Burke, *Legal Aspects of Ocean Exploitation, id.* at 1, 10–13.

7. Mouton, *supra* note 3 at 24.

8. Mero, *op. cit, supra* note 6 at 289.

9. McDougal and Burke, *op. cit, supra* note 2, at 704–24; Young, *Offshore Claims and Problems in the North Sea*, 59 Am. J. Intl. L. 505, 517–22 (1965).

10. See, generally, Report of the Panel on Oceanography, President's Science Advisory Committee, Effective Use of the Sea 44–45 (June, 1966) ; see also, Interagency Committee on Oceanography, Undersea Vehicles for Oceanography 6–9 (ICO Pamp. No. 18, October 1965).

It is reported that "Information about currents can also be deduced from the photographs (of the sea floor) and samples." Emery, Merrill, and Trumbull, *Geology and Biology of the Sea Floor as Deduced from Simultaneous Photographs and Samples*, 10 Limnology and Oceanography 1, 9 (1965).

11. The basis for this statement consists of information from several American oceanographers, all acquired in personal conversation. In addition one widely known American oceanographer disclosed that he canceled plans for survey work involving the shelf regions off ten countries, estimated to take two summers to complete. The basis for this cancellation was the expectation that it would take longer to secure the permission, if it were given at all, than to do the surveys.

On procedures for securing consent see Interagency Committee on Oceanography, U.S. Oceanic Research in Foreign Waters (ICO Pamp. No. 25, January, 1966).

225

12. It is, apparently, the U.S. view that such states are entitled to require that consent be received. *Id.* at 7. This would mean, of course, that since the obligation does not stem from the convention those party to it may also require consent for research by those affiliated with non-party states.

13. Van Panhuys and van Emde Boas, *Legal Aspects of Pirate Broadcasting: A Dutch Approach,* 60 Am. J. Intl. L. 303, 337 (1966).

14. *Id.* at 338.

15. *Id.* at 303–4, 326–27.

16. *Id.* at 308.

17. Taken from *id.* at 340–41.

18. *Id.* at 330–35.

19. See, generally, UNESCO, Intergovernmental Oceanographic Commission, Preliminary Report of UNESCO and IMCO on the Legal Status of Unmanned and Manned Fixed Oceanographic Stations (Doc. No. NS/IOC/INF/34) (1962) ; *id., Report of the Director-General of UNESCO in consultation with the Secretary-General of IMCO on the Legal Status of Oceanographic Research Stations* (Doc. No. UNESCO/IOC/INF–60) (1964) ; UNESCO, Intergovernmental Oceanographic Commission, IOC Working Group on Ocean Data Stations, Second Meeting (DOC. No. AVS/9/89E–ODS) (March, 1966).

20. UNESCO, Intergovernmental Oceanographic Commission, *Preliminary Report, supra* note 19, at 10.

21. International Law Commission, 1955, Report 3.

22. It should be noted in this connection that the report of the second meeting of the IOC Working Group on Ocean Data Stations states that in preparation of a single legal code for ocean data stations "it will be desirable to consider" the question of "Rules pertaining to installation of stations on the Continental Shelves of other States." *Supra* note 19, at 9.

23. UNESCO, IOC, *Preliminary Report, supra* note 19, at 5–6.

24. *N.Y. Times,* Feb. 7, 1966, reports on the projected use of this device in archeological investigations by Dr. Harold E. Edgerton of MIT. On the subject generally see Bass, *The Promise of Underwater Archeology,* 32 The American Scholar 241 (1963) ; *id.,* The Asherah: A Submarine for Archeology, 18 Archeology No. 1, Spring, 1965, p. 7.

25. Mourad, *Marine Geodesy,* Battelle Technical Review, Feb. 1965, 5, at 6.

26. Legal aspects of marine geodesy will be considered in somewhat more detail in a paper for the First Marine Geodesy Symposium, co-sponsored by Battelle-Columbus and the U.S. Coast and Geodetic Survey, Sept. 28–30, 1966.

27. In a statement before a Congressional committee the Legal Adviser of the State Department stated: "In view of the recent developments in international practice, action by the United States at this time to establish an exclusive fisheries zone extending nine miles beyond the territorial sea would not, in the view of the State Department, be contrary to international law." *Hearing on S.2218 before the Subcommittee on Merchant Marine and Fisheries of Senate Committee on Commerce,* 89th Cong., 2d. Sess. 20 (1966).

28. See the account in Lawrence, *Military-Legal Considerations in the Extension of the Territorial Sea,* 29 Military L. Rev. 47; Statement of W. M. Chapman Respecting H.R. 5175, the Law of the Sea and Public Policy in *Hearings on National Oceanographic Program Legislation before the Subcommittee on Ocean-*

ography of the House Committee on Merchant Marine and Fisheries, 89th Cong., 1st Sess. 388, 394 (1965).

29. JOHNSON, EUROPEAN FISHERY LIMITS IN DEVELOPMENTS IN THE LAW OF THE SEA 48 (British Institute of International and Comparative Law, Spec. Pub. No. 6, 1965); Mouton, *The Establishment of Rules of International Law on a World Basis or a Regional Basis,* with Particular Reference to Limits on Fisheries, 12 European Yearbook 79 (1966).

30. CHRISTY AND SCOTT, THE COMMON WEALTH IN OCEAN FISHERIES 187 (1965).

31. *Hearings,* supra n. 28, at 401.

32. See, for example, statements by various Committee members and witnesses in *Hearings, supra* n. 27.

33. "New Dimensions for the United Nations," 17th Report, Commission to Study the Organization of the Peace 42 (1966).

34. *Id.* at 44. For similar recommendations see the White House Conference on International Cooperation, *National Citizens' Commission Report of the Committee on Natural Resources, Conservation and Development* 7 (1965).

Discussion of Harlow, Sullivan, and Burke

1. A state, for security requirements, may temporarily suspend the right of innocent passage for all foreign vessels through its territorial sea. These restrictions, in cases such as weapons testing, gunnery practice, and the like, need not apply to the entire territorial sea. Innocent passage itself may be open to question. For example, would passage be innocent if a foreign ship was using electronic gear to monitor the coastal state's radio broadcasts, chart the sea floor, or interfere with normal radio communications? Actually a state has the right, according to one speaker, to protect itself against hostile acts in the waters adjoining its coasts, regardless of whether such acts occur within, or beyond, the limits of its territorial sea. A complication here, of course, is the definition of the term "hostile."

Countries have, in the interests of testing atomic weapons or other military devices, utilized parts of the high seas for short periods of time to the virtual exclusion of use of that area by other countries. Foreign ships could proceed through the designated area, but at considerable risk; in practice, if ships navigate through the area in defiance of notice, military operations are suspended until the navigation is completed. In some instances fishermen have been compensated for the loss resulting from the fishing activities they were forced to suspend during the operations. The United States also has aircraft identification zones which extend out over the high seas and which in a sense infringe on the freedom of action of civil aircraft in that within these zones they must identify themselves.

2. When considering the use of straight baselines in archipelagos, discussants noted that there has been "quasi-compliance" by the United States in certain straight baseline delimitations. For political reasons we have tended to avoid test cases, while at the same time withholding recognition of the legality of such claims. When navigation by U.S. ships has been made within the straight baselines, the foreign country involved

has not attempted to make arrests. Discussion of the use of straight baselines in archipelagos brought out the point that one of the keys as to whether islands could or could not be enclosed within the baseline has been not only the distance from the coast, but also whether or not the waters between the islands and the mainland can be treated as inland waters. Yet up to now there has been no real agreement on what are the criteria of the regime of internal waters.

3. With respect to Mr. Sullivan's paper, it was pointed out that for the past twenty-five years the Coast Guard has been operating manned weather stations in the ocean, which transmit meteorological data on assigned frequency. The Navy also maintains manned buoys. Among the problems in the future will be not only the status of unmanned, transmitting buoys, but also the assignment to them of transmission frequencies.

Chapter Fifteen:

JURISDICTIONAL, ADMINISTRATIVE, AND TECHNICAL
PROBLEMS RELATED TO THE ESTABLISHMENT
OF CALIFORNIA COASTAL AND
OFFSHORE BOUNDARIES

In view of the monumental two-volume work *Shore and Sea Boundaries* by A. L. Shalowitz (retired from the United States Coast and Geodetic Survey), it might appear presumptuous to suggest that there are new as well as continuing problems in this field that have not been analyzed nor resolved within practical limits currently. Despite the scope of Volume I of the aforesaid work, "Boundary Problems Associated with the Submerged Lands Cases and the Submerged Lands Acts," published in 1962, followed by Volume II in 1964, these volumes could not include analyses of the practical application of the Convention on the Territorial Sea and the Contiguous Zone,[1] which became effective September 10, 1964, nor the Supplemental Decree of the Supreme Court of the United States on January 31, 1966, in *United States* v. *California*.[2]

In 1937 attention was focused on the interrelationship of jurisdiction and coastal and offshore boundaries by the introduction of a Congressional resolution seeking to "establish the title and possession of the United States to the (coastal) submerged lands . . . and all petroleum deposits underlying the same. . . . "[3] For California the questions of jurisdiction and boundaries were affected in 1947 by an Order and Decree of the Supreme Court in *United States* v. *California*,[4] in 1953 by the Submerged Lands Act,[5] and currently in 1966 by the Supplemental Decree.

Shore and Sea Boundaries states that in proceedings before a Special Master (1948–52), "Valuable oil reserves in the vicinity of Huntington Beach (Orange County, California) made the determination of the inland waters of San Pedro Bay a crucial question."[6] This basis for interest by the federal government was exemplified further in an announcement in November, 1965, by the Department of the Interior that bids would be sought for oil and gas leases on California outer continental shelf lands, three months before the Supplemental Decree on January 31, 1966, establishing the geographic limits of state and federal jurisdiction in the California offshore area.

By specification of criteria and definitions from the convention, the court has eliminated a series of uncertainties, including the comparative value of a geographic mile (or marine or nautical) and an English mile, as well as establishing the absolute magnitude of the geographical mile and criteria for location of the coastline, generally at the line of mean lower low water. However, evaluation of the application of these definitions and precise distance standards along the California mainland coast and around the off-lying islands and rocks has already produced problems and questions, as well as the recognition of the need for development of topographic and hydrographic survey technology.

Although this review will relate only to the application of the effective Convention on the Territorial Sea and the Contiguous Zone, it must be noted that application of the provisions of the Convention on Fishing and Conservation of the Living Resources of the High Seas to establish adequate controls for California coastal waters is of extreme current importance.

Some of the boundary location problems that have been identified are listed in the following:

1. As stated in *Sovereignty of the Sea,* "With respect to the geographic situation along the world's seacoasts it must be granted that distribution of land and water and shoreline configuration produce a pattern which in no place is a duplicate to that of any other place. It is little wonder, therefore, that the application of an effective jurisdictional pattern to so complicated a physical setting encourages biased interpretations and meets with so much controversy." [7]

Administrative and jurisdictional problems were already in the open in California through what must be a unique set of conditions for a determination of governmental regulatory jurisdiction. Pacific Southwest Airlines (PSA), as a California intrastate air carrier since 1949, has always been subject only to the regulatory control of the California Public Utilities Commission. Following the Supplemental Decree defining the submerged lands of the state as located " . . . within three

231

geographical miles seaward from the coastline. . . . " [8] it has been alleged that PSA is now subject to Federal Civil Aeronautics Board jurisdiction as an interstate air carrier. This allegation of extension of jurisdiction is based on the analysis that in flying the direct routes established for sixteen years between San Diego-Los Angeles, and Los Angeles-San Francisco, PSA planes are approximately twelve nautical miles offshore opposite Oceanside, California (Figure 10), and approximately four nautical miles offshore when crossing Santa Monica Bay (Figure 11). Thus on a flight San Diego-Los Angeles-San Francisco, a PSA plane leaves and re-enters the state of California (and the United States) twice, and therefore purportedly is now subject to a jurisdictional classification of interstate air carrier.

This problem could possibly be resolved inefficiently for PSA by the assignment of new longer air routes landward of the high seas. The allegation of extension of jurisdiction, however, appears to be based upon a misinterpretation of the effect of the 1965 decision in *United States v. California,*[9] which will be considered in greater detail hereinafter.

2. "Both to the hydrographer and the topographer the low-water line is one of the most uncertain and difficult features to delineate." [10] " 'Mean lower low water' means the average elevation of all daily lower low tides occurring over a period of 18.6 years. . . . " [11]

It is a reasonable estimate that only a minority of USC & GS tide gauge stations on the California coast have recorded measurements over a complete tidal cycle of 18.6 years. The precision with which the elevation of a tidal datum plane may be established depends on the extent of tide gauge observations, ranging from a value correct to within 3.0 inches from one day of observations to a value correct within 1.2 inches from one month of observations.[12] Within these limits the relative rise of sea level along the Pacific Coast at 0.06 inches per year is not of particular short-term significance, but does represent another element of instability in the absolute location of the mean lower low-water line.[13]

" 'Low-tide elevation' means a naturally formed area of land surrounded by water at mean lower low water, which is above the level of mean lower low water but not above the level of mean high water." [14] This definition corresponds with earlier practice by the USC & GS in designating "rocks awash." Modern practice by the USC & GS identifies

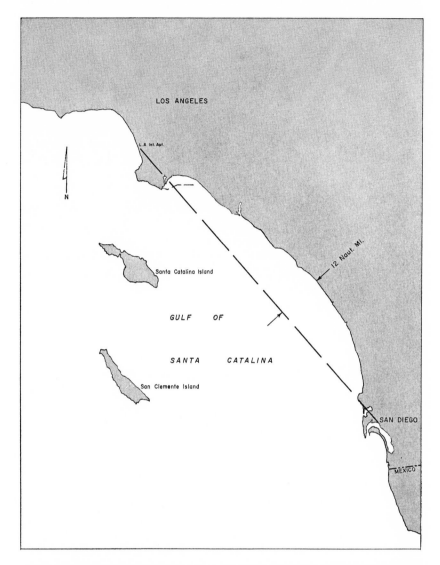

Fig. 10.—The generalized direct air route flown by P.S.A. between San Diego and Los Angeles.

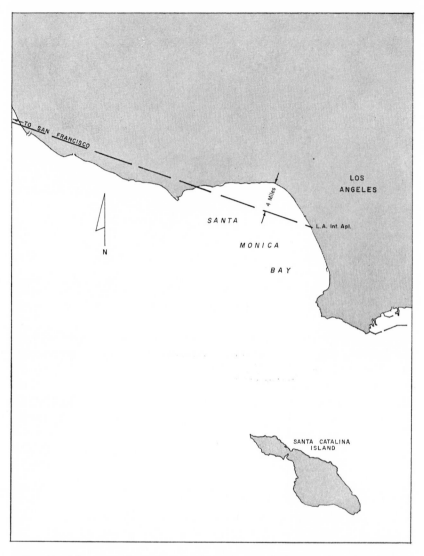

Fig. 11.—The generalized air route flown by P.S.A. between Los Angeles and San Francisco.

"rocks awash" on the Pacific Coast as including rocks with an elevation down to two feet below mean lower low water. The current USC & GS Hydrographic Manual provides that when it is not practicable for a hydrographer to land on a rock, its height is to be estimated for identification upon the survey chart. This practice was employed in the preparation of the 1933–34 charts published for the California coast, which makes the applicability of low-tide elevations and the slightly submerged rocks as shown on the hydrographic surveys very uncertain as base points for location of the coastline.

3. What are the results of difficulties in delineation and lack of precision in the location of the line of mean lower low water? With the current level of survey technology sufficiently precise locations (horizontal control) can be determined for both onshore and offshore features such as islands and rocks. However, inasmuch as the location of the coastline is determined by the intersection of the plane of mean lower low water with the land forms, similar precision is now required for the determination of elevations (vertical control). As pointed out in the previous section, heretofore it may not have been considered necessary to determine a precise elevation for an offshore low-tide elevation. Actually, it is not currently possible to make elevation determinations of sufficient precision, particularly for the most distant offshore features, to permit positive identification of low-tide elevations as valid base points, nor to establish accurately the coastline for all of the off-lying islands. Such determinations, even for islands, will become feasible only after extensive tidal datum determination projects, whereas the need for offshore state boundary establishment is immediate to permit the federal government to proceed with the leasing of the seaward outer continental shelf lands for the development of oil and gas. In this connection the inaccuracies of boundary location due to current technological limitations could result in misallocations of areas of large economic significance.

4. What structures or elements are contained within the " . . . outermost permanent harbor works that form an integral part of the harbor system within the meaning of Article 8 of the Convention of the Territorial Sea and the Contiguous Zone"? [15]

5. If the coastline includes a breakwater as part of the "outermost permanent harbor works," what is the nature of the transition from the seaward end of the breakwater coastline to the mainland coastline? The

235

outermost permanent harbor works for the ports of Los Angeles and Long Beach is a breakwater, as shown on Figure 12. Identification of the coastline requires a continuation of the baseline marking the seaward limit of inland waters at the easterly end of the breakwater to a juncture with the mainland coastline.

This juncture could be accomplished through any one of a number of possible alternatives, including: (1) A median line could be drawn from the mainland coastline to connect with the end of the breakwater baseline, by analogy with the criteria in the Convention for division of the territorial sea between adjacent states, " . . . the median line every point of which is equidistant from the nearest points on the baselines from which . . . measured." [16] (2) The baseline on the seaward side of the breakwater could be projected easterly to an intersection with the mainland coastline. However, a more realistic result would appear to be obtained by determination of the juncture of the limits of the territorial sea utilizing the easterly end of the Los Angeles-Long Beach breakwater and the most easterly Anaheim Bay jetty (Figure 12) as basepoints and then delineating this limit as a straight line parallel to the straight baseline between harbor works.

6. What criteria should be recommended for establishment of boundaries for division of the territorial sea in negotiations with adjacent coastal states (nations)? The adoption of the convention has focused attention on the need for establishment of the offshore international boundary on the Pacific Coast between the United Mexican States and California. On the upland the boundary was established by the Treaty of Guadalupe Hidalgo of 1848, but the text description of the boundary line starts at the coast and proceeds inland.

Section I, Article 12, of the Convention provides:

1. Where the coasts of two States are opposite or adjacent to each other, neither of the two States is entitled, failing agreement between them to the contrary, to extend its territorial sea beyond the median line every point of which is equidistant from the nearest points on the baselines from which the breadth of the territorial seas of each of the two States is measured. The provisions of this paragraph shall not apply, however, where it is necessary by reason of historic title or other special circumstances to delimit the territorial seas of the two States in a way which is at variance with this provision.

2. The line of delimitation between the territorial seas of two States lying opposite to each other or adjacent to each other shall be marked on large-scale charts officially recognized by the coastal States.

236

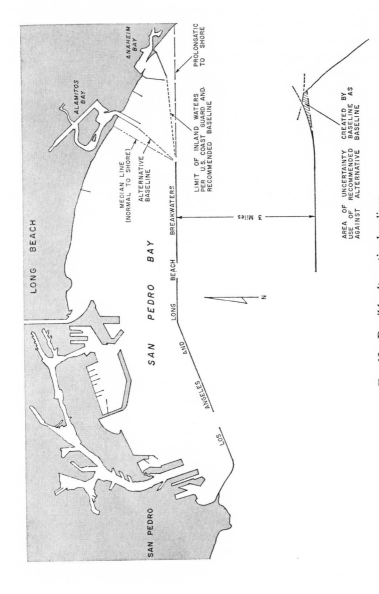

FIG. 12.—Possible alternative baselines.

Mexico is not currently a signatory to the convention. Mexico claims a nine mile territorial sea, compared with the three mile territorial sea claimed by the United States. A map incorporated into the Treaty of Guadalupe Hidalgo (Figure 13) shows the boundary line projecting into the Pacific Ocean as an extension of the upland boundary. This extension is not included in the treaty text and therefore may be questioned as to validity as a binding agreement line.

Possible alternative locations for the international boundary are shown on Figure 14, depicting the anomalous condition of Mexican territorial sea contiguous to, and seaward of, California submerged lands.

7. Finally (at least for this review), a problem must be pointed out that seems to have been ignored by many persons considering the effect of the 1965 decision in *United States* v. *California.*[17] The court in that decision expressly refused to consider the seaward location of California's political boundaries as being relevant to the question there involved. Rather, it decided that the seaward extent of the state's proprietary ownership extended only to the outer limit of the territorial waters of the United States as defined in the convention.

As appears to be clear from the 1960 decisions in *United States* v. *Texas* and *United States* v. *Florida,*[18] it is entirely possible for the political boundaries of a state to extend six geographical miles beyond the outer limits of the territorial sea. If California has properly interpreted the state constitutional boundaries, as approved by Congress, the state political jurisdiction for domestic purposes extends three geographical miles seaward of the off-lying islands and includes all intervening waters. Although this jurisdiction cannot, of course, be exercised in a matter which would violate international law and must take into consideration the express terms of the Outer Continental Shelf Lands Act,[19] it may well be effective for many purposes. For example, if a gambling ship operated by United States citizens should be anchored within Santa Monica Bay, but more than three geographical miles from shore, California would certainly assert the applicability of the state criminal laws and the enforceability by state officers.

The seaward extent of California's governmental power and the circumstances under which this power may be exercised are very much open questions, not settled by Supreme Court decisions, and must receive the most careful attention by state governmental authorities and legal counsel.

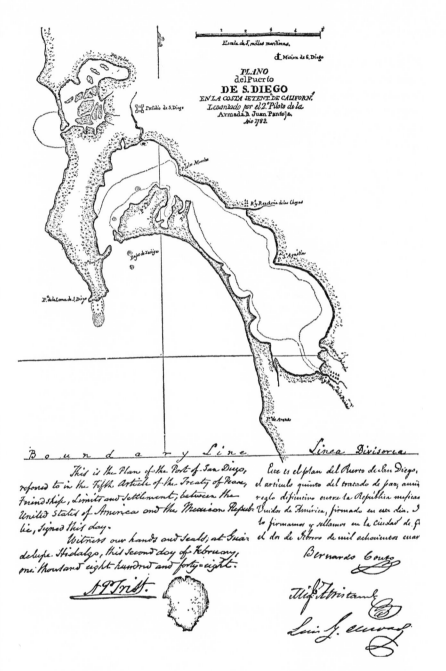

FIG. 13.—Exhibit incorporated in the Treaty of Guadalupe Hidalgo, 1848.

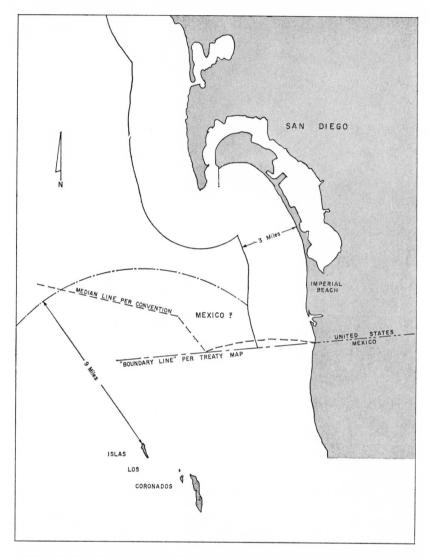

Fig. 14.—Possible alternative locations of the international boundary between the United States and Mexico in the territorial sea.

1. U.N. Doc. A./CONF.13/L.52 (hereinafter referred to as the "Convention"). TIAS 5639.

2. United States v. California, 382 U.S. 448 (hereinafter referred to as the "Supplemental Decree").

3. S.J.Res. 208, 75th Cong., 1st sess., August 20, 1937.

4. United States v. California, Order and Decree, 332 U.S. 804, 805.

5. Public Law 31, 83d Cong.

6. Aaron L. Shalowitz, *Shore and Sea Boundaries,* I (Government Printing Office, 1962), 55 n. 50.

7. U.S. Department of State, *Sovereignty of the Sea,* Geographic Bulletin No. 3 (1965), p. 3.

8. Supplemental Decree, p. 5.

9. United States v. California, 381 U.S. 139.

10. *Shore and Sea Boundaries,* II (1964), 183.

11. Supplemental Decree, p. 2.

12. *Shore and Sea Boundaries,* II (1964), 63.

13. *Ibid.,* p. 59.

14. Supplemental Decree, p. 2.

15. Supplemental Decree, p. 2.

16. Convention, Section I, Article 12.

17. United States v. California, 381 U.S. 139.

18. 363 U.S. 1.

19. Public Law 212, 83d Cong.

Discussion of Boundary Problems and Delimitation

1. The problems of state jurisdiction in coastal waters were discussed, with particular reference to California. There are many aspects of regulations and inspection criteria for geological and geophysical exploration on the continental shelf which can, through agreement, be handled to the mutual satisfaction of the Department of the Interior and the individual states, regardless of where the state/federal boundary line on the shelf happens to be. It does not necessarily follow, because the territorial jurisdiction of the state extends three miles out, that criminal jurisdiction and other state jurisdictions terminate at that point. Conditions vary considerably in different parts of the United States, and additional research is needed in defining how far into the sea state jurisdiction extends, and for what purposes.

2. When considering the extent of the territorial sea, discussants noted that the waters between the individual Hawaiian islands were held by the Supreme Court to be international in nature, beyond the three mile limit. The same is true between the southern California islands and the mainland, although the islands lie within the state's historic boundaries as they were ratified by Congress at the time of the Act of Admission. The baseline from which California's three mile offshore boundaries are measured was decided by the Supreme Court to be the mean lower low water line as shown on the Coast and Geodetic Survey charts. By constructing breakwaters and jetties California might be able to extend the outer limits of its jurisdiction; but structures of this type require the approval of the U.S. government through the Army Corps of Engineers.

3. A presentation of boundary lines drawn on Coast and Geodetic Survey charts was presented by officials from the survey. These lines did not represent official U.S. policy, but were attempts at experimentation, according to the articles of the Geneva Convention on the

Territorial Sea and the Contiguous Zone. These articles pertain to international boundaries and are not necessarily germane to boundaries between individual states. Although earlier in the Law of the Sea Institute Conference it was stated several times that one should not draw a precise line unless absolutely necessary the Coast and Geodetic Survey officials disagreed, feeling that boundaries of the states' jurisdiction should be delimited on maps and charts as accurately as possible, even before the need for such precision arises.

4. In the case of boundaries between individual states the principle of the median line is followed. However, disagreements may come up as to the exact position of the median line and the question arose as to how such disagreements should be settled—by the State Department, by Congress, by the Supreme Court, or by agreement between the states themselves? One opinion held that boundaries between the states is a matter for Congress to decide. Congress may determine the location of the boundaries or give consent to the states to make an agreement or compact between themselves.

5. One technical point which was raised involved the use of tidal datum planes. In some areas along the Gulf Coast the tide is at one time of the month semidiurnal, that is, high or low twice daily, and at other times of the month, high or low only once daily. There is also considerable difference among the various high waters or low waters (mean low, lower low, lowest low, etc.) ; as a result it is extremely difficult to establish a permanent baseline along this coast from which the outer limits of the territorial sea can be determined. There are islands along the Louisiana coast which tend to move up and down with relation to sea level. These are mostly piles of damp shell and sand lying on top of oyster beds, and no matter how often they are surveyed their configuration cannot be precisely established. There are also meteorological variables which show up in tidal observations.

243

Chapter Sixteen:

THE LAW OF THE SEA CONFERENCE,
1958-60, AND ITS AFTERMATH*

In developing my topic for discussion, I shall focus not on the width of the territorial sea but on the legal problems of the continental shelf, particularly the legal problems posed by the rapidly developing offshore oil and gas operations of the petroleum industry, such as in the North Sea.

The invaluable guidelines and policies embodied in the 1958 Geneva Convention on the Continental Shelf have, of course, been the principal response under international law to the legal problems raised by development of the natural resources of the continental shelf. In addition to examining this convention, and several other international agreements relating to the continental shelf, I should like to review a variety of problems in connection with the continental shelf which have arisen under United States domestic law, both state and federal.

Until quite recently man expended natural resources as though they were inexhaustible. Finally, however, in the last few decades, people have begun to realize that the supply of many minerals and foodstuffs essential not only to our economy but also to civilization as we know it, is finite in quantity. Two results of this realization have been the widespread initiation of conservation programs and the exploration of new areas in search of mineral resources.

The quest for untapped resources took man to the sea; there the search has been quite rewarding. In addition to fishery resources, enormous quantities of oil and gas, in particular, have been uncovered in offshore fields along the continental shelves of several countries.

These valuable finds, like the discoveries of gold in California and Alaska, have led to disputes provoking cries of "claim-jumping." In this instance, however, many of the "claim-jumpers" are not individual prospectors or, for that matter, large corporations, but cities, states, and even nations. Problems of international law, of federalism, and of private law have arisen in the aftermath of practically every offshore find, varying in intensity in direct proportion to the value of the discovery involved.

These problems have necessarily required legislation—on the international level, treaties—for their solution. Sometimes the "solution" has been less a panacea than a Pandora's box, but quite frequently it has proved feasible.

Perhaps the best solutions, some that might well serve as models for settling future disputes, have been those agreed upon at the international level, particularly the Geneva Convention on the Continental Shelf, to which thirty-five states have become parties.

There is an understandable reluctance on the part of national governments to enter into agreements with other countries binding them irrevocably to future action or inaction. Circumstances, science, and technology change, and nations should not always assume obligations into the indefinite future for better or for worse. As a general rule, therefore, most nations prefer to work out *ad hoc* arrangements with other countries rather than to enter into formal agreements which might prove unduly restrictive in the light of later knowledge.

This natural inclination to avoid any rigid treaty is especially pronounced when the dimensions of the subject matter of a potential treaty are relatively unknown and, accordingly, where the eventual effect of agreement can least be gauged. When the activity sought to be regulated by treaty has just commenced, so that customs and practices with respect to it have not crystallized, treaties—which draw much of their text and support from customs and practice—will seldom be found.

Since exploration of the continental shelves is still in the early stages, it is not surprising to find merely a few international agreements defining and distributing rights among the various coastal nations. In addition, it is only to be expected that where no significant offshore discoveries have been made there will be no treaties.

I. *The Convention on the Continental Shelf*

Fortunately, however, a number of thoughtful principles were promulgated in the Convention on the Continental Shelf, a product of the 1958 Geneva Conference on the Law of the Sea, and in the other conventions

245

there adopted.[1] These principles can feasibly be invoked as guidelines in settling disputes involving any body of water dividing governments, even though the Convention binds only those nations signatory to it, and even though by its terms it applies only to geological continental shelves.

The convention codifies the basic premise, suggested in President Truman's September 28, 1945, Proclamation concerning the continental shelf, that each nation has sovereign rights over the exploration and exploitation of the natural resources [2] of its continental shelves.[3] From this starting point it proceeds to define the term "continental shelf," [4] to specify procedures for dividing a shelf between nations whose claims might otherwise overlap [5] and to make suggestions for accommodating exploitation of undersea resources with other offshore activities, such as the laying and maintenance of submarine cables, fishing, research, and navigation.[6]

Article 1 of the Convention defines "continental shelf" as that body of land off the coast of a continent which extends from the coastline to the point (1) where the sea is 200 meters or (2) "where the depth . . . admits of the exploitation" of the "shelf," whichever is farther.[7] This dual standard accords the coastal nation a minimum area of sovereignty to 200 meters depth, and a maximum that is limited only by the actual extent of the shelf and technical ability in the exploration of the shelf itself.

Article 6 of the convention sets forth three procedures for dividing the shelf among littoral nations. These three procedures might be analogized to contract, legislation, and litigation.

The first and preferred procedure is agreement among the nations concerned, strongly advocated by the convention.

In the absence of such agreement, however, the convention declares that the "principle of equidistance" is to be applied. By this principle all claimant nations would have exclusive rights from the baselines from which their territorial seas are measured to that point at which equidistant lateral lines drawn from their baselines would meet.

The third procedure is an optional protocol, not ratified by the United States, which provides for the compulsory settlement of disputes by submission to the International Court of Justice or to an arbitral tribunal.[8]

The prophylactic character of the Convention on the Continental Shelf is underscored by several concrete suggestions which evidence a

246

farsighted anticipation of and attempt to avoid certain areas of dispute which might arise in the future.

Significant in this respect is the provision in Article 6(3) that boundaries should be fixed by reference to permanent points on land, obviating the possibility that future coastline changes might provoke disagreement. The provisions of Articles 4 and 5 which attempt to achieve an accommodation between exploitation of the resources of the continental shelves and other undersea activities should also reduce future disputes.

While the convention is laudatory in its attempts to foresee and avoid disputes over the continental shelves, several questions remain un-answered. Three may be found in the definition of "continental shelf" in Article 1 of the convention.

Article 1 encompasses in its definition of "continental shelf" that portion of offshore lands constituting a part of the continental shelf and more than 200 meters under the sea "where the depth . . . admits of the exploitation" of the shelf. The language is susceptible of at least two interpretations: (1) that the outer boundaries of the shelf are dependent upon the actual technological ability of the particular nation concerned, and (2) that boundaries are determined by the technological ability of the most advanced nation.

Arguments can be made supporting either interpretation. Thus, it can be said that to extend the offshore boundaries of a less developed nation to the farthest range capable of exploitation by the most advanced nation is uneconomical and unproductive. To accord undeveloped nations equal rights with technologically advanced nations, the argument runs, is perhaps unfairly to deprive the world of large supplies of natural resources.

Consideration and application of the basic principle on which the convention was founded at Geneva in 1958 refutes this argument. The convention was predicated on the notion that each nation, whether technologically advanced or not, has sovereign rights over its portion of the continental shelf.[9] The convention explicitly provides that its rights are not diminished by failure to exploit;[10] indeed, allowing off-shore sources of minerals and foodstuffs to lie fallow might be a prudent conservation measure in the best interests of the entire world.

Wise or not, however, each nation's portion of the continental shelf is its alone, to exploit or not to exploit as it sees fit. The principle of the equality of nations compels the conclusion that the definition of "continental shelf" is to be the same for each country, that differences in technological expertise are not to be reflected in boundary lines.

A practical difficulty inherent in the contrary view is that it opens the door to dispute. To say that the limits of the continental shelves vary according to each littoral nation's technology is to allow those boundaries to move laterally as well as seaward. A nation slower than its neighbors in developing its petroleum drilling facilities could thus find itself frozen out—a result clearly not intended by the convention and repugnant to the ideas underlying the principle of equidistance. Such a result might impel a nation to repudiate the convention.

Moreover, the degree of technological advancement of most nations in fact bears little relation to the extent of exploration and exploitation sponsored and undertaken by them. Petroleum exploration affords an excellent example.

Most international petroleum activity is conducted by British, Dutch, American, Japanese, and Italian corporations and joint ventures working in concert with local governments and local interests. Many nations that might be classified as comparatively undeveloped technologically have nevertheless had the astuteness to employ the technological skills of other countries to engage in mutually rewarding enterprises. Thus the argument that the limits of the continental shelves are determined by actual technological advancement founders on the facts as well as on the spirit of the convention itself.

A second unresolved problem of the definition of "continental shelf" contained in Article 1 of the convention is the extent of its application to offshore areas that are not, geographically speaking, continental shelves at all, for example, the Persian Gulf. The International Law Commission, which prepared an initial draft of the convention, clearly intended the definition to encompass many such areas and to go beyond the geological definition of continental shelves. The conference did not depart from the Commission's intent by its use of the term "continental shelf" in preference to the alternative term "submarine areas," which was suggested by some persons but discarded.

A third problem unresolved by the definition of "continental shelf" in Article 1 concerns the situation where submerged areas of a depth less than 200 meters, situated fairly close to the coastline, are separated from that part of the continental shelf adjacent to the coast by a channel deeper than 200 meters. The question arises as to whether such a channel delimits the coastal nation's area of sovereignty.

248

Norway is faced with just this situation in the North Sea.[11] Norway has taken the position that this channel is only a depression in its continental shelf and has claimed its full rights under the principle of equidistance. Its claim has apparently been accepted by all other countries concerned.

Norway's position may be justified by the history of the convention, but some may argue that the solution is not so clear as it could be. The International Law Commission's comments to Article 1 state that the shallow area close to the coast "could be considered as adjacent to . . . the shelf." Unfortunately, however, the Commission's comments leave the question open by declaring that

> It would be for the state relying on this exception to the general rule to establish its claim to an equitable modification of the rule. In case of dispute it must be a matter for arbitral determination whether a shallow submarine area falls within the rules here formulated.

Although understandably a wide channel might effectively detach the coastal area from the continental shelf, the Commission's presupposition that the channel is "narrow" would seem to obviate such a problem. The better practice might be to disregard all channels of less than a certain width, especially where the land lying beyond the channel seems geologically to be a part of the continental shelf.

II. *Other International Agreements*

To date, international agreements affecting undersea boundaries have been executed with respect to only three specific areas—the Gulf of Paria, the Persian Gulf, and the North Sea—only one of which, the North Sea, is superjacent to land properly classified as a "continental shelf" in the geological sense. It is appropriate to discuss here the agreements relating to these areas and the effect on them of the Convention on the Continental Shelf.

The North Sea.—The North Sea has thus far been a fertile site for offshore exploration. It is auspicious that undersea boundaries there will probably be determined in large part pursuant to the principles of the Convention on the Continental Shelf inasmuch as the North Sea lies above a continental shelf and five of the seven nations bordering on the North Sea—the United Kingdom, Denmark, the Netherlands, Germany, and France—have signed the convention.[12]

249

As far as can be determined, however, only two countries, the United Kingdom and Norway, have formally agreed on their entire common boundary beneath the North Sea, although Germany has reached agreement with the Netherlands on part of their joint boundary.

A number of other agreements, still in the draft stage, are being negotiated.[13] The United Kingdom has announced its intention to enter into further bilateral boundary agreements.[14] Nations that have not entered into formal agreements are laudably employing the median lines as a boundary.[15]

The United Kingdom–Norway agreement follows closely Article 6 in adopting as the common boundary between the two nations a line "every point of which is equidistant from the nearest points of the baselines from which the territorial sea of each country is measured."[16] This agreement is brief and for the most part taken up with the description of the dividing line which, as suggested by Article 6(3) of the convention, is shown on a chart annexed to the agreement.

A unique and quite ingenious provision in this agreement states that, should the boundary cross a mineral deposit which can be exploited from only one side the parties shall consult with their licensees to determine how the exploitaton shall be carried out and how the proceeds therefrom shall be divided.[17]

The Gulf of Paria Treaty.—Some sixteen years before the signing of the Convention on the Continental Shelf, the principle of equidistance was used to set the undersea boundaries between Venezuela and Trinidad, then a British possession. The Gulf of Paria Treaty, the first undersea boundary agreement, divided the Gulf of Paria at the midpoints and each signatory party agreed not to claim in the other's area.[18] The treaty was, happily, not repudiated by Trinidad when it gained its independence and remains in force.[19]

Since the land beneath the Gulf of Paria is not properly part of a continental shelf, and because the only two nations whose coastlines abut on the gulf have apparently settled the boundary between them, there seems to be no room for the application of Article 1 of the convention on the Continental Shelf here.[20]

Yet even here the convention provides a useful tool for settling other types of disputes. For example, Articles 4 and 5 offer methods of accommodating the exploitation of the undersea resources of the Gulf of Paria to other offshore activities.

The Persian Gulf.—The Persian Gulf, surrounded by or overlying some of the largest proven oil reserves in the world, appears to be a most fruitful area for offshore drilling and there have, in fact, been significant efforts in that direction.[21] It is thus imperative, both for the countries involved and for the economies of many nations, that principles be formulated to provide for dispute-free exploitation of the abundant reserves which are thought to lie below the gulf.

Unfortunately, Iran is the only nation bordering on the Persian Gulf which has signed the Convention on the Continental Shelf. Unfortunately, too, it conditioned its signing on two reservations, both of which run counter to the precepts of the convention.[22]

The first reserves to Iran the right to refuse to allow submarine cables or pipelines on its portion of the shelf. The second reservation states that in special circumstances the boundary determined according to Article 6 may be measured from the high-water mark. The significance of the high-water mark reservation is that the shore of parts of the Persian Gulf coastline of other countries slopes gradually. There is a difference of opinion as to whether the traditional low-water mark or the high-water mark should determine the shore. By this latter reservation, therefore, Iran has left the way open for it to claim substantially more of the sea bed and subsoil than the convention would normally allow.[23] This reservation may well be the source of future disputes.

The only agreement in force in the Persian Gulf area at this time is between Saudi Arabia and the government of Bahrein. Neither is a party to the Convention on the Continental Shelf, but their agreement in large part follows the principle of equidistance adopted by Article 6 of the convention for the delineation of shelf boundaries between nations whose claims would otherwise overlap. Thus, the boundary runs "on the basis of the middle line" between the mainland of Saudi Arabia and the Island of Bahrein between points which are, as suggested by Article 6(3), set out on a map attached to the agreement and in some cases defined by latitude and longitude as well.

A departure from the principle of equidistance, but a solution clearly sanctioned by the convention's exhortations to agreement, is the provision that a certain six-sided area which would otherwise be partly within the area belonging to Bahrein shall "be in the part falling to the Kingdom of Saudi Arabia," but that one-half of all revenues arising from oil exploitation in that area shall be granted to Bahrein.

251

The nations bordering on the Persian Gulf would do well to follow the example of the Saudi Arabia–Bahrein agreement within the framework laid down in the Convention on the Continental Shelf. Otherwise, prospecting for new fields in the shallow waters of the gulf may cause friction between countries competing for fields in disputed areas.[25]

In the North Sea, most of the nations, particularly the United Kingdom and Denmark, have been negotiating to fix their undersea boundaries, or at least to evolve working relationships which will enable them to get about the business of leasing. Additional commercial finds of oil or gas in the North Sea will doubtless spur the progress of agreements.

There appears less hope for early agreements in other parts of the world, which so far lack the impetus to treaty impelled by the rich mineral finds made in the North Sea.

However, with the convenient framework provided by the Convention on the Continental Shelf, those nations which wish to do so will find it easier to conclude boundary agreements today than in the days when the only model for such an agreement was the Gulf of Paria Treaty, with its necessarily rather local geographical provisions. It is to be hoped that more nations will accede to the convention itself.

Undersea boundary agreements in those areas where they are most urgently needed—where commercial exploitation of the undersea area is contemplated or already in progress—must inevitably add to the attractiveness of additional investment in such exploitation. The enhanced political stability of fixed and reliable boundaries invariably facilitates commercial operations.

III. The United States Continental Shelf

Conflicting state and federal claims to ownership of the surrounding shelf have complicated the situation in the United States. It has taken more than a decade to reach the present state of federal-state coexistence in this area, and a number of problems remain to be solved.

The first stage of development of the present federal-state relationship was the Supreme Court's rulings in *The Tidelands Cases* of 1947 and 1950[26] that the states had no claim to the United States Continental Shelf.

The second stage was the 1953 enactment of the Submerged Lands Act,[27] which vested in the coastal states complete ownership of lands beneath navigable waters.[28] That act defined navigable waters as those within a state's coastal boundaries. It limited coastal boundaries to three geographical miles beyond the coastline (except in the Gulf of Mexico where, under certain conditions, boundaries might extend up to three marine leagues seaward).[29]

The third stage was the Supreme Court's determination in 1960 that, of the Gulf Coast states, Texas and Florida were entitled to three marine leagues and Louisiana, Alabama, and Mississippi were limited to three geographical miles.[30]

The fourth stage, which has yet to be completed, is the determination of the shoreward boundary of the three mile or three league marginal belt of the continental shelf owned by the coastal states.[31]

The upshot is that, while state law applies to submerged lands between the coastline and the three mile or three league coastal boundary, the continental shelf lying seaward and outside of the submerged lands owned by the states is under the sole jurisdiction of the federal government.

This state of the law is codified in the Outer Continental Shelf Lands Act.[32] That statute, enacted by Congress in 1953, declares it to be the policy of the United States "that the subsoil and seabed of the Outer Continental Shelf appertain to the United States and are subject to its jurisdiction, control, and power of disposition." [33]

Adopting the rule of *The Tidelands Cases*, Section 2(a) of the act provides that the law applicable to the outer continental shelf is federal law, "to the same extent as if the Outer Continental Shelf were an area of exclusive Federal jurisdiction located within a state." [34]

Section 4 of the act proceeds to delineate the hierarchy of laws and regulations that govern the outer continental shelf lands.[35] It provides that, in addition to the act itself and the regulations of the Department of the Interior promulgated thereunder, all federal laws generally,[36] and the Longshoreman's and Harbor Worker's Compensation Act[37] and the National Labor Relations Act[38] specifically, are applicable to the outer shelf.

This act also gives the Coast Guard and the Secretary of the Army authority to regulate certain activities on the outer shelf.

Finally, it declares that the laws of the adjacent states, both civil and criminal, as of August 7, 1953, are adopted as the laws of the outer shelf so far as consistent with the laws and regulations already in effect or thereafter adopted.[39]

253

The assimilation of adjacent states' laws at one stroke cut through a number of knotty legal problems which were inherent in several alternate courses proposed during the debates on this section of the act.[40]

Potential problems remain, however. For example, although adoption of state laws as of August 7, 1953, freezes the law at that point and thus avoids the problem of a possible unconstitutional delegation of the federal legislative power,[41] as to future state legislation it will result in eventual obsolescence of the law unless there is periodic legislative review.[42]

Another area sure to provoke controversy concerns the extent to which state laws are made applicable by the Outer Continental Shelf Lands Act. There are really two questions inherent in this inquiry: first, is the act itself applicable? and second, if so, is the particular state law sought to be applied inconsistent with federal law?

A step toward a permanent solution to the first question was taken in *Guess* v. *Read*.[43] There the Fifth Circuit, affirming a decision by Judge Wright, held that state law did not govern where an accident occurred at sea beyond the boundary of the state but within the area subject to the operation of the Outer Continental Shelf Lands Act.

The case concerned a helicopter crash into the open sea more than three miles from the Louisiana shore. The widow of a man killed in the crash brought an action under the Death on the High Seas Act[44] and sought to join insurance carriers under the Louisiana Direct Action Statute.[45]

The court noted that the provisions of the Outer Continental Shelf Lands Act which assimilated state law intended that law to be applied only to the subsoil and sea bed of the outer shelf and to artificial islands and fixed structures erected on the shelf and concluded that the area of applicability of state law did not include the sea and air above the shelf.[46]

The provisions of the act that the high seas character of the waters above the outer shelf be unaffected by the act were cited as bolstering the Court's conclusion. It was suggested, however, that a different result might have been reached had the helicopter crashed directly upon a drilling platform.[47]

The case is consistent with the clearly expressed intent of the act to restrict the operation of state laws to state territorial waters except where made otherwise applicable by the act.

In the case of *Pure Oil Co.* v. *Snipes*,[48] decided only a month after *Guess* v. *Read*, the Fifth Circuit further restricted the scope of the Outer

254

Continental Shelf Lands Act and its adoption of state law by choosing to apply the federal maritime doctrine of *laches* rather than a state statute of limitations to an accident occurring on a fixed drilling platform on the outer shelf.

The court stressed the maritime aspects of the case. It noted that while plaintiff had fallen from the platform into the water below sustaining injuries en route, a substantial part of his disablement was traceable to infection contracted from the waters beneath the platform and that "there can be nothing more maritime than the sea." [49]

The pervasive regulations of the United States Coast Guard dealing with outer shelf activities [50] as well as the adoption of the Longshoreman's and Harbor Worker's Compensation Act were adduced to show a statutory intent that federal maritime law govern the suit.

It should be noted that the Louisiana one-year statute of limitations had expired only ten months before the suit and there was no showing of surprise or prejudice which would suffice to support a defense of *laches*.

An instance in which state law was held applicable on the outer shelf is *Corrosion Rectifying Co.* v. *Freeport Sulphur Co.*[51] This was an action on a contract made on an artificial island seven miles off the Louisiana coast. A verdict was rendered for the plaintiff in the trial court and one of the issues on appeal was whether attorneys' fees were allowable as an element of damages.

The Texas court first held that the issue of attorneys' fees was a matter of substantive law for choice of law purposes and that, under Texas' conflict of laws rules, the law of the place of making the contract controlled.[52]

In ascertaining what law applied to the artificial island the court construed Section 4 of the Act to adopt the laws of Louisiana, the adjacent state.[53] No conflict was found with federal law and, following Louisiana law, attorneys' fees were not allowed.

Compensation laws pose especially difficult problems in their application to the outer shelf, for there are a number of such statutes potentially applicable. Although the Longshoreman's and Harbor Worker's Compensation Act [54] is the only federal compensation law specifically mentioned in the Outer Continental Shelf Lands Act as applying on the outer shelf, other federal compensation laws are not thereby excluded.

Indeed, the Jones Act [55] and the Death on the High Seas Act [56] have been frequently applied on the outer shelf.[57] A considerable body of case law has been generated by the interactions of these laws with

255

each other and with state workmen's compensation laws.[58] Which law applies may depend upon where the accident which gives rise to the cause of action occurs, whether in a state's territorial waters, on the outer shelf, or on the seas or in the air over the outer shelf. If on the outer shelf, it may also be significant whether the drilling platform where the accident occurs is fixed or floating.

Some guidelines can be discerned. It appears that state workman's compensation laws do not apply on the outer shelf,[59] being pre-empted by the plethora of federal laws there in force. Also, the Death on the High Seas Act by its terms applies only "on the high seas beyond a marine league from the shores of any state," [60] and could not be invoked in the territorial waters of any state except perhaps Texas and Florida.[61]

In California, matters are further complicated by the presence of a third body of potentially applicable law, municipal law. The state of California has made a number of grants of offshore lands to the littoral municipalities without reserving any mineral rights.[62] As a result, much of the offshore land in California and most of the present producing area is subject to the law of adjacent municipalities as well as to state law.

The effect of the laws of the littoral municipalities on the submerged lands within the state boundaries depends on whether the state has granted those lands to the municipality, as appears from a comparison of the two cases of *Monterey Oil Co.* v. *City Court of City of Seal Beach* [63] and *Higgins* v. *City of Santa Monica*.[64]

In the *Monterey* case petitioner, the operator of an oil rig located one and one-half miles offshore from the city of Seal Beach, successfully applied for a writ of prohibition to prevent the city court from exercising jurisdiction in a criminal prosecution for violation of an ordinance which declared unlawful drilling for oil within the city limits. The court found no proprietary municipal interest in the offshore lands and hence no power to prohibit drilling on the lands. The court also noted that the state had fully occupied the field relative to the control and leasing of state-owned submerged lands and an ordinance in that area was therefore invalid.[65]

In the *Higgins* action, the facts were the same as in the Monterey case except that the state had granted the adjacent submerged lands to the city.[66] The Supreme Court of California held that the ordinance was constitutional and a valid exercise of the city's discretionary powers. Petitioner's argument that, by the enactment of certain statutes relating to state-granted submerged lands, the state had wholly occupied the field and invalidated the ordinance,[67] was rejected, the court declaring:

> Although the statutes show a preemption by the State with respect to the mode and manner in which a city may execute oil leases to tide and submerged lands granted to it by the State, there has been no preemption of the field of determining whether or not such lands should be developed for oil or gas.[68]

It may be concluded that, absent a grant, the powers of the littoral municipalities in the submerged lands are to be exercised at the sufferance of the state and are subject always to being overridden by the state and by federal law.

A very important area of current conflict between state and federal laws concerns the seaward boundaries claimed by five states. Four states, Alaska,[69] New York,[70] Maine,[71] and Virginia,[72] have enacted statutes purporting to extend the outer boundaries of their states to submerged lands and the superjacent seas "to the extent that jurisdiction is claimed by the United States of America, or to the extent recognized by the usages and customs of international law or by agreement to which the United States of America or the state is a party." The fifth state, Florida, claims three marine leagues off the Atlantic Coast.[73]

It would appear that the claims of Alaska, Maine, New York, and Virginia are in direct conflict with the ruling of the Supreme Court in *The Tidelands Cases* [74] and with the doctrine of the Submerged Lands Act.[75] If so, then the states are entitled to only three miles (or, in some cases, three marine leagues) from the coast line, and the applicable statutes are invalid.

It is argued that Florida's claim stands on better reasoning: Although Florida has been awarded a boundary of three leagues only in the Gulf Coast, the same consideration which impelled the Supreme Court to grant it three marine leagues there, the fact that Florida's claims were approved by Congress, would seem to support Florida's claim in the Atlantic as well.

IV. *Conclusion*

We have come a long way since President Truman's September 28, 1945, Proclamation concerning the United States continental shelf, and, as more and more deposits of minerals and foodstuffs are discovered beneath the sea, it will become increasingly important that methods exist for the dispute-free exploitation of the ocean's resources, particularly those underlying the continental shelf.[76]

On the international level, the Convention on the Continental Shelf is an important step in that direction. It is hoped that more and more nations will accede to its terms.

Insofar as the United States continental shelf is concerned, the aim must be to define the respective jurisdictions of the cities, states and federal government with clarity, for the risk of litigation can effectively impede offshore exploitation.

<hr />

* The writer wishes to express his gratitude to his associates Robert P. Borsody, Lester L. Cooper, Jr., and John E. Donnelly for assistance in the preparation of this study.

1. TIAS 5578 (April 20, 1958) (effective June 10, 1964), U.N. Doc. No. A/CONF. 13/L. 55 (1958, 52 *Am. J. Int'l L.* 858 (1958). As of June 28, 1966, thirty-five states were parties to this Convention. Information supplied by the United Nations Treaty Service on June 28, 1966.

Three other conventions were signed at the same time in Geneva: the Convention on the Territorial Sea and the Contiguous Zone, April 29, 1958. TIAS 5639 (effective Sept. 10, 1964), U.N. Doc. No. A/CONF. 13/L.52, 52 *Am. J. Int'l L.* 834 (1958); the Convention on the High Seas, April 29, 1958, TIAS 5200 (effective Sept. 30, 1962), U.N. Doc. No. A/CONF. 13/L.53, 52 *Am. J. Int'l L.* 842 (1958); and the Convention on Fishing and Conservation of the Living Resources of the High Seas, April 29, 1958, U.N. Doc. No. A/CONF. 13/L.54 and Add. 1, 52 *Am. J. Int'l L.* 851 (1958). See generally Amador, *The Exploitation and Conservation of the Resources of the Sea* (1959); Auguste, *The Continental Shelf* (1960); Campbell, "International Law Developments Concerning National Claims to and in Offshore Areas," 33 *Tul. L. Rev.* 339 (1959); Dean, "The Geneva Conference on the Law of the Sea; What was Accomplished," 52 *Am. J. Int'l L.* 607 (1958); Dean, "Achievements at the Law of the Sea Conference," 1959 *Proc. Am. Soc'y Int'l L.* 186; K. L. Koh, "The Continental Shelf and the International Law Commission," 35 *B.U.L. Rev.* 522 (1955); M. M. Whiteman, "Conference on the Law of the Sea; Convention on the Continental Shelf," 52 *Am. J. Int'l L.* 629 (1958).

2. The term "natural resources" is defined by Article 2(4) as follows: "The natural resources referred to in these Articles consist of the mineral and other non-living resources of the sea-bed and subsoil together with living organisms belonging to sedentary species, that is to say, organisms which at the harvestable stage, either are immobile on or under the sea-bed or are unable to move except in constant physical contact with the sea-bed or the subsoil."—Convention on the Continental Shelf, Art. 2(4).

3. Convention on the Continental Shelf, Art. 2(1). The Convention does not, however, purport to affect the *res communes* character of the superjacent sea and air. See Dean, 52 *Am. J. Int'l L.* 607, 620 (1958).

4. Convention on the Continental Shelf, Art. 1.

5. Convention on the Continental Shelf, Art. 6.

6. Convention on the Continental Shelf, Arts. 4, 5.

7. Convention on the Continental Shelf, Art. 1.

8. U.N. Doc. No. A/CONF. 13/L.57, 52 *Am, J. Int'l L.* 862 (1958).

9. Article 2(1) of the Convention expressly declares that "The coastal state exercises over the continental shelf sovereign rights for the purpose of exploring it and exploiting its natural resources." Convention on the Continental Shelf, Art. 2(1).

10. Thus, the Convention states that: "The rights referred to in paragraph 1 of this article are exclusive in the sense that if the coastal state does not explore the continental shelf or exploit its natural resources, no one may undertake these activities, or make a claim to the continental shelf, without the express consent of the coastal state."—Convention on the Continental Shelf, Art. 2(2). The thesis that the coastal state's rights are not dependent upon use is reinforced by Article 2(3), which stipulates that "The rights of the coastal state do not depend on occupation, effective or notional, or on any express proclamation."—Convention on the Continental Shelf, Art. 2(3).

11. For a bathygraph of the portion of the North Sea adjacent to Norway see Shawcross, "The Law of the Continental Shelf," in *Discourses to the Twentieth International Geographical Congress* 42 (Stamp & Cox, [ed.] 1964). See generally *id.* at 40; 253 *H. L. Deb.* (5th ser.) 916–17 (1963).

12. Information received from the French Information Service, New York, on May 20, 1965; *Times* (London), April 22, 1965, p. 12, col. 1.

13. For instance, the United Kingdom and Denmark have negotiated a draft treaty defining their North Sea boundaries which is at present undergoing further study. Letter from Danish Embassy of May 3, 1965.

14. 253 *H. L. Deb.* (5th ser.) 912–13 (1963).

15. *Times* (London), May 15, 1964, p. 7, col. 1. For a map depicting North Sea boundaries based on the delimitation procedures contained in Article 6 of the Convention see Gombos, "Continental Shelf Act," 1964 *L. Soc'y Gaz.* 475, 476; Shawcross, *supra* n. 11, at 41; Enright, "The North Sea—Oil's Biggest Gamble to Date," *Oil and Gas J.,* May 10, 1965, p. 125. See generally *id.* at 125–63.

16. *Cmnd. No.* 2626 (Norway No. 1, 1965).

17. *Id.,* Art. 4.

18. Treaty Relating to the Submarine Areas of the Gulf of Paria, Feb. 26, 1942, *Cmnd. No.* 6400 (T.S. No. 10, 1942), 4 Tratados Publicos y Acuerdos Internacionales de Venezuela 719, *Laws and Regulations on the Regime of the High Seas* 44–46 (ST/LEG/SER. B[1]) (U.N. Pub. Sales No. 1951, V. 2) [hereinafter cited as *Laws and Regulations*]. 205 LNTS 121. For a map showing the agreed boundary see Auguste, *The Continental Shelf* App. 1 (1960). See generally Cosford, "The Continental Shelf 1910–1945," 4 *McGill L. J.* 245, 256–62 (1958).

19. Letter from the Venezuelan Embassy Information Service of April 30, 1965; letter from the Embassy of Trinidad and Tobago, of May 28, 1965.

20. The Trinidad government did not sign the Convention. Venezuela did sign on October 30, 1958, and made the following statement: "In signing the present Convention, the Republic of Venezuela declares with reference to Article 6 that there are special circumstances to be taken into consideration in the following areas: the Gulf of Paria, in so far as the boundary is not determined by existing agreements, and in zones adjacent thereto. . . . " This statement appears to recognize the continuing applicability of the Gulf of Paria treaty.

21. See *Wall Street J.,* April 30, 1964, p. 1, col. 1; *N.Y. Times,* July 4, 1965, §3, p. 1, col. 1.

22. The text of the reservations is as follows: "In signing this Convention on the Continental Shelf, I am instructed by the Iranian Government to make the following reservations:

"(a) *Article 4:* With respect to the phrase 'the coastal State may not impede the laying or maintenance of submarine cables or pipe-lines on the continental shelf,' the Iranian Government reserves its right to allow or not to allow the laying or maintenance of submarine cables or pipe-lines on its continental shelf.

"(b) *Article 6:* With respect to the phrase 'and unless another boundary line is justified by special circumstances' included in paragraphs 1 and 2 of this article, the Iranian Government accepts this phrase on the understanding that one method of determining the boundary line in special circumstances would be that of measurement from the high water mark."

23. See Shawcross, *supra* n. 11. See generally Young, "The Legal Status of Submarine Areas Beneath the High Seas," 45 *Am. J. Int'l L.* 225, 236–37 (1951).

24. The text of this agreement appears at 7 *Int'l & Comp. L. Q.* 519–21 (1958). The agreement was signed in Ridyadh on February 22, 1958. Although Bahrein is a British protectorate, the United Kingdom is not a party to this agreement; it has, however, indicated its approval. E. Lauterpacht, "The Contemporary Practice of the United Kingdom in the Field of International Law—Survey and Comment, VI," 7 *Int'l & Comp. L. Q.,* 514, 518–19 (1958).

Iran and Saudi Arabia signed an agreement in Teheran In December, 1965, relating to their Persian Gulf boundary; the details of this agreement have not, however, been reviewed by the writer.

25. A portent of trouble is the fact that there were a number of almost simultaneous declarations in 1949 to the effect that the adjacent subsoil and sea bed "appertained" and were "subject to the jurisdiction and control" of the declarant nation. These declarations, collected in *Laws and Regulations* at 22–30, were made by Saudi Arabia, and nine Arab states under the protection of the United Kingdom—abu Ihabi, Ajman, Bahrein, Dubai, Kuwait, Qatar, Ras al Khaimah, Sharjah, and Umm al Qaiwain. See generally Auguste, *The Continental Shelf* 68–70 (1960); Liebesny, "Legislation on the Sea Bed and Territorial Waters of the Persian Gulf," 4 *Middle East J.* 94 (1950).

26. *United States* v. *California,* 332 U.S. 19 (1947); *United States* v. *Louisiana,* 339 U.S. 699 (1950); *United States* v. *Texas,* 339 U.S. 707 (1950). These decisions have been the subject of considerable comment, much from the affected coastal areas and much of it adverse. See generally Bartley, *The Tidelands Oil Controversy —A Legal and Historical Analysis* (1953); Note, "Submerged Lands: A Case Study in Federal Power," 3 *Baylor L. Rev.* 115 (1951); Bingham, "Juridical Status of the Continental Shelf," 26 *So. Cal. L. Rev.* 4 (1952); Clark, "National Sovereignty and Dominion Over Land Underlying the Ocean," 27 *Texas L. Rev.* 140 (1948); Hardwicke, Illig & Patterson, "The Constitution and the Continental Shelf," 26 *Texas L. Rev.* 398 (1948); Illig, "Offshore Lands and Paramount Rights," 14 *U. Pitt. L. Rev.* 10 (1952); Illig, "Tidelands, An Unsolved Problem," 24 *Tul. L. Rev.* 51 (1949); Keeton, "Federal and State Claims to Submerged Lands Under Coastal Waters," 25 *Texas L. Rev.* 262 (1947); Thomas, *"United States* v. *California*: Paramount Rights of the Federal Government," 26 *Texas L. Rev.* 304 (1948); Trigg, "National Sovereignty Over Maritime Resources," 99 *U. Pa. L. Rev.* 82 (1950); 50 *Mich. L. Rev.* 114 (1951). The area of submerged lands owned by the states could be significantly enlarged in some instances by the application of the straight baseline concept. Such an argument was advanced by the state of California in an attempt to establish its seaward boundaries around its

offshore islands. However, the Supreme Court has concluded that "states may not use such baselines to extend our international boundaries beyond the traditional international limits against the expressed opposition of the United States. The choice . . . is one that rests with the Federal Government and not with the individual States."—*United States* v. *California,* 381 U.S. 139, 167–68 (1965). In an attempt to bring enlarged areas of submerged lands under state jurisdiction, Senator Bartlett (D. Alaska) has introduced legislation requiring the Federal executive to employ straight baselines. See, S. 1954, 89th Cong., 1st sess. (1965).

27. 67 Stat. 29–38 (1953), 43 U.S.C. §§1301–15 (1958).

28. 67 Stat. 30 (1953), 43 U.S.C. §1311(a) (1958).

29. 67 Stat. 29 (1953), 43 U.S.C. §1301(a), (b) (1958). To justify a boundary of three marine leagues, either the boundary had to exist at the time the state was admitted to the Union or else it had to have been approved by Congress.

30. Florida's Gulf Coast claims were upheld in *United States* v. *Florida,* 363 U.S. 121 (1960), on the ground that Congress had approved its three league boundary described in the Florida Constitution of 1868, *Fla. Stat. Ann.* §§411, 413 (1962), under a submission to Congress required by a reconstruction act passed March 2, 1867, 14 Stat. 428. Claims of other states were resolved in *United States* v. *Louisiana,* 363 U.S. 1 (1960). The Texas three league boundary was allowed because that was the boundary Texas had maintained as a sovereign nation before admission to the Union. No opinion was expressed by the court in either decision on the location of the coastline of any of the states.

31. The Submerged Lands Act defines this boundary, the coastline, as the ordinary low-water line or the seaward limit of inland waters. 67 Stat. 29 (1953), 43 U.S.C. §1301(c) (1958). There has been considerable difficulty and delay in fixing the precise location of this line, especially in California and Louisiana, but recent Supreme Court rulings have laid a definitive framework for the definition of the California and Louisiana coastlines (see footnote 32 *infra*), and in so doing have adopted principles that should aid in the resolution of the coastlines of other states as well. See *United States* v. *Louisiana,* 382 U.S. 288 (1965) ; *United States* v. *California,* 381 U.S. 139 (1965). The Louisiana decision defined only a portion of that state's coastline, but it has been stated that clarification of the remainder will soon be sought. See *Wall Street J.,* Dec. 14, 1965, p. 32, col. 1. In the interim, leasing in the unsettled area has continued, see e.g., 29 Fed. Reg. 2703 (February 26, 1964), for state and federal agreements have settled the ultimate disposition of revenues received from the area, see A. W. Lewis, "The State-Federal Interim Agreement Concerning Offshore Leasing and Operations," 33 *Tul. L. Rev.* 331 (1959). See also 67 Stat. 467 (1953), 43 U.S.C. §1336 (1958) ; *La. Rev. Stat.* §30:179.11 (Supp. 1964) ; *Cal. Pub. Res. Code* §6301.5 (1963) ; *Alaska Stats.* §38.05.137 (Supp. 1964).

32. 67 Stat. 462–71 (1953), 43 U.S.C. §§1331–43 (1958).

33. The territorial extent of the outer continental shelf is not defined in the act. Both the Senate and House Committee Reports on the bills regard the outer limit as coinciding with the beginning of the continental slope which is described as occurring at a depth of approximately 600 feet, see S. Rep. No. 411, 83d Cong., 1st sess. 3–4 (1953) ; H.R. Rep. No. 413, 83d Cong., 1st sess. 2 (1953), and the press release accompanying President Truman's Proclamation of September 28, 1945, Presidential Proclamation No. 2667, 59 Stat. 884 (1945), the so-called Truman Doctrine, also defines the shelf as extending to the 600-foot line. It may be, nevertheless, that the Government's ratification of the Convention on the Continental Shelf operated automatically to extend United States jurisdiction "to the seabed

and subsoil of the submarine areas . . . outside the area of the territorial sea, to a depth of 200 metres or, beyond that limit, to where the depth of the superjacent waters admits of the exploitation of the natural resources of the said areas," pursuant to the terms of Article 2(1) of the Convention.

34. 67 Stat. 462 (1953), 43 U.S.C. §1332(a) (1958). A detailed analysis of the Outer Continental Shelf Lands Act, with well-grounded insight into the legislative background of the Act, is contained in Christopher, "The Outer Continental Shelf Lands Act: Key to a New Frontier," 6 *Stan. L. Rev. 23* (1953). See also Brumfield, "State and Federal Laws and Regulations on Offshore Leasing, Drilling and Production," in *Oil and Gas Operations: Legal Considerations in the Tidelands and on Land,* 226 (Slovenko ed. 1963) (hereinafter cited as *Oil and Gas*).

35. 67 Stat. 462–63 (1953), 43 U.S.C. §1333 (1958).

36. See note 34 *supra* and accompanying text. The specific denomination of certain federal laws as applicable to the outer shelf does not mean that any other federal laws are not applicable. See 67 Stat. 463 (1953), 43 U.S.C. §1333(g) (1958).

37. 44 Stat. 1424–46 (1927), 33 U.S.C. §§901–50 (1958).

38. 49 Stat. 449–57 (1935), 29 U.S.C. §§151–68 (1958).

39. State tax laws, however, were exempted from this blanket adoption. See 67 Stat. 462 (1953), 43 U.S.C. §1333(a)(2) (1958).

40. See Christopher, "The Outer Continental Shelf Lands Act: Key to a New Frontier," 6 *Stan. L. Rev. 23,* 37–41 (1953). Opposition was expressed during the debates to states sharing in revenues from the outer shelf, see 99 *Cong. Rec.* 7479 (1953), and there has been some concern that the absorption of state laws would provide a foothold for states to lay claim to a share, see Christopher, *supra* at 43. However, the Act specifically states that adoption "shall never be interpreted as a basis for claiming any interest in . . . the outer continental shelf . . . or the revenues therefrom." 67 Stat. 462–63 (1953), 43 U.S.C. §1333(a)(3) (1958).

41. Cf. *Washington* v. *W. C. Dawson & Co.,* 264 U.S. 219 (1924); *Knickerbocker Ice Co.* v. *Stewart,* 253 U.S. 149 (1920). Yet the Federal Assimilative Crimes Act, 62 Stat. 686 (1948), 18 U.S.C. §13 (1958), which provides for the adoption of future as well as existing state criminal law, has been held constitutional. *United States* v. *Sharpnack,* 355 U.S. 286 (1958). See generally Annot., 2 *L. Ed.* 2d 1686 (1958).

42. Moreover, as Circuit Judge J. Skelly Wright noted when a judge of the Eastern District of Louisiana, peculiar problems of double jeopardy may arise if the states continue their practice of punishing offenses occurring off their coastline, since a crime on the outer shelf, if punishable by a state government, could be punished by the federal government under the same law for an additional penalty. Wright, "Jurisdiction in the Tidelands," 33 *Tul. L. Rev.* 175; 183–84 (1958).

43. 290 F. 2d 622 (th Cir. 1961), *cert. denied,* 368 U.S. 957 (1962).

44. 41 Stat. 537–38 (1920), 46 U.S.C. §§761–68 (1958).

45. *La. Rev. Stats.* §22:655 (1959). This statute allows a plaintiff to sue defendant's insurer without having exhausted his remedies against the defendant.

46. 290 F. 2d at 625.

47. *Ibid.*

48. 293 F. 2d 60 (5th Cir. 1961).

49. *Id.* at 65 n. 6.

50. Falling into the sea is a hazard expressly recognized by those regulations. *Id.* at 66–67 & n. 11, citing 33 C.F.R. §§143.15–1, –5 (1956).

51. 197 F. Supp. 291 (S.D. Tex. 1961).

52. *Id.* at 292–93. Under Texas law attorneys' fees were allowable and under Louisiana law they were not.

53. *Id.* at 293. The Court noted that although there was scant authority on the interpretation of Section 4, 67 Stat. 462–63 (1953), 43 U.S.C. §1333(a)(2) (1958), *Guess* v. *Read,* 290 F. 2d 622 (5th Cir. 1961), *cert. denied,* 368 U.S. 957 (1962), furnished a hint that Louisiana law would apply in a situation such as this.

54. 44 Stat. 1424–46 (1927), 33 U.S.C. §§901–50 (1958). The Director of the Bureau of Employees' Compensation, United States Department of Labor, has promulgated regulations concerning the extension of the Longshoreman's and Harbor Worker's Compensation Act to the outer continental shelf which are contained in Title 20, Code of Federal Regulations, subchapter H and subpart H of subchapter A.

55. 38 Stat. 1185 (1915), 46 U.S.C. §688 (1958).

56. 41 Stat. 537–38 (1920), 46 U.S.C. §761–68 (1958).

57. For comment on the possible exposure of employees to pay compensation under several laws and the exposure of employees to risks and dangers, some of them unique, see Reese, "Status of an Employee in the Tidelands: The Employer's Viewpoint," *Oil and Gas* 520; Kierr, "Status of an Employee in the Tidelands: The Employee's Viewpoint," *Oil and Gas* 509.

58. A number of thoughtful articles have illuminated this rapidly developing field of law. See generally Carrere, "Recent Developments in Personal Injury Law in the Tidelands," 32 *Tul. L. Rev.* 274 (1958); Eikel, "Legal Procedures in Maritime Personal Injury Litigation," 33 *Tul. L. Rev.* 323 (1958); Lyman, "Barge and Dredge Workers as Seamen Under the Jones Act," 32 *Tul. L. Rev.* 202 (1958); Sims, "General Principles Applicable to Maritime Injuries," *Oil and Gas* 496; G. W. Stumberg, "Some Aspects of Offshore Injuries," *Oil and Gas* 570; John Minor Wisdom, "Injuries to Maritime Workers: Landlubbing Longshoremen and Seagoing Roughnecks in the Muddy Waters of the Fifth Circuit," *Oil and Gas* 559.

59. See *Goodart* v. *Maryland Gas Co.,* 139 So. 2d 567 (Ct. App. La. 1962); cf. *Ross* v. *Delta Drilling Co.,* 213 F. Supp. 270, 272 (E.D. La. 1962).

60. 41 Stat. 537 (1920), 46 U.S.C. §761 (1958); cf. *Bergeron* v. *Aero Assoc.,* 213 F. Supp. 936 (E.D. La. 1963).

61. See note 30 *supra* and accompanying text.

62. See Krueger, "State Tidelands Leasing in California," 5 *U.C.L.A. L. Rev.* 427, 429 (1958). Mr. Krueger's article contains a comprehensive discussion of the California laws covering offshore oil activities, including the text of selected statutes, regulations and forms used in leasing. See also *Cal. Pub. Res. Code* §§6871.1, –.2 (Supp. 1963).

63. 120 Cal. App. 2d 31, 260 P. 2d 846 (Dist. Ct. App. 1953).

64. 62 Cal. 2d 24, 41 Cal. Rptr. 9, 396 P. 2d 41 (1964).

65. A parallel civil action involving a building permit ordinance was decided on the same day and with the same result. *Monterey Oil Co.* v. *City Court of City of Seal Beach,* 120 Cal. App. 2d 41, 260 P. 2d 851 (Dist. Ct. App. 1953).

66. By Cal. Stats. 1917, ch. 78, p. 90, as amended, Cal. Stats. 1949, ch. 616, p. 1114.

67. The statutes adverted to were *Cal. Pub. Res. Code* §§7058.5, –59, –60.

The argument was also made that the city, as trustee of the lands granted by the state, had an obligation to see that the trust was as productive as possible.

The court disposed of this contention by drawing a distinction between a trust with a profit purpose and a trust with a safeguarding purpose, and finding the city's trust to be of the latter type. *Higgins* v. *City of Santa Monica, supra* at 28–29, 41 Cal. Rptr. at 12, 396 P. 2d at 44.

68. *Id.* at 32, 41 Cal. Rptr. at 14, 396 P. 2d at 46.

69. *Alaska Stats.* §44.03.010 (1962) provides: "The jurisdiction of the state extends to waters offshore from the coast of the state as follows:

"(1) The marginal sea to its outermost limits as those limits are from time to time defined as recognized by the United States of America by international treaty or otherwise.

"(2) The high seas to the extent that jurisdiction is claimed by the United States of America, or to the extent recognized by the usages and customs of international law or by agreement to which the United States of America or the state is a party.

"(3) Submerged lands including the subsurface of submerged lands, lying under the waters mentioned in this section."

70. *N.Y. State Law* §7-a (Supp. 1964).

71. *Me. Rev. Stats. Ann.* tit. 1, §2 (1964).

72. *Va. Code Ann.* §7-1.1 (Supp. 1964).

73. *Fla. Const.* art 1. A 1955 Florida law set the East Coast boundary of the state at "three geographical miles" from the coast. *Fla. Stats. Ann.* §6.11 (1961).

74. See note 26 *supra* and accompanying text.

75. See note 27 *supra* and accompanying text. Section 6(m) of the Alaska Statehood Act, 72 Stat. 343 (1958), 48 U.S.C. note preceding §21 (Supp. 1963), specified that the Submerged Lands Act should apply to Alaska as a state, and it has been held that Alaska "is entitled to such powers as have been given to all states by the Submerged Lands Act." *Organized Village of Kake* v. *Egan,* 174 F. Supp. 500, 503 (D. Alaska 1959), *aff'd,* 396 U.S. 60 (1961) ; *accord, Kirkpatrick* v. *Commissioner, Dept. of Nat. Resources,* 391 P. 2d 7 (Alaska 1964) ; cf. *United States* v. *Alaska,* 201 F. Supp. 796 (D. Alaska 1962).

As a matter of fact, Alaska has already come to grips with the federal government over territorial claims but on a different issue. In 1963 Alaska planned to lease portions of Cook Inlet and Yakutat Bay after favorable survey reports in those areas. The United States filed suit to block the leasing, claiming that the state is without authority to lease beyond the three-mile line in bays having a headlands closure greater than ten miles, *United States* v. *Alaska,* No. A–51–63 (D. Alaska). The case is currently pending. Alaska, however, hews to the twenty-four mile closure view which has support in international law. See 1 Hyde, *International Law Chiefly as Interpreted and Applied by the United States* 473 (2d ed. 1945). The state has recently provided statutory authority for co-operative leasing agreements with the United States in the disputed areas, *Alaska Stats.* §38.05.137 (1964).

76. Economic activity in the United States continental shelf regions in calendar 1964 (or fiscal 1965) is estimated at $21.4 billion. Natural resources (oil, gas, fish, and so forth) taken from the United States continental shelf regions for the year reported amounted to about $1.2 billion and cargo salvage is estimated at $6 million. The remaining $20.2 billion is made up of income, investments, and expenditures associated with the services, missions, and activities of private and governmental pursuits. (*U.S. Department of Commerce, Development Potential of U.S. Continental Shelves,* pt. II, at 4 [April, 1966].)

Henry Reiff
Ralph Johnson
L. F. E. Goldie
John Mero
Alexander Melamid

Chapter Seventeen:

A SYMPOSIUM ON THE GENEVA CONVENTIONS AND
THE NEED FOR FUTURE MODIFICATIONS

REIFF:

Our topic is a vast subject. A good index of the proceeding would reveal several hundreds of suggestions for clarifications, correction, amplification, or revision of several new conventions. I for one on the panel can offer only a few observations and suggestions. I shall proceed by a process of enumeration and brief description and leave the argument in support until later, if I am asked to provide it.

I. *Observations and Suggestions*

A. *Structuring of a Future Conference*

An effort should be made in the preparatory work to provide for arranging the composition of the committees or at least the subcommittees to reflect differentials in interest, experience, and expertise of the participating nations. This is not a suggestion to use weighted voting in the conference: very likely it will be desired to continue to use the principle of one state one vote in both the committee system and in the plenary sessions, with majority and two-thirds requirements as before. What I suggest is the constituting of committees or at least the subcommittees along the lines of the patterns adopted in the Intergovernmental Maritime Consultative Organization for its Council and Maritime Safety Committee, Articles 17 and 28, respectively. Thus the sixteen members of the Council are selected from nations with (a) the "largest" interest and (b) "substantial" interest in *providing inter-*

national shipping services and with (a) the "largest" interest and (b) "substantial" interest in *international seaborne trade*. The Maritime Safety Committee similarly reflects categories of interest. Article 28 reads: "The Maritime Safety Committee shall consist of fourteen Members elected by the assembly from the Members, Governments of those nations having an important interest in maritime safety, of which not less than eight shall be the largest ship-owning nations, and the remainder shall be elected so as to insure adequate representation of Members, Governments of other nations with an important interest in maritime safety, such as nations interested in the supply of large numbers of crews or in the carriage of large numbers of berthed and unberthed passengers, and of major geographical areas."

Similar methods of categorization of interest are used in a number of commodity conventions, e.g., the Coffee Agreement, which groups the participants into producers and users.

B. *With Respect to Fisheries*

In the foreseeable future, we shall probably still have to rely upon bilateral and multilateral agreements dealing with stocks or regions, made by the interested parties.

The Northwest Atlantic Fisheries Convention is a particularly serviceable model. Two questions may arise with regard to such agreements: (a) An increase in the number of parties to the point of overloading the fisheries. In such a case, what criterion could be used to restrict the number of participants? (b) The securing of acquiescence in the regimes by non-parties. Would it be possible to include in the general convention on fisheries an obligation by non-parties not to interfere with the treaty arrangement? If so, does this lead to an extension of the doctrine of abstention?

C. *Some Thoughts on Obligations and Duties*

Thus far the contributors to this volume have stressed rights under the Geneva conventions and generally in use of the sea. I should like to emphasize some obligations and duties. This is justified, I believe, by our increasing emphasis on the sea as *res communis*.

266

1. *Law of nuisances.*—I think that it is time to consider a law of nuisances that obligates an individual state not to create nuisances and that grants it some authority in their eradication. There is a need for systematic preliminary study in this regard. We already have some doctrinal examination of the notion in the Trail Smelting Case between the United States and Canada. No doubt, considerable materials could be gathered together to help in the formulation of such a law.

Thus far we have dealt with nuisances piecemeal. A good example is the Convention on Oil Pollution of Navigable Waters (1954). Another is the obligation in Article 25 in the High Seas Convention with respect to pollution of the seas by means of radioactive wastes. One of the objectives of the Nuclear Test Ban Treaty also seeks to avoid contamination of the sea by fall-out.

Such a nuisance law could set up criteria of reasonable care, with principles derived from private law. We already have an example in the Convention on the Protection of Submarine Cables.

Other types of activities might, with proper definitions, be considered under a nuisance law, such as: dumping of refuse or debris on fishing grounds; "pirate" radio stations; failure to notify the emergence into the sea of floating islands; the dumping of live ammunition or lethal gases in offshore areas where they may create hazards for both fisheries and exploitation of the continental shelf; the disposal of hulks at sea in places which may interfere with fisheries, submarine cables, or exploitation of the continental shelf; and so forth.

2. *Navigational safety.*—It may be possible to create some firm obligations to light coasts and provide for navigational safety and to chart coasts, with an ancillary duty to file navigational charts (but not charts indicating territorial water boundaries, or contiguous zone boundaries, or continental shelf boundaries) with the Intergovernmental Maritime Consultative Organization or the Cartographic Office of the United Nations. Obligations such as these might have a salutary effect on excessive claims to territorial seas.

[AUTHOR's NOTE: In discussion after the panel, it was pointed out that national hydrographic services supply each other with their charts and also file their charts with the International Hydrographic Bureau at Monaco. At a recent date, however, only thirty-nine governments were members (*International Scientific Organizations,* p. 383), among them, naturally, the more enterprising and responsibility-assuming governments. The creation of a "firm obligation" to chart and file charts, as well as to promote navigational safety along coasts, should, however, be additionally considered by IMCO or a future law of the sea conference.]

D. *Additional Minor Suggestions*

1. *Clarification of the law relating to treasure trove or archeological discoveries in the continental shelf, or beyond, seaward of territorial waters.*—Consideration should also be given to protection against vandalism in connection with archeological sites or relics. The sovereign rights of the coastal state are restricted to exploring the continental shelf and exploiting its natural resources. Both the convention and the law of salvage should be clarified with respect to both treasure trove and archeological research.

2. *Coastal land fills.*—There is considerable activity going on in various parts of the world—Hong Kong, Japan, the coasts of Florida, outside harbors, along shore—aimed at creating additional land areas for airports, residential, industrial, and other purposes. These land areas reach into the territorial sea. They are not mere "permanent harbour works" envisaged by Article 8 of the Convention on the Territorial Sea. If the rule of riparian boundary law is used to determine the baseline from which the breadth of the territorial sea is measured, then artificial modification of the low-water line creates no new baseline. Thus far no serious problem of jurisdiction seems to have arisen internationally, but it has arisen in relation to the offshore claims of the federal government and the state of California. (Shalowitz, *Shore and Sea Boundaries,* I, 101–4.) Internationally, however, certain complexities could arise if the creation of such coastal land becomes significant enough. Thus, if the riparian rule for the original low-water line is used, it is conceivable that new land created on a proper coast could extend so far into the territorial sea as to eliminate it as a jurisdictional area, leaving the coastal state with only the contiguous zone as measured from the original low-water base line. If the riparian rule is not used and a new low-water line is recognized at the outer limits of the artificially created land, then the coastal state is in a good position to extend its territorial sea and contiguous zone seaward. In areas where

the land-fill faces a wide-open sea, it would seem no great harm to the regime of the high seas would result, provided navigational safety is assured. In narrow straits, however, if such land fills were feasible, problems would speedily arise with respect to use of the strait. It may be premature to deal with this type situation of land fills at any immediately forthcoming conference: there are other, numerous and more important, problems to be solved. But the phenomenon may grow and require attention at some future date.

3. *Sport fishing.*—Increased leisure has led to enormous increases in sport fishing in recent decades. Well-managed clubs and tournaments provide by rule for non-wasteful disposal of the fish taken. Otherwise, however, there must be considerable waste. Some attention might be given this matter in any revision of the convention on fisheries.

4. *Artificial reefs.*—Attention should be given to the hazards to navigation represented by artificial reefs constructed in aid of sport fishing, particularly when these are situated beyond the territorial sea.

5. *Fixed geographical stations.*—The International Oceanographic Commission has asked the IMCO to prepare a convention on both manned and unmanned installations. Certainly, general interest in the sea is now sufficiently high to justify a forthcoming conference on the law of the sea to give its approval, by resolution or otherwise, to such a convention.

6. *Navigation lanes through oil fields.*—The increased size of oil fields located on the continental shelf and the rapidly proliferating number of tankers that serve them suggest the desirability of giving some attention to the possible hazards to navigation that these operations represent.

II. *Continued Leadership of the United States*

The United States has a commendable record, which extends over nearly all of the past century, in advancing rational use of the sea, a record that is replete with progressive proposals, commitments, and instances of co-operation. This nation is in an excellent position to furnish leadership to the world in this important area, and it should by all means continue to do so.

269

JOHNSON:

Instead of discussing possible new conventions to follow the 1958 Geneva conventions on the law of the sea, I should like to comment on the proposals by the Commission to Study the Organization of Peace, by Christy and Scott, in their book *The Common Wealth in Ocean Resources,* and others, suggesting that either the mineral or fishery resources of the sea, or both, be turned over to the United Nations or some other international organization. Although some of the objectives of these proposals are widely lauded, I am convinced that unless the proposals themselves are made more realistic they will never be anything more than "pie in the sky."

Professor Burke has carefully described the existing political and power structure in the world and demonstrated why these proposals are quite unrealistic at the present time. However, this is not to say that the political and power structure of the world cannot change. In the past, we have seen such changes brought about by wars, by industrial expansion, by changes in the population, and similar major events; such events may again occur, or may now be taking place. I would point, for example, to the war in Vietnam, and to the potential starvation that may result from the anticipated population explosion. Man's attitude toward the United Nations, or to the distribution of the resources of the sea may undergo a significant change when it appears that ten or twenty million people, or more are likely to starve in a given year.

The goals of these several proposals appear to be:

1. To encourage production of the greatest possible amount of food and other resources from the sea.

2. To cause a larger share of these resources to be distributed to the less developed countries.

3. To prevent overcapitalization of high seas fishing and mineral extraction capacity by the various nations involved in ocean resource development.

4. To provide the United Nations with a reliable source of funds for its budget.

Goal No. 2, providing a greater percentage of the ocean's resources for the less developed countries, appears to be either implicit or explicit in all of the proposals. Apparently, this goal is to be achieved by giving the United Nations control over the resources of the sea along with the power to issue licenses for substantial fees, or tax the profits made from ocean resource development. As if this were not difficult enough in itself, the area of yet greater difficulty concerns how these profits might be distributed by the United Nations after they are collected. It is one thing to say that the United Nations ought to collect or receive such profits, but it is quite another to design an acceptable distribution system of those profits after they are in hand. What criteria would be used? Would this wealth be used only for emergency donations? Would it be distributed on the basis of gross national product per number of citizens? Would it be distributed on the basis of "need" and if so how would this be determined? Would it be turned over to some administrative agency under the authority of the General Assembly to hand out as their discretion dictated? Would the General Assembly itself acting something as the Congress of the United States make the distribution as they saw fit? These are exceedingly difficult questions.

It seems to me that this distribution problem is one of the most troublesome points in the whole proposal, however none of the proposals I have seen has made any attempt to solve it. It is one of the very early subjects which must be taken up if these ideas are to get any further than mere speculation.

A second problem that is basic to the various proposals concerns the distinction between those resources that are already being exploited, and to which the nations of the world would claim "vested rights," and those that are not yet claimed or vested. It would seem improbable in the extreme to think the fishery or mineral resources of the sea that are now being exploited would voluntarily be turned over by the nations of the world to some international agency. As an outside possibility one might think that the yet unexploited or unclaimed resources might be turned over. Then the question is, What resources are now subject to vested rights or claims and what not? How does one define or separate those resources or geographical areas which are not now being exploited or claimed from those which are being exploited or claimed? Some of my students and I, this last year, diligently tried to compose language which would make this separation. We could not do it. Such language must be widely understandable not only in English but in the numerous other languages of the world. In our seminar we tried various phrases that had some meaning in American law, such as "appropriated," "vested rights," "historic rights," and others. None

271

was adequate. With regard to fisheries, one is faced with the special fact that several powerful nations of the world have large distant water fishing fleets. These nations might be expected to claim "vested or historic" rights through the development of these fleets to fish stocks in all the high seas fishery areas of the world. Remember that the key to the success of such fleets is their mobility, their ability to move from one stock of fish or geographical area to another. They were not designed to fish a single stock of fish or a single geographical area but were designed on the "expectancy" that they would be able to roam the high seas and go where the fish are. It would seem unlikely that such nations would lightly agree to give up the right to fish *any* area of the high seas.

An easier problem it would seem, would concern the nations with coastal fisheries only. Conceivably one might argue that they have historic or vested rights only to the stocks of fish and geographical areas in which they have operated in the past. Not that this would be easy, but it would be easier than handling the problem of the nations with the distant water fishing fleets.

As between fisheries and minerals, it is likely that the mineral problem would be more easily approached than fisheries. Because fewer minerals of the sea have been exploited in the past there are fewer "vested" or "historic" claims to them.

Possibly a better way to approach the whole subject would be to turn it around and ask which of the mineral and fishery resources of the sea are clearly *not* subject to any historic or vested claims at present. If this approach were used the quantity of fishery and mineral resources turned over to the United Nations would likely be smaller than otherwise, but in the context of political reality such a proposal might have more chance of succeeding.

In conclusion, it might be worth a special effort by the proponents of these proposals to try to identify the national interests of the U.S., the U.S.S.R., Japan, and the other major sea powers that would be served by carrying out such proposals. Maybe such national interests do exist which are not now readily perceived (although I, myself, have a great difficulty in conceiving of them). For example, what will be the relationship of the population explosion (and the world's growing need for food) to the concept of "sovereignty" and to the development of international organizations in the coming years. I could not say that the proponents of these proposals should look forward to the results of such studies with great optimism; however, it should be remembered that historically the humanitarian or generous act of one generation often becomes the act of necessity for the next.

GOLDIE:

There can be little basis, if any at all, for disagreeing with the widespread acclamations which the four Geneva conventions on the law of the sea in 1958, and their attendant protocol and resolutions, have received. Nor can we cavil at such statements as:

> The United Nations Conference on the Law of the Sea held in Geneva from February 24 to April 28, 1958, is unquestionably the most important international conference ever held on this subject, and one of the most significant attempts ever made by governments of the world to codify international law.[1]

The only addendum that I would like to make is that the conventions' significance derives, not only from the amount of important codification achieved, but also from the inclusion of new concepts falling under the rubric of "the progressive development of international law." Although all the conventions contain many fascinating points of discussion, and formulations which invite proposals for modification, I shall restrict my discussion to some specific issues which call for modifications to the Convention on the Continental Shelf. Furthermore, the discussion which follows will be restricted to the problems of offshore boundaries and zones and special problems of offshore control.

I.

Several different definitions of the continental shelf region have been offered. The geographer Bourcart, for example, in his leading treatise, *Géographie du fond des mers: Etude du relief des océans,* has defined the shelf as being the submarine land masses that lie beneath the shallow sea areas between the shores and the *rupture du pente,* or "break of slope"—that is, the first substantial falloff, whatever the depth. Bourcart has also described this zone as the "ocean rim."

Bourcart's concept is predicated on a vision of the continental land masses and insular areas beyond the continental regions as standing, as it were, on vast pedestals above the ocean abyss. Lying off-shore, but underneath the oceans, and between the shores and the depths, a shallow shoulder extends for some distance seaward. This terminates in a steeper slope and plunges into the ocean abyss. At the point where the slope becomes steeper and plunges downward, Bourcart saw the terminating point of the continental shelf. Here definition reflects geographical reality. Other geographers, taking the view that there is a tendency, in many parts of the world, for the *rupture du pente* to coincide with the two hundred meter bathymetric contour line, have proposed that, for the purpose of obtaining a useful working definition, the geographical continental shelf should be defined as extending from the shore to this isobar, without consideration of the actual break in slope. We should, perhaps, note that the International Committee on the Nomenclature of the Ocean Bottom Features of the International Association of Physical Oceanography at Monaco (a member of the International Council of Scientific Unions) favors the latter mode.

Following the majority of oceanographers, ocean biologists, and ocean zoologists, the International Law Commission proposed, and the 1958 Geneva Conference on the Law of the Sea accepted, the 200 meter bathymetric contour line as one of the two criteria for determining the existence of the legal continental shelf (as distinct from the geographical). Article 1 of the 1958 Geneva Convention on the Continental Shelf states:

> For the purpose of these articles, the term "continental shelf" is used as referring (a) to the seabed and subsoil of the submarine areas adjacent to the coast but outside the area of the territorial sea, to a depth of 200 metres or, beyond that limit, to where the depth of the superjacent waters admits of the exploitation of the natural resources of the said areas; (b) to the seabed and subsoil of similar submarine areas adjacent to the coasts of islands.

Can the two tests, that of the 200 bathymetric contour line and that of exploitability, be taken in conjunction? The history of the Conference shows that the exploitability test was inserted into Article I to have a supplementary and subordinate function. It was intended to permit a coastal state to exercise sovereign rights over continental shelf activities carried out on the continental slopes and in the continental borderland in the continuation of activities begun, or connected with those carried out, in the zone between its territorial sea and the 200 meter bathymetric contour line. The test was thus a practical measure, and one intended to give a practical solution to day to day problems which would arise if the 200 meter bathymetric contour line were accepted as a complete and final cutoff line.

Both of the tests for determining the submarine regions to be designated the "continental shelf" of the coastal state for the purposes of the convention are admittedly fictitious. Be that as it may, the definition of the continental shelf by reference to the 200 meter bathymetric contour line may, especially, perhaps, in the seclusion of the study, the atmosphere of the classroom, and that of the courtroom, give an impression of having at least a tenuous connection with Bourcart's geographical shelf. In any given case the coincidence of the break in the slope with the 200 meter line will be accidental. The geographical and the legal shelves may, in concrete situations, be widely divergent; but there is a general and perhaps abstract congruence. On the other hand the test of exploitability has no claim to verisimilitude with geographical reality. It is clearly quite independent of the geographical and oceanological concept of the pedestal upon which the land masses rest—the geographer's notion of the part the continental shelf plays in the depiction of the world's oceanographic features. Indeed this test is as free of any empirical connection with the geographical shelf as are the much-criticized 200 miles seaward "continental shelf" claims of Peru, Ecuador, Chile, and Costa Rica. Like these claims, furthermore, the exploitability test provides no criteria limiting the claims short of median lines, or perhaps *thalwegs,* in the abysses in the middle of the oceans.

Certain present-day developments, although now almost entirely in their experimental phases, underscore this point. Direction drilling for oil and gas, Captain Jacques-Yves Cousteau's Conself I, II, and III, the United States Navy's Sea-Lab, the developments in submersibles by the aerospace industry, Edwin Link's Man-in-Sea Project, the discovery of the beckoning wealth of mineral nodules (as well as subsoil minerals including petroleums) existing at great depths on the ocean's floor, all point to the pending obsolescence of the 200 meter bathymetric contour line test. They place emphasis on the exploitability test. These two tests (i.e., depth and exploitability) may be seen as not only distinct, and mutually exclusive, but also in potential competition. For, whereas the 200 meter bathymetric contour line was chosen as a test because

275

it clearly and unequivocally indicated the outer limits of the submarine areas wherein states could exercise their rights, the exploitability test, largely thanks to its indeterminacy, permits the assumption of sovereign rights without consideration of depth. It is, hence, a test which may be available to excuse extensions to rights beyond the limiting depth of 200 meters vertically, and horizontally beyond the land-encircling 200 meter bathymetric contour line. This points to the final paradox: The test which was conceived in 1958 as having a subordinate function promises, in the next decade, to supplant that to which it had been originally attached as a supplementary and supernumerary concept.

In addition to the expected effect upon claims to "offshore boundaries and zones," the impending transfer of contemporary experimental developments to industry will affect current activities connected with the North Sea's bed and subsoil. As the common continental shelf of its littoral states, this provides another warning against a facile adoption of the exploitability test. At the outset we should note that the North Sea states have departed, in some cases to quite a considerable degree, from "what the law allows," when the "law" is taken to be the Convention on the Continental Shelf. It was tempered, if not with mercy, then at least with equity. Thus, on at least one interpretation of Article 1 (and this arguably, the interpretation most consistent with the apparent intention of the framers of the convention at Geneva), the United Kingdom could have validly asserted sovereign rights over the whole of the North Sea's sea bed and subsoil lying above a depth of two hundred meters from the surface of the sea and which lies to the north of a parallel of latitude subtending westerly from the most southerly point on the south bank of the Norwegian Trench lying at the depth of 200 meters. Alternatively a British claim could have been asserted to a slightly smaller area which may be seen as lying above a depth of 200 meters and to the north of a section of a parallel of latitude drawn westerly from the most northerly point of a boundary line running south from the southerly 200 meter bathymetric contour line of the Norwegian Trench, and establishing a north-south boundary between the British and Danish submarine zones of the North Sea.

Application of either of these alternative systems of measurement predicated on the 200 meters of depth criterion would entail the exclusion of Norway from what we have been led to believe to be the impending North Sea oil and gas bonanza. In contrast with these possibilities, the British proclamations made due allowance for a Norwegian claim extending at least as far west as a median line between the two states. Was this an acknowledgment of a possible valid Norwegian claim predicated on the exploitability test? A study of contemporary British publications, both official and unofficial, would lead to a negative reply. The British restraint arose from the pragmatic desire to proceed as quickly as possible and to avoid time-consuming disputes, and an acknowledgment that equity would appear to be on the side of opposition to a greatly extended British claim reaching to the Norwegian Trench.

Because, however, some writers have sought to predicate the Norwegian claim upon the exploitability test, and have done so with considerable persuasiveness, it becomes clear that, to these writers at least, the test is no longer subordinate and supplemental. Analysis might be helped, I would suggest, by asking the question: What would be the effect upon Norway's claim to share in the wealth of the North Sea's bed and subsoil if the exploitability test were deleted from the legal definition of the continental shelf? I submit, none. In the actual circumstances of the North Sea states' situation, the government of the United Kingdom, in terms of equity, comity, and respect for Norwegian claims, unilaterally promulgated a claim only out to a line some miles *west* of a true median between the Norwegian and British coasts. (The claim was not asserted as far to the east as the median line would allow so that later adjustment could be worked out, if necessary, in terms of unclaimed areas.) It might be argued that such a respect for the equities might not obtain in other, and perhaps less developed, or friendly regions. My submission is not that Anglo-Norwegian diplomatic relations provide a substitute whereby parties might ignore claims in terms of "exploitability" on the one hand, and "continuity" on the other, but that the hard facts of proximity on the same shelf, and a need to observe standards of good neighborliness (involving self-restraint) provide the guidelines of settlement. In this context, it should be observed, an adherence to the exploitability test as provided by Article 1 could provide a vehicle for the manifestation of chauvinistic self-assertiveness.

In his excoriation of the then developing legal doctrines of the continental shelf (in his important article "Plateau Continental et Droit International"),[2] Professor Scelle pointed out that such developments may do no more than excuse an ever-increasing series of claims into the common domain of the high seas, both upward to embrace the superjacent sea and the superambient air, and outward further into the oceans until a *thalweg* in the abyss is reached. He envisaged the free high seas as finally being enclosed in the territories of the coastal states. I submit that these encroachments need not occur, provided the definition of the legal continental shelf given by the 200 meter bathymetric contour line (in preference to the test of the break in slope of the realist, or geographical concept of the continental shelf, only because of the definitional difficulties and legal problems which may be involved in any concrete situation) is rigorously adhered to. On the other hand, the exploitability test, now included in Article 1, encourages the overthrow of the simple, if formalist, concept of the shelf which the 200 meter line provides. It need not provide an essential argument in the development, and recognition, of Norway's claim to share in the riches of the North Sea's continental shelf. It will encourage those encroachments into the oceans, made feasible by recent scientific and technological developments, against which Professor Scelle forewarned us. My first proposed modification of the Continental Shelf Convention is, accordingly, that the exploitability test should be deleted from Article 1.

If, despite the arguments in the preceding pages, the exploitability test is not to be eliminated as a legal definition of the continental shelf's extent, or if it is to be retained, with a view to possibly providing (on mistaken premises, I submit) solutions for problems arising in such areas as the North Sea, the Mediterranean, the Caribbean, the Persian Gulf, the Red Sea, and the Arafura Sea, then Article 1 should be modified. It should be redrafted so that the two tests can function side by side, each in its own area of effectiveness. Such a redrafting should eliminate the present ambiguities and sources of conflict between the tests by spelling out the scope of the rights which are to depend on the test of depth plus continuity (the 200 bathymetric contour line test) and the scope of the rights which are to depend on the exploitability test. Furthermore, we should be told the conditions which permit valid reliances on the 200 meter depth once the first bathymetric contour line of that depth has been passed and when an adjacent shallow sea area of less than 200 meters—for example, a submarine mount—is reached, and when reliance should be placed on exploitability. Secondly, the Convention should clarify the conditions of when, and whether, rights dependent upon the depth of sea are to prevail over those supported by exploitability, and vice versa. Thirdly, the Convention should clearly state whether the exploitability test allows a state to

278

leapfrog deep areas (on an analogy, perhaps, with the World War II military strategy of "island hopping"). Does it permit the United States, for example, to assert a claim to the Cortes Bank, a submarine mount some two hundred miles from the coast of California—and Mexico's Baja California del Norte? Although this paragraph points to the need for the modification of Article 1 in the event of the retention of the exploitability test, the difficulties this discussion points to, namely those attendant on the inclusion of equal and conflicting criteria, are equally strong arguments in support of the elimination of the exploitability test altogether.

II.

Although the deletion of the exploitability test from Article I of the Geneva Convention on the Continental Shelf would solve the problems just indicated, such a deletion would give rise to others—especially in view of the fact that man can now exploit, and will soon be able to live and work for extended periods, below the depth of 200 meters. The question may be asked whether the elimination of the exploitability test would, on balance, create greater difficulties than its retention. How could legal titles over appropriated resources be secured if states may not extend their legal systems into areas where the resources are being won? How can access to resources beyond the continental shelf regions be limited and regulated so as to prevent the supervention of the anarchy which so frequently attends claims based on the doctrine of occupation? Finally, how, in the absence of a state exercising regulatory powers ("sovereign rights"), or in the absence of an international authority (for example, as suggested as one of three possible developments by Drs. Christy and Scott in their book, *The Common Wealth in Ocean Fisheries* and advocated by the Commission to Study the Organization of Peace in its Seventeenth Report),[3] can the taking of sea bed and subsoil resources below the 200 meter bathymetric contour line be regulated, so as to prevent overcapitalization and overproduction and costs of congestion? In reviewing these questions I would suggest they are so complex and ramifying that to rely simply on the exploitability test for their solution would be illusory. They require no less than a treaty regime which would assure exclusive titles regarding the taking of mineral resources from the sea bed and subsoil of the oceans below the two hundred meter depth. This treaty regime should be governed, I suggest, by additional articles to those already existing in the Geneva Conventions. They may be cast into the form of a fifth convention, the "Convention on the Resources of the Seabed and Subsoil of the High Seas." (Alternatively the articles I am suggesting could be formulated as additional articles to the Convention on the High Seas.) However characterized, these articles should be formulated so as to assure firm titles to minerals recovered from the sea bed and subsoil of the oceans beyond both the territorial limits of states and their continental shelves. The underlying theory, I suggest, should be an equivalent, among the signatory states, to a regime of recognition, or of "Full Faith and Credit" to be accorded by the authorities of all the states who are parties to the resources won from the bed and subsoil of the deep oceans. To be more explicit: my intention, in what is to follow, is to propose the principles of a regime governing the assurance of titles created under the municipal law of each state by their recognition in the courts of all the others through an international agreement and by means of establishing, under public international treaty law, conflict of law obligations of recognition.

Before I spell out the principles of such a regime I should utter two warnings. The first is that the doctrine of occupation, in whatever guise of "first come first served" it may appear, should be conscientiously eschewed. Any analogies which one may be tempted to discuss between the proposed articles and the occupation provisions of the Berlin Convention on the Congo, 1885, for example, are illusory. The second is that I feel the moment to be not yet ripe to invest in an international agency discretionary powers of granting territory to states, or the right to win and appropriate resources to individuals. Here the emphasis is on the power to *grant*. Perhaps I should add that my own feeling is that the accordance of such a granting power, if only it were currently feasible, would be highly advantageous, and would be in the interests of humanity. Be that as it may, rather than enter into frustrating conflicts now, the main policy goals of secure titles, limited access to a resource to insure the prevention of over-capitalization, overproduction and congestion, and the avoidance of "first come first served" tactics and the ensuing conflicts, could be gained if regional agencies (with, necessarily, a central index in the United Nations Secretariat) could be established to carry out *evidentiary* (notice) and *recording* functions. We might, perhaps, and with great profit, note that at least one United

Nations agency, namely the International Telecommunication Union (ITU) performs a similar function to the one I am proposing. Its function is, moreover, relative to those increasingly valuable property interests, radio frequencies—increasingly valuable because they are becoming increasingly scarce. Minimally therefore, the proposed draft articles would include, in broad terms:

1.   The recognition of a right inuring in signatory states to acquire, and have recorded, specialized zones of jurisdiction and control whereby they would be enabled to give legal title over resources appropriated from the sea bed and subsoil to their citizens (whether individuals or corporations) under their own municipal laws. Such zones of special jurisdiction would, in addition to clothing physical appropriations with legal rights, enable the recording state, under whose jurisdiction the zone was recorded, to protect the enterprises working the areas within its competence from piracy, theft, violence, trespasses of all kinds, and a general disregard of the legal validity and consequences of appropriations made in the zone.

2.   The establishment of international recording agencies, organized on regional bases, with a central index in the United Nations Secretariat. When activated by a state with a valid claim, these agencies would have power to issue instruments defining the recording state's Zone of Special Jurisdiction.

3.   (a) On an analogy with the Guano Islands Act of 1856,[4] the originating initiative could well be left to the citizens of the signatory states. In fact a two-step function is envisaged. First, an individual or an enterprise would record, with the state of its nationality (presumably with the consulate closest to the location of the resource), its claim to a sea bed resource beyond the continental shelf (and, *a fortiori,* beyond the territorial limits) of any state. This would be a municipal law claim, operating only within the law of the state with which that claim had been recorded. (b) The country with which the claim to explore for, and exploit, the resource had been recorded would then record, in its own turn, its international claim to exercise jurisdiction and control over the individual's (or enterprise's) activity with the agency indicated in §(2) above. The decision to lodge an instrument of international recordation would be left to the state concerned. The provisions I am

281

proposing would not impose an obligation to record, as a result of a private citizen's initiative, upon a signatory state—simply a right. But once a state has recorded, then its laws would govern the winning of the resource.

4. The system of recordation of the title to the property taken from the sea bed and subsoil as a result of the private individual's or corporation's initiative should be determined by the law of the state exercising jurisdiction and control. To accord immediate legal validity to these titles in the courts of other signatory states would *not* be a function of international treaty rules. In enacting their domestic legislation the states adhering to the international regime could choose to follow principles of recordation of title or of registration under analogies with the Torrens or other systems. Whatever the form of the domestically created titles, the international regime would call for their recognition, in terms of an international parallel to a federal Full Faith and Credit clause, in the courts, and by the authorities, of all the other signatories to the international convention (whatever domestic system of recordation and/or registration the state called upon to recognize a title in any case may follow).

5. Although, in their municipal laws, states might, on an analogy with the mining laws of many states of the United States and of Australia, as well as with a number of the provinces of Canada, accord priority between competing claimants on the basis of "pure race" concepts, I submit that the international recording systems should bear closer analogies to the "race notice" principle than to the "pure race" principle. (The dispute between the United States and Great Britain in 1867-77 over the Western Australian Lacepede Islands gives strength to this proposal.)

6. The authority of a state exercising the jurisdiction and control permitted in these articles should be limited to the working of the specific resource which had been initially recorded (or registered) with it. Thus recordation with the appropriate international regional agency of a state's claim to exercise jurisdiction and control over the winning of manganese nodules by one of its citizens (whether an individual or a corporation), would not give it any authority whatever to exercise sovereign rights over nearby sulphur deposits or oil pools—let alone fisheries in the superjacent sea. Thus the zone of special jurisdiction would receive its first limiting characteristic—that of purpose.

7. Secondly, the special jurisdiction should be limited as to time. A state's authority over a submarine area should not survive the period that area is actually worked. Thus the termination of the exploration and/or the exploitative activity of an individual or corporation should terminate the state's jurisdiction and control.

8. Thirdly, states' sovereign rights over recorded zones of special jurisdiction should be limited as to areas. What the precise areas should be is, clearly, dependent upon a great number of variables, e.g.: concentration of the resource, the cost of winning, processing and marketing it, the reserves required, and the projected demand. Again, states should be obligated to require and supervise rigorously the prompt working of claims recorded (or registered) with them, prevent the possibility of conspiracies between individuals or corporations to enter claims under fictitious names, and exclude "dummying" activities. The convention should, further, establish requirements of minimum times within which a resource should be proved, and the minimum investment allowable for both exploration and exploitation in order to keep a claim fresh and valid. Finally, states which record instruments giving notice of their sovereign rights over the working of a resource with the appropriate international regional agency should be required to exercise effective control over the working. Indeed, I suggest that an inability to exercise effective control should be a valid excuse for states to deny recognition of title to appropriations not subjected to the effective control of the recording state.

9. The Convention should contain assurances that charges in the international recording agency for the recordation of the requisite instruments should not defray any costs other than those incurred by that agency for purposes of administering its recordation system.

10. So far the issue of military activities and national defense have not been canvassed. My suggestion is that these activities should fall within a distinct regime (or number of regimes) from those suggested for the proposed convention. The defense regime should also be indicated here. My suggestion is that, on an analogy with the relevant Trusteeship Articles of the United Nations Charter, states seeking to establish *fixed* defense installations on sea mounts and on the sea bed should give notice to the effect that such areas are taken for defense purposes and are not to be viewed as being any longer within the general regime of the sea bed and its subsoil. Upon such an announcement

283

the state in question may, further, establish security zones. The rights asserted would be analogous to those in the Australian Defence (Special Undertakings) Act, No. 19 of 1952 (proclaiming the Porto Bello Islands to be a "prohibited area" for the conduct of atomic tests), rather than the Notice to Mariners concept followed by the United States and the Soviet Union in their nuclear weapon testing areas on the high seas. (Naturally the proclamations of defense areas would be accompanied by notices to mariners.) Naval submarines would not, of course, fall within this regime. They will have to take their chances, as heretofore, as they clandestinely move about under the cover of the seas.

In concluding this outline of the Draft Articles on the Resources of the Sea Bed and Subsoil, I would like to add the observation that individuals, corporations, and, indeed, states should be perfectly free to invoke, or not to invoke, at their discretion, the foregoing principles. They might, conceivably, prefer to carry on a specific submarine activity outside this regime and in secret. If, for example, states do not invoke the procedures suggested above, then their citizens may still mine in the sea bed and subsoil beyond continental shelf regions and outside the zones of special jurisdiction of other states; but only on the basis of the general international law privilege of taking the resource. Should, for example, a dispute as to title come before the courts of a third state (or before an international tribunal) over a shipment of oil taken from a sea-bed operation outside continental shelf regions (as defined by the 200 meter bathymetric contour line), between a state (or its citizens) asserting ownership under the general and traditional privilege of appropriating items of the sea's wealth and a state (or its citizens) which was acting under the regime proposed in this paper, then, analogously with the "race-notice" recording statutes with which we are all familiar, the rights established under the regime should prevail over those derived from traditional concepts and practices permitting appropriations on, or under, the high seas.

Again, a state placing a higher value on secrecy with respect to an installation on the sea bed than on the regime envisaged in §(10) above could stay outside that regime and rely on whatever protections general international law might allow. Primarily, reliance would, clearly, be not on any legal concepts, but upon secrecy and camouflage—in the widest sense. (This is, of course, the present position.) Outside the regime a state could not demand the immunities and protections, nor the exclusive

284

rights, which the regime would afford, any more than today the U.S. Navy can demand exclusive rights on the high seas when its exercises excite the curiosity of Russian trawlers. In brief, a state opting to bring a fixed submarine installation into the regime gains immunity, but at the cost of the secrecy of that installation's general location—but not of its exact location, nor of its characteristics. If the state prefers the shield of secrecy, it will stay outside the regime; but at the cost of immunity if the secret should be broken, or the installation discovered.

Finally, I would like to suggest that a treaty regime embodying the principles I have just suggested would achieve two important objectives. First, it would secure titles to appropriated goods, and by limiting access to any given resource, tend to reduce overcapitalization and losses due to overproduction and congestion. Second, it would meet, and answer, by offering a more certain alternative, the usual arguments supporting the exploitability test—namely the need to secure titles to resources taken from beyond the shelf region and to prevent a free-for-all on the continental slopes and in the continental borderland. The regime I have suggested spells out in detail how those evils may be averted. It does not suffer from the weaknesses of the disabling indeterminacy inherent in Article 1's exploitability test.

III.

Article 2(4), which purports to define the natural resources of the shelf, the exploration and exploitation of which fall within the coastal state's "sovereign rights," is as follows:

> The natural resources referred to in these articles consist of the mineral and other non-living resources of the sea bed and subsoil together with living organisms belonging to sedentary species, that is to say, organisms which, at the harvestable state, either are immobile on or under the sea bed or are unable to move except in constant physical contact with the sea bed or subsoil.

Commenting on this paragraph, a leading participant in its drafting, Sir Kenneth Bailey of Australia, has commented:

> In an attempt to work out a scientific and legally exact definition, the Australian delegation at Geneva was encouraged to organize a Commonwealth working party, in which marine biologists were associated with lawyers. There resulted the definition which is now to be found in the convention. I am myself too long in the tooth as a lawyer to wish to be dogmatic about the meaning that will

be given hereafter to any form of words, however meticulously prepared. This definition, however, certainly resulted from a most heartening piece of Commonwealth co-operation. It is the earnest hope of its draftsmen that it will be found in practice to *exclude* the shrimp and the sole from the natural resources of the continental shelf just as unequivocally as it *includes* the mother-of-pearl shell, the pearl oyster, the beche-de-mer, the trochus and the green snail, as well as the sacred chank of India and Ceylon. If it turns out to do these things, Australia has good ground for being pleased with the result, and for being grateful for staunch support from her associates in the Commonwealth and also from the United States, France, Norway and others.[5]

Sir Kenneth Bailey indicates that the framers' intention was, on a perhaps extended analogy with crops as *partes soli,* as for example, formulated in *Duchess of Sutherland* v. *Watson*,[6] to include sessile creatures only, and to exclude shrimp, and one may infer, crabs (including the Alaska king crab?), lobsters, langoustes, and other edible and mobile crustaceans from paragraph (4) as well as demersal fish (indicated by the reference to one species, i.e., the sole). That paragraph, unfortunately, while clearly formulated in its indication of what is included, does not indicate (unlike Sir Kenneth Bailey's explanation) what is explicitly excluded from its scope. A significant fact in the history of paragraph (4)'s drafting is that the Fourth Committee had originally accepted a proviso to the paragraph, and it ran " . . . but crustacea and swimming species are not included in this definition." The plenary session of the 1958 Geneva Conference rejected it.[7]

With this point of history in mind, Sir Kenneth Bailey's exclusion of the shrimp and the sole (i.e., crustaceans and demersal fish) would appear to rest upon a negative implication to be derived from the words which the conference permitted to remain in paragraph (4). Apart from questioning the propriety of detecting a negative implication after the plenary session had deleted the express negative proviso, one should, I think, point out that negative implications have traditionally been, in the context of interpreting federal constitutions no less than that of treaties, uncertain guides. Indeed, in the subsequent history of paragraph (4), its negative implication has fared little better than most others—especially those which have been casualties in the constitutional histories of the United States and of Australia.

For example, in 1962, the dispute, journalistically and graphically labeled "The Lobster War," arose between Brazil and France with the arrest on January 2, 1962, of the French vessel, the "Cassiopée." [8] The occasion of this "war" was the enterprise of Breton fishermen who, moving from their more traditional lobster-fishing grounds off the Atlantic coast of North Africa, began fishing the langoustes which inhabit the Brazilian continental shelf. Maintaining that the lobsters were not only sojourners on the national continental shelf, but resources of it, Brazil decreed a prohibition of the French fishermen. France claimed that the langoustes were a resource of the high seas, and if found beyond Brazilian territorial waters, might be lawfully fished by all off the continental shelf. Was France right? If we assume Sir Kenneth Bailey's illustration of "the shrimp" was a stylistic device indicating all crustaceans of the sea bed, then langoustes would fall outside the scope of paragraph (4) no less certainly than shrimp. (Arguing by the usual lawyers' device of analogy from shrimp to langoustes would produce a similar result.) Clear as Sir Kenneth Bailey's position may be on langoustes, on December 10, 1964, an amicable settlement was reached between the conflicting interests of both countries—the Breton lobstermen on the one hand and the Brazilian group which sought its government's intervention in the first place on the other. By this accord, twenty-six French vessels were permitted to fish for five years in the prohibited zones; but they were obliged to give tribute in lobsters and fish to the private Brazilian group for the privilege.

Professor Rousseau considers that the agreement, being "purement professional et corporatif," leaves unsolved "la problem juridique . . . entre les deux gouvernments." [9] But does it? May not the ad hoc solution create difficulties—should France refuse to acknowledge that the disputed crustaceans are indeed to be viewed as resources of Brazil's continental shelf? May not the Breton lobstermen have, by the undertaking to deliver a percentage of their catch off the Brazilian continental shelf, placed themselves in an unfavorable position, namely one analogous to "contractual licensees" in the common law? And may not France, by not intervening to prevent this resolution of the immediate problem, be viewed as having tacitly acquiesced in the Brazilian claim?

A second and perhaps less ambiguous development is to be found in the United States note, dated November 25, 1964, in the exchange of notes constituting the Japanese–United States Agreement on King Crab Fishing off Alaska, Washington, 1964. It stated, *inter alia*:

> The Government of the United States of America is of the view that the king crab is a natural resource of the continental shelf over which the coastal state

287

(in this case the United States of America) has exclusive jurisdiction, control and rights of exploitation.[10]

True it may be that the Japanese have not agreed with us on this specific point. Not yet. But before 1958 they were disputing with equal tenacity that the mother-of-pearl oyster on Australia's continental shelf was not a natural resource of that country's continental shelf either. Surely, once one type of animal (and the creatures listed by Sir Kenneth are animals—any analogy between them and emblements on dry land is biologically, but of course, not necessarily legally, false) is viewed as a natural resource of the shelf, then interest groups and nations will press analogies from one sessile animal to another, and perhaps not quite so sedentary, creature. The green snail, one could argue, since it moves about on the sea bed, is closer to the king crab than the mother-of-pearl oyster which during its adult life remains fixed to one spot. Perhaps a criterion of some limiting value may be that of the Article 2(4) test of immobility at the moment of harvesting. This would exclude crustaceans. But what is its value? Whereas the immobility of the oyster may result from its being affixed to the sea bed, the immobility of the chank and the green snail, like that of the shrimp, the langouste, and the king crab may be no more than an immobility occasioned by fright at the immediate prospect of being harvested.

The addition of biological resources to the category of the "natural resources" of the shelf has led to confusion, and to encroachments on the freedom of fishing on the high seas. These will continue, as more and more species will be brought within the category, on one ground or another, of "resources of the continental shelf." To prevent an "enclosure movement" from developing further, I would like to propose that the resources of the continental shelf which are to be subjected to a coastal state's sovereign rights should be limited to mineral resources. Article 2(4) is an inappropriate place for formulating the rights of coastal states over sedentary fisheries. I am not, for a moment, advocating that the rights of all states in such fisheries should be abolished. In place of overloading the concept of the continental shelf and that of "its" resources (thereby rendering the notion of the resources of the continental shelf more indeterminate than its limitation to minerals would require), I would suggest the revival (subject to an alteration to be proposed at the appropriate point) of the International Law Commission's 1951 Draft Article on Sedentary Fisheries.[11] That Article states:

288

> The regulation of sedentary fisheries may be undertaken by a state in areas of the high seas contiguous to its territorial waters, where such fisheries have long been maintained and conducted by nationals of that state, provided that non-nationals are permitted to participate in the fishing activities on an equal footing with nationals. Such regulations will, however, not affect the general status of the areas as high seas.

If this provision were followed the rights of states to whom historical sedentary fisheries appertain, such as those of Tunis, Libya, Ceylon, India, the Persian Gulf, and Australia, would be preserved. On the other hand, the limited terms of the article would prevent continued accretions of species which could be caught within the indeterminate phrase "natural resources of the continental shelf," but which do not fall into the above article's definition of historic sedentary fisheries, and would prevent extending the denotations of the continental shelf theory from sessile forms to all the other creatures of the benthos (including demersal fish, e.g., plaice and flounder, which are nektonic but inhabit the benthic division), and to wrecked ships, sunken bullion, and perhaps eventually to the whole nektonic division of the seas, including pelagic fish and animals.

There is one point of disagreement I should like to register with the Sedentary Fisheries Article as formulated in 1951. I submit that the proviso "provided that non-nationals are permitted to participate on an equal footing with nationals" should be deleted. In its place the phrase "with non-nationals enjoying, subject to the principle of abstention, such historical privileges as they may have acquired by long usage" should be inserted. The traditional concept of the rights of coastal states over historic sedentary fisheries was well expressed in the "Examination of Legal Principles" of the British in the *Bering Sea Arbitration*,[12] which was as follows:

> . . . [And] so as to oysters and coral beds when they are within the waters over which international law recognizes an exclusive fishery right, this right becomes equivalent to a right of property because they are attached to the soil. But in animals which move from this area into the high sea no such property can be acquired.

The traditional view, which the British Case outlined, held that both *imperium* and *dominium* were vested in the coastal state. The present-day climate of opinion would not, so it seems to me, be amicable to divesting coastal states of either one. Secondly, the principle of abstention

289

may be invoked (with, probably, more effect by smaller and newer countries with few developed resources than by the United States or Canada) to call for recognizing a coastal state's exclusive rights in a sedentary fishery. The principle of abstention has been defined in the following terms:

> According to this principle when a country has fully developed a fishery and, as a result of continuing scientific study, is regulating it so as to obtain the maximum sustained yield, newcomers who are parties to the treaty agree to abstain from fishing the stocks concerned.[13]

IV.

My final suggestion is that the provisions in Article 5(8) regarding free scientific research should be modified. That paragraph provides:

> The consent of the coastal state shall be obtained in respect of any research concerning the continental shelf and undertaken there. Nevertheless, the coastal state shall not normally withhold its consent if the request is submitted by a qualified institution with a view to purely scientific research into the physical or biological characteristics of the continental shelf, subject to the proviso that the coastal state shall have the right, if it so desires, to participate or to be represented in the research, and that in any event the results shall be published.

Although I am in full agreement with Article 5(8)'s provisions requiring the publication of results, and permitting the participation of the coastal state, either actively or by means of an observer, or representative, I feel that that paragraph is too weakly formulated. I submit that there should not only be an obligation of "not normally withhold[ing] . . . consent" on the part of the coastal state; but further a positive duty of supporting, or at least refraining from interference with, bona fide scientific researches carried out on its contiguous and adjacent shelves, and of restraining its nationals from so interfering. These obligations should, of course, be subject to the coastal state's essential requirements in connection with national defense. In addition, possible threats to, or restrictions on, future scientific research should be a criterion for granting or withholding the recordation of claims by a state of exploration and exploitation licenses to individuals and business enterprises. My proposal here is that exploration and exploitation policies, no less than conservation policies, should be developed which take ac-

290

count of the enormous value of scientific research to the development of the shelf regions.

Secondly, what should be the position of scientific research beyond the shelf? In regions unaffected by exploitative activities (in connection with either minerals or fish including sedentary species), the traditional situation could continue for the time being at least. When, on the other hand, exploitations take place outside the scope of the draft articles I have outlined, then the exploiting entities or individuals should be required so to conduct their enterprises as neither to interfere with, nor diminish the value of, any neighboring scientific activity. A right to collect damages for such interference should be provided. Also preventive procedures should be available. Similarly, in the event of scientific activities' being conducted near an exploitation which has been registered under the procedure I have proposed, then the economic activity should not be carried on in any manner which might unreasonably impair the value of the scientific activity. The state which recorded the claim with the United Nations agency should, however, have all the privileges and rights—participating in the activity or sending observers—which have already been recognized as inuring, in the Continental Shelf Articles, to the coastal state. In addition, the results of the research should be published. Thus the policy of Article 5(8), with the additions I have proposed thereto in connection with the continental shelf region, should be extended to zones in the deep oceans, whatever the depth, where states have established their control and their sovereign rights. Again, the conductors of the scientific research should be able to obtain preventive relief from unjustified interferences, and obtain damages for breach of this obligation. This benefit should be theirs on account of the inclusive nature of their activity.

In connection with fixed defense installations under the sea, the preceding principles should not apply. I would like to suggest that here, again, when an undersea area is dedicated for defense purposes the state in question should be entitled, on an analogy with Article 82 of the United Nations Charter (the "strategic areas" provisions in Chapter XII "International Trusteeship System"—apart from the authority therein of the Security Council in Article 83), to proclaim the area as a zone to be used solely for defense purposes. The effect of such a proclamation would be to take the area proclaimed outside the articles I have suggested—including those according privi-

291

leges and immunities to scientific research. As with the other proposed draft Articles regarding defense installations on the sea bed, these defense areas provisions are not intended to be relevant to submarines in motion. They would, however, be relevant to submarine pens on the sea bed.

Finally, a state might choose not to proclaim a defense area under these proposals. In such a case it would choose to rely on secrecy and be exposed to the possibility of discovery. Furthermore, should scientific research develop in the area, the claims of the state relying on secrecy rather than on the treaty regime should be subordinated to priorities and claims favoring research under the treaty regime. A state has a choice between the immunities provided by the articles as a matter of law and those which may be obtained from secrecy. The attendant benefits of both are different. In choosing one or another the state balances its conveniences. It must, however, choose, it cannot, in my suggestion, have the advantages of both, nor can it escape the restrictions of either.

1. Franklin, "The Law of the Sea: Some Recent Developments," 1, 53 *Naval War College Blue Book Series* (1961).

2. 58 *Revue Général de Droit International Public* 5 (1955).

3. Christy and Scott, *The Common Wealth in Ocean Fisheries* (Baltimore: Johns Hopkins Press, 1965) ; and Commission to Study the Organization of Peace, *New Dimensions for the United Nations: The Problems of the Next Decade,* 41–46 (17 Report, 1966).

4. 11 Stat. 119, 48 U.S.C. §§1411–1415 (1958).

5. 1 *Adelaide Law Review* 1, 11 (1960).

6. 5 *Sc. L. Rptr.* 158, 40 *Sc. Jur.* 119 (Ct. of Sess., 1868).

7. See 6 United Nations Conference on the Law of the Sea, Geneva, 1958, *Official Records (4th Committee)* 136 (U.N. Doc. No. A/CONF. 13/42, 1958), 2 United Nations Conference on the Law of the Sea, Geneva, 1958, *Official Records (Plenary Meetings)* 15 (U.N. Doc. No. A/CONF. 13/38, 1958), and Whiteman, "Conference on the Law of the Sea: Convention on the Continental Shelf," 52 *American Journal of International Law* 629, 638 (1958).

8. See 67 *Revue Général de Droit International Public* 133 (1963).

9. 69 *Revue Général de Droit International Public* 120 (1965).

10. 4 *International Legal Materials* 157, 158 (1965).

11. See "Draft Articles on the Continental Shelf and Related Subjects," Part II, Related Subjects, Article 3, U.N. Doc. No. A/1858, in 2 International Law Commission, *1951 Yearbook,* 143 (U.N. Doc. No. A/CN.4/SER.A/1951/Add. 1, Sales No.:1957, V.6. Vol. 11, 1957).

12. Cd. 6921 (1893–94) 110 *Parliamentary Papers* 759, 822.

13. Van Cleve and Johnson, "Management of the High Sea Fisheries of the Northeastern Pacific," 1, (No. 2) *University of Washington Publications in Fisheries, New Series* (1963). See also Canada and United States, *Proposal, Additional Article and Article 58* (U.N. Doc. No. A/CONF.13/C.3/L.69), 5 United Nations Conference on the Law of the Sea, 3rd Committee, *Summary Records of Meetings and Annexes* 155 (U.N. Doc. No. A/CONF.13/41, Sales No. :58V.4 Vol. V, 1958), and *Comment, id.,* 156.

MERO:

I am not an attorney but an engineer, concerned primarily with the development of the various resources of the ocean. My particular field of interest is the development of the mineral resources of the sea. In many cases, in fact in most cases, practical law is quite a negative thing. Engineers seldom bring attorneys in on matters until there is trouble and legal assistance is needed. However, in resource development in the sea, there is an opportunity for the law fraternity to indulge in some creative lawmaking—to design a system of law which will actually encourage the formation of what can be a very substantial industry and provide substantial material resources for all of the people of the world. As an example I shall cite the legal system that Australia has, as versus the one in the United States, concerning the granting of mineral exploration concessions off their coast. The system in Australia encourages groups to take concessions, with the result that about 65 per cent of the coast of Australia is taken up in mineral exploration concessions; and a great deal of activity is going on in that nation at this time to develop an offshore mining industry. In the United States the competitive bidding system that we have does not encourage the initiation of exploitation or exploration of offshore mineral resources. We have no mining industry off our coast to speak of. A properly designed legal system can be a boon in initiating new industries such as offshore mining.

Viewed in the context of the atmosphere in which it was formulated, the Geneva Convention on the Law of the Sea is truly a remarkable document, and I can think of no major revisions to this document which would necessarily encourage exploitation of the resources of the sea, especially the mineral resources. I do, however, feel that some of the definitions of this convention could be tightened a little. For example, the statement of this convention that the "seabed and subsoil

293

of the submarine areas adjacent to the coast but outside the area of the territorial sea to a depth of 200 meters, or beyond that limit to where the depth of the superjacent waters admits of the exploitation of the natural resources of the area," as the definition of the continental shelf, or the definition of that area to which an adjacent nation may lay claim to the resources of the ocean floor, can be most misleading.

The outer edge of the continental shelf, or at least the distance in the sea to which a nation may lay claim to the resources of the sea floor, should be fixed and stated and not left indefinite for future adjustments that may be protested. There is nothing that companies or groups fear more than having political boundaries moved back and forth over a property in which they have invested a great deal of money to develop. Especially when capital investments in such developments may run into hundreds of millions of dollars.

It was probably not the intention of the delegates of that convention to imply that a nation may lay claim to the deep sea floor a thousand miles or so off its coast simply because some national of that nation is mining material from the ocean floor, but the present wording of the convention indicates that such is so. Possibly one can say that the distance to sea which a nation can make claims hinges upon the word adjacent, but how far is adjacent. The moon is really adjacent to the earth as far as distances in space are measured.

I think that all ocean miners would like to see some definite lines on a map indicating the point off a nation's coast at which that nation's control ends and which is considered, for purposes of mineral exploitation, open ocean. This line can be drawn somewhere between the 200 meter depth contour and the 2,500 meter depth contour lines. In practically all cases, the distance between these two lines is not great. The 2,500 meter contour then would be the outer limit to which any nation may make claim to mineral resources of the ocean floor. Such a line would include most basins and shoals off any nation's coast, such as the deeps within the California borderland area or the trenches off Norway. But it would also leave free for exploitation by the rest of the nations of the world the bulk of the remainder of the ocean floor. We might also include provisions for individual groups to lay claim to a certain area surrounding some fixed point on the surface of the earth in which that group has exclusive exploitation rights for a period of time, providing the group spends a certain amount of time and effort in exploring the deposits and then developing them. If such work were not carried out, the claim would lapse and the territory claimed would go back to the general domain. Such claims should not be parceled out indiscriminately, and the claiming groups must do the exploration and development work themselves.

Thus, we would provide a means for the ocean miner to secure some measure of security that he has exclusive rights to mine in an area in which he has spent a great deal of time, effort, and money in finding and developing. Whether the miner chooses to lay claim to such an area with right of protection to his claim from possible poachers should remain optional, but at the miner's option. If he does lay claim, of course, he should expect to pay a fee for it and the ensuing protection. And I would suggest that the administration of this claim be laid in the hands of the United Nations. I would also suggest that nationals of no nation be allowed to claim an aggregate area containing more than about fifty years' reserves of minerals as measured by domestic consumption in that nation. Such a law, I think, would prove a boon to ocean resource exploitation and probably would remove one of the risks from an extraordinarily risky business and one which normally infuriates engineers, that is, having their elegantly conceived and expensively executed ventures fail because of uncontrollable political situations.

You may notice that I have a small ax to grind in this particular case, but I feel it is rather justified because mineral resource people have not been represented in the past at various law of the sea conferences.

MELAMID:

A geographer opened this conference—and now another geographer is closing it. In between, we looked at many maps and heard many geographical definitions. Almost everything that could be said about the Geneva conventions has been said. So there is nothing left for me to do but try to torpedo the whole system.

If you want to, you can interpret the Geneva conventions as a series of loopholes connected by loopholes. Let's start out with a concrete case: median lines determine the division of offshore areas. The Geneva convention, under the heading of "special circumstances," permits deviation from median lines. West Germany is now pleading "special circumstances" to obtain more favorable boundaries in the North Sea; of course Holland and Denmark are opposed to these pleas. Many other countries also can plead "special circumstances." Median lines are to be determined from base lines, and I do not think anybody has yet dared to count the number of "special circumstances" that might be pleaded to establish base lines far from shores. In fact, the Geneva convention permits the loading of "special circumstances" on "special circumstances." As a result, if one wants to (and there are quite a few nations that want to) one can continually base his arguments on special circumstances, but then what happens to the conventions?

I have tried to explore the possibility of turning matters over to the UN but the idea just does not work. I have seen the United Nations in operation, and their administration of territory is pretty bad. The way the UN is constituted and the way trends are, I cannot see any improvement. I would like to comment on Professor Johnson's argument about the creation of what is known among geographers as neutral territory, or known among lawyers as condominia, out in the water. From the studies I have made, I have become dissatisfied with the administration of neutral territories. They work best only if administered by a third party, such as an oil company, and this is usually not regarded as a desirable solution. Overall, I am opposed to any modification of the Geneva conventions which suggests giving more power to the UN or which suggests an increasing use of condominia.

As a result of these considerations there is no doubt that we must work with the existing arrangements, even if they are full of loopholes. Let's be happy that we have at least these Geneva conventions. I doubt whether the international community of states would agree on such conventions today if we had to establish them in the political climate of the 1960's.

Under these circumstances, what can we do? One thing I would suggest is a series of sample studies. Professor Goldie said that the world is different; everything is an exception. As a geographer I have to teach and to generalize, and we can make some generalizations for example regarding coastlines. Some are sinking, some are rising, some suffer from four tides a day, some from one and a half, as in Louisiana. We can set up a series of case studies and then pass them to a committee—of ourselves preferably—for evaluation.

296

What I do believe is that we should not turn over the problem of "special circumstances" to an international body, but rather keep the existing conventions and reduce the loopholes, particularly by case studies of certain types of coastlines. When we have done this, I suggest that we then go out beyond the continental shelf, for my reading of the petroleum press suggests we will soon be ready to drill for oil in mid-ocean.

Other model studies can follow covering other groups of geographical or economic phenomena so that we can establish watertight rules for the application of the Geneva conventions. Further conferences, like this one, will be of great importance in this work. For this reason I recommend that we meet at regular intervals so that we can make this convention work for the benefit of mankind.

Discussion:

1. One system for handling the exploitation of the minerals of the sea bed beyond the continental shelf limits would be through a world-wide recording and registration system. Individual states might register and place the world on notice of their entitlement to exercise jurisdiction and control over a specific working on the sea bed beyond the 200-meter isobath. Or the claims could be registered with the United Nations, although the UN would not necessarily formulate the laws under which the mining companies would operate. The mining companies might themselves decide how much territory they would need in order to operate efficiently. Structures on the sea floor would, of course, have to be designed so as not to interfere unnecessarily with fishing or other uses, and should be charted, particularly in the interests of submarines and other underseas vehicles.

The registering of claims to the sea bed beyond the shelf might be opposed by defense officials who would feel that this might restrict the freedom of action of underseas vehicles.

Much of the confusion about the exploitation of the mineral resources of the sea will remain unresolved, according to one speaker, until one basic problem has been settled. Do these mineral resources belong to

297

all nations, so that exploitation by one sovereign must somehow be shared with the other sovereigns? Or do they belong to no nation, so that exploitation by any one sovereign in no way connotes sharing with other sovereign nations? Private enterprise and technologically advanced nations, it was suggested, will lean to the no nation–no sharing concept, while underdeveloped nations will subscribe to all nations–all sharing concept.

2. A summary statement on the conference noted two underlying problems faced by the discussants. The first involves the production of the resources of the high seas—the search for a regime which will permit the most effective operation of the fishing and mining industries, and of the other users of the sea. The second problem concerns the distribution of the wealth of the sea, a matter on which considerably more study is needed than is currently in progress.

A final theme which ran through the entire conference was the desirability of seeking a third law of the sea conference. Are there sufficiently important problems at this time to warrant such a conference? Might the United States end up having lost more than it gained at a third conference? Is there sufficient flexibility in the present Geneva conventions to allow for existing technological, economic, and political changes? The conference took no stand on this issue, but it seemed probable that the question would be raised again at subsequent conferences.

Clark M. Eichelberger
Francis T. Christy, Jr.

Chapter Eighteen:

COMMENTS ON INTERNATIONAL CONTROL
OF THE SEA'S RESOURCES

EICHELBERGER:

I am grateful to Dr. Burke for initiating discussion of this topic and for making it possible for some of the materials prepared by the Commission to Study the Organization of Peace to be incorporated in the proceedings of the first annual conference of the Law of the Sea Institute. I wish to add a few words of explanation to the discussion and to express disagreement on a number of points.

I wish, first of all, to thank Dr. Burke for his very fair analysis. He was good enough to point out that the Commission will publish a book in the fall of 1966 that may fill in some of the gaps he noticed during his study of the report. The Commission to Study the Organization of Peace, of which I am Chairman, is a research affiliate of the United Nations Association. It was started in 1939. We made suggestions about what should take the place of the League of Nations, and we have been working ever since. The report that Dr. Burke has referred to deals with what we think are the major crises before the United Nations in the near future. Let me say in the first place that he made certain criticisms of the report which I think will be met when our full book is produced. On the other hand, if I am accused of putting forward utopia I hardly think a proposal which many people think is a rational one for meeting a condition of anarchy which could mean rivalry for large part of the surface of the earth can hardly be called utopian. He points out, I think quite rightly, that such a plan as we propose cannot be subject to the parliamentary majority of the General Assembly. I point out that we do not mean that. We believe that there must be a special agency; the agency must be weighted in favor of those with the greatest interest; the agency must function with the efficiency of the International Bank. It will take a long time to work out such an agency, but we believe that the principle must now be established. However, when Dr. Burke said that the parliamentary majority of the General Assembly of the United Nations as now constituted could not set up such an agency then I would have to disagree.

I hope you will permit me to take time to give an illustration or two. The United States and Great Britain announced to the General Assembly a few years ago that they were negotiating a treaty for an international atomic energy agency, and that the subject was too involved to be sent to the General Assembly. They said they would inform the members of the United Nations after it was agreed to. The Assembly disagreed, took over the discussion, and the agency was finally created with some wisdom from the smaller powers. The atomic agency limped for a while, until all of a sudden the governments became afraid of the danger caused by a proliferation of nuclear materials. The U.S. government is now moving rigorously to place all of its bilateral agreements under agency inspection. It is even submitting some of its own reactors to such inspection in order to show that we are claiming no privileged position. Suddenly the atomic energy agency is coming into its own.

The General Assembly in 1961 unanimously proclaimed that the celestial bodies were not subject to appropriation, that the law of the charter applied to outer space, and later an Assembly resolution announced that the nations agreed that atomic weapons could not be carried on space ships. Now the Soviet Union and the United States, afraid that a resolution of the General Assembly was not sufficient, have each proposed a treaty which will accomplish all of these objectives. These treaties will probably be consolidated and be ready for the General Assembly. But I wonder what kind of reaction there would be to the outer space treaty if the General Assembly had not had the courage to proclaim that celestial bodies were not subject to appropriation and that space ships could not carry weapons of mass destruction?

Just a point or two more. In the first place, there could be a resolution of the General Assembly that the seas are not subject to appropriation by any state. And then in the course of time the General Assembly could declare that the resources of the sea which are the common property of mankind, should be subject to licensing and proper control by a special agency that would be set up. Then we would hope that there might be an agreement, first in a proclamation by the General Assembly and then agreement by the powers most concerned, a vast new area of weapons development might be avoided.

I am not going into the economics of the problem. Mr. Christy covered that most thoroughly in his paper. But there were several papers read that have caused me some concern. A distinguished international lawyer said there was no vacuum in the deep sea; any state could explore and stake out a claim. If any states attempted exploration nearby, they could harmonize their problems. That is a concept of international law that is essentially European and American. I think the Russians, because they are a privileged people, also go along with it. International law can be so interpreted to defend those that are the strongest and to protect a privileged position. What if the rest of the world rejects it?

For illustration, international law protected the right of the British and others to maintain colonies that were swept aside in the movement for decolonization. Mr. Chapman in his paper gave what I think was a most alarming and brilliant discussion of anarchy of the sea. He pointed out that there had been conflict before and that we could expect equal conflict in the future. But I ask, Is it necessary for us to have that? Can we not have our economic interests adequately protected, and at the same time have a rational economic order? Our forefathers were able to take what they wanted in this country and so were the Canadians because there was nothing in their way but defenseless Indians. We cannot take what we want from the sea in the same way without the Russians, or the Japanese, or others wanting to do the same thing. Why can we not all enjoy what we want through a rational order?

We have heard from Dr. Burke about those that are able to go out and establish colonies in the sea, but I ask how many nations are able to do it? The United States, the Soviet Union, the United Kingdom, Japan, maybe the Scandinavian countries in combination. But what of the vast part of the world that has suddenly come to independence, the underdeveloped parts of the world that need resources?

I ask us to lift our sights today. Five-sevenths of the surface of the earth is composed of the sea. As yet it has not been claimed by sovereign powers. Shall we say this vast area will be an area of anarchy in which a new struggle for colonial riches, and thus a new power struggle, will prevail? We believe that the privilege of men to explore the ocean's bed and to exploit its resources can be better guaranteed, and these resources saved from depletion, by co-operation than by anarchy. It should not be

301

necessary for a few maritime powers to embark on another power struggle on another frontier, nor to arm the sea in order to make its bounties available for the benefit of all mankind.

CHRISTY:

During the discussions at the Law of the Sea Institute, there emerged several objections to the suggestions for "internationalization" of the sea's resources.[1] Because debate on this subject is likely to continue, it will be useful to attempt a classification of the objections and to point out some of the areas where further research is needed and where further discussion will be fruitful. Generally, the objections fall into three categories, although there is some overlap. The three categories are: (a) that there is no need for international authority; (b) that international authority would be detrimental to the interests of the United States; and (c) that there is no practical means for achieving international authority.

I. The Need for International Authority

With respect to the fisheries of the high seas, international controls are already well established. What is needed is a different form of control—an authority that can regulate the amount of effort. The case for this has already been presented and need not be repeated here. The objections are largely concerned with the difficulties of implementation.

With respect to minerals lying on, or under, the sea floor beyond the depth of 200 meters, the question of need for an international authority hinges upon one's views as to which governmental body can best provide the guarantee of exclusive rights that will be required by the mineral industries. Any industry that is considering the very heavy and risky investments that deep ocean mining will require must be assured of exclusive rights to the property before undertaking the investment. The question is whether the exclusive rights can best be guaranteed by an individual nation-state or by an international body such as the United Nations.

302

Both of the critics, William Burke[2] and Northcutt Ely,[3] admit that a greater degree of international control than now exists may be necessary in the future. Burke rejects "blueprints for utopia" and indicates that the difficulties of implementation (discussed later) will prevent any immediate achievement of the long-range objective. Ely feels that there is no need for international administration until conflict appears; that laws and regulations governing such administration cannot be written with precision until there is a history of use; and that when the need occurs, international law can crystallize as rapidly and as effectively as it did for the continental shelf.

In the "search for appropriate jurisdiction to assure exclusive occupancy of a segment of the seabed," Ely's preferred solution is to permit the explorer to appropriate the segment under the jurisdiction (and protection, I assume) of his flag. If conflict develops during exploitation, then the flag nations "are likely to arrive at an accommodation," and only if that fails will it be necessary to create a "licensing scheme for administration by the United Nations."

It is difficult to separate the question of need for an international approach from the question of the distribution of the sea's wealth. The United States has technological advantages over most, if not all, other nations when it comes to mining deep sea minerals. If the United States will guarantee and protect a firm's exclusive rights to a segment of the sea bed, the firm may feel that it can operate more freely than under an international licensing system administered by the United Nations. Under this flag-nation approach, the initial advantage (and perhaps temporary) is likely to go to the mineral firms that are involved. And by the time conflict develops, these firms, and the United States, may have acquired "historic rights" that will permit them to exert considerable influence on the system that will be developed for administering and distributing the sea's minerals.

This view assumes that the United States (and other coastal states) would be willing to guarantee and protect a citizen's claim to exclusive use of a resource beyond the edge of the continental shelf. This assumption, or hope, is one of the issues that should receive considerable debate and study in the future. What are the costs and benefits (political as well as material) associated with the flag-nation approach as against the international approach? How would interests (transportation, military, fisheries) other than minerals be affected? What would be the effect of establishing either approach as a precedent? How

303

are other nations likely to view the flag-nation approach as against the international one, and what would be the influence of their views on the decision? When conflicts develop, can these best be worked out by multilateral agreements, or under the aegis of an international body already established to administer the licensing of exclusive rights?

In addition to questions about which governmental body could best guarantee exclusive rights, questions were raised about the inability to be precise about rules and regulations covering potential enterprises and about the ability of international law to meet speedily the problems when they arise. I think that the question of precision is irrelevant to the issue of international authority. To be sure, deep sea mining of minerals is only a potential development, and it is difficult to speculate on the needs of an industry with respect to the spatial and legal scope of its rights. But this difficulty in precision holds true for both a flag-nation approach and an international approach. In either case, the desire for precision will have to be subordinated to the need for flexibility. And in either case, it will be useful to acquire as much knowledge as possible about the needs of an industry for exclusive rights to a mining area. That principles can be advanced in the absence of precise knowledge of conflict is indicated by the Geneva Convention on Fishing and Conservation of the Living Resources of the High Seas which anticipates conflict and prescribes certain rules of behavior to deal with it.

Whether or not international law can crystallize rapidly enough to meet future conflicts between flag nations is questionable. The analogy of the continental shelf law does not appear to me to be a satisfactory one. It is remarkably imprecise. While it guarantees the right of a coastal state to its shelf resources, it leaves completely open the question of resources beyond the edge of the shelf where the real conflicts are likely to occur.

In summary, a guarantee of exclusive rights is essential for the development and exploitation of deep sea minerals. The basic issue for future discussion and research is whether this guarantee can best be secured under an international authority or by individual nations.

II. *The Interests of the United States*

Although it was not stated explicitly, it is clear that some of the objections to "internationalization" of sea resources arise from fears that this approach would be detrimental to the interests of the United States. This is essentially the question of the distribution of the sea's wealth, the question of "who gets what."

The distribution of fisheries' wealth has already been discussed, although no estimates of the effect of different systems on the United States economy were made. Such estimates cannot be made without a good deal of research, and this is one of the many tasks facing the social sciences. It is worthwhile to mention, however, a few of the elements important to this evaluation. First, it should be pointed out that the catching end of the fishery industries makes only a negligible contribution to the economy of the United States. The annual gross revenue to U.S. fishermen is about $400 million—less than that from potatoes, for example. And because of the wasted applications of redundant effort, the net contribution to the economy is very small.

Second, unless there is rationalization of fisheries, it is unlikely that any high seas regime will do much to increase the contribution of fishing industries to the U.S. economy.

And third, it should be made clear that "internationalization" will *not* mean that the profits to individual fishermen and firms will be taken by the international authority. Under this system, where duplicating effort is prevented from entering the fishery, it would be the *surplus* profit (the economic rent) that would be removed. This surplus profit is now dissipated because the fishery attracts too much capital and labor. With internationalization, the dissipation would be prevented and the economic rent would be produced in the form of taxes, leases, or license fees paid by the fishermen. And for this payment, the fishermen would be receiving the right to participate in a fishery that is free from congestion and redundant amounts of capital and labor. There would be fewer participants and each would receive a greater share of the total supply. The fee would be similar to the purchase, by a farmer, of property—property that carries the right of exclusive use. Under this form of control, the net gain to the U.S. would depend upon the willingness of the U.S. fishermen to invest in this form of property. Given the technological advantages of the U.S. and the freedom from congestion, the net contribution to the U.S. economy is likely to be larger than it is at present.

For minerals, the problems of congestion and excess applications of effort are not fully relevant, because the necessity for exclusive rights and the ease of describing the property is much clearer than it is for

305

the fugitive fisheries. Deep sea mining operations will call for extremely large investments carrying great risks. It is unlikely, at present, that individual firms would be willing to bid very much for exclusive rights to mine a property at the bottom of the deep sea; nor is it likely that it would be in the best interests of the world community to impose a use fee at this time.[4] However, just as there is a market for property on the continental shelf, there will, most likely, develop a market for property on the deep sea bottom; at least, within the United States and other free enterprise systems. In free enterprises, the market guides the allocation of resources, and individuals and firms acquire these on the basis of their willingness to pay for them. Thus even if there is a flag-nation approach to the distribution of the sea's minerals, the individual firms would have to bid for, or buy, their rights to exclude others (and, in addition, buy the protection of their flag). As the value of deep sea mining increases, the value of this form of property right is also likely to increase.

Under internationalization, the right to exclude others would be acquired in the world market, with individual firms or nations bidding for the privilege. It is difficult to say whether the open world market would require higher bids by U.S. firms than the domestic market. This would depend upon the comparative advantages among nations. It is likely, however, that the capital intensiveness and technological requirements of deep sea mining would give the edge to the United States firms, so that their bids would not have to be higher under a world market than under a U.S. market.

The major difference would be that under internationalization, the payments would go to the world community, which would seem appropriate if these resources are considered to be the property of the world community.

In the above discussion, I have assumed that the property right is limited and specific; that it refers to the mining of certain minerals over a certain length of time and for a fixed area. This is not the appropriation of full property rights, nor the acquisition of sovereignty over a segment of the sea bottom. Under a flag-nation approach, however, it may be difficult to limit and maintain the specificity of the right. Military interests, the possible development of other resources and uses of the sea bottom, or perhaps a sense of imperialism, may provide incentives to extend the rights and claim full sovereignty. To the extent that this is permitted, it is likely to lead to what President Johnson

306

has referred to as a "new form of colonial competition among the maritime nations." [5]

In summary, it is not at all clear that the United States interests, over the long run, would be less well off under a system of internationalization than under a flag-nation or open-access approach. The payments made to the international authority would be payments to assure efficiency and to guarantee exclusive rights. The gains from these are likely to outweigh the amount of the payments. Aside from the purely economic aspects of the evaluation, the future discussion will also have to take into consideration the social and political values of alternative regimes. Evidence of the importance of these relatively intangible values lies in the further remarks of President Johnson: "We must be careful to avoid a race to grab and to hold the lands under the high seas. We must ensure that the deep seas and the ocean bottoms are, and remain, the legacy of all human beings."

III. *The Means for Achieving International Authority*

The need for international authority cannot really be considered without reference to the means of achieving it. It is possible, although I do not hold this view, that the costs of achieving an international high seas regime may outweigh the benefits to be obtained. In large measure, the objectors to the United Nations approach have taken this position. The difficulties are, indeed, great. As some critics have pointed out, not a single state of the United States has been able to achieve a rationalized fishery. How then, can we hope to rationalize international fisheries where the obstacles are so much greater?

William Burke states that "although there is an evident need for establishing international institutions, endowed with adequate authority, policies, and procedures for coping with a rapidly changing situation, it would be a mistake to attempt to place too much confidence in the capacity of the international political system to respond to the new demands."

He then specifies three of the major obstacles that would have to be overcome: the necessity for reconstituting the General Assembly of the UN so that it will more accurately reflect the distribution of power, wealth, and skill, and thereby be able to deal more adequately with the problems of international ocean authority; the difficulties of accommodating military uses of the ocean and, as urged in the Report of the

307

Commission to Study the Organization of Peace, of preventing military appropriation of the sea bottom; and the fact that there is "minimal effort now devoted to inquiry into economic criteria for the exploitation of fishery resources."

These obstacles are certainly difficult, but they are not insurmountable. The Commission to Study the Organization of Peace has recommended reconstitution of the General Assembly, and will be working toward this goal. Military uses of the sea bottom will, of course, be difficult to accommodate, but that does not mean that the machines of war should be condoned. It may be true, as Mr. Burke states, that the "prohibition of military activity hardly seems to be a necessary consequence of organized international exploitation of the ocean," but it is clear that military uses, potential or actual, have considerable influence on national policy; viz., the (somewhat specious) military objections to extensions of the three mile limit. One of the major, and most irreconcilable, problems in the study of ocean policy is that the military "requirements" are not made public. This means that the evaluation of alternative regimes must proceed as if there were no military uses.

But Burke's major objection appears to be one of strategy—that "the bare recommendation of this objective [internationalization] hardly advances the prospect of achieving it. Serious recommendations of this sort would gain far greater influence if accompanied both by acknowledgment of the obstacles which must be surmounted and by suggested strategies by which the campaign must be conducted." This would, of course, be desirable, but the advancement of the principles and the delineation of the need without presentation of the details is hardly a sufficient basis for discarding the suggestions as "blueprints for utopia."

I believe that an international approach through the United Nations is both necessary and desirable. Others hold contrary views. But all who seek to exploit the oceans and all who look forward to the orderly, rational, and beneficial development of ocean resources should make every effort to explore and discuss as openly as possible, the alternative goals, the methods of achieving these, and the difficulties that will have to be overcome.

---

1. As a member of the Commission to Study the Organization of Peace and of the Committee on Natural Resources Conservation and Development for the White House Conference on International Cooperation, I have participated in,

and supported, the recommendations for United Nations' authority over high-seas resources. Early suggestions for international authority over fisheries were presented by Anthony Scott and me in *The Common Wealth in Ocean Fisheries* (Johns Hopkins Press, 1965), and have been carried forward in my paper, "The Distribution of the Seas' Wealth in Fisheries," presented at this conference. For minerals as well as fisheries, see the chapter by David B. Brooks and me in the forthcoming book by the Commission to Study the Organization of Peace.

2. William T. Burke, "Law and the New Technologies," *supra,* pp. 204–27.

3. See the papers prepared by Northcutt Ely for the American Institute of Mining, Metallurgical and Petroleum Engineers; for the Marine Technology Society; and *supra,* pp. 174–79.

4. This is debatable. The production of manganese nodules could have a deleterious effect on some of the less developed, raw-material producing countries. Some restraint in production may facilitate adjustment by these countries.

5. President Lyndon B. Johnson, "Remarks of the President at the Commissioning of the New Research Ship, the Oceanographer," July 13, 1966.

Chapter Nineteen:

REFLECTIONS ON THE MEETING OF THE
LAW OF THE SEA INSTITUTE

I. *Introduction*

During the week of June 27, 1966, the Law of the Sea Institute of the
University of Rhode Island conducted its first summer conference,
ostensibly on the subject of offshore boundaries and zones. This topic
merely served as a frame of reference and a springboard for a wide-
ranging discussion of the problems involved in using the oceans in
ways other than the traditional ones of surface transportation and fishing.
The conference also provided a forum for those (the fishing, oil, and
other mineral industries as well as the Navy) with vital economic and
other direct interests in the oceans to present, for the record, well-
articulated rationalizations of their positions. This airing of positions
was a particularly valuable contribution, since it suggested the outlines
of the future debate and struggle over ocean resource policy. The debate
also put the question of internationalization of the oceans' resources in
much sharper focus. The tone of the conference suggested clearly that
any move in the direction of international control must be based on
specifics and that the position taken by the White House Conference
(the Commission to Study the Organization of Peace, 17th Report, May,
1966) must be built up in much greater detail before it can become
operational. Finally, by bringing together experts from many different
disciplines (law, marine biology, physical oceanography, economics,
and administration), the conference illustrated again the difficulties in
communication between groups of experts. The running argument
between the physical scientists and economists over the definition of
optimization of resource use is illustrative of the many real difficulties
(in addition to merely semantic problems) introduced into the dis-

cussion by differences in training and outlook, i.e., which variables are considered important.

The historical background of the meeting was the Geneva conferences on the law of the sea in 1958 and 1960. The positions taken by the United States at that time on the desirable extent of the territorial sea, the uses of the high seas and the continental shelf were reasserted with no significant shift in position by Arthur Dean, the head of our delegation at the Geneva conferences. The representatives of the Department of State also supported specific aspects of this position in the debate (although the position of the Navy was ambiguous on several key points, specifically on the use of the deep ocean). The cornerstone of this position is a territorial sea of six miles (as against the old rule of three) with an exclusive fishing zone of another six. In addition, the unilateral Truman Proclamation of 1945 is the basis for exclusive claim to the mineral resources of the continental shelf. In general, our national position is to minimize the width of the territorial sea over which any nation may exercise sovereignty and at the same time to reserve (primarily for mineral exploitation) the use of the shelf for our nationals. This approach to use of the oceans is consistent with the position of most, but not all, of our fishing interests (the most obvious difference is that between the tuna and salmon fisheries) and the oil and other mining companies.

> In preparing this paper I confess to a point of view based on the interests of U.S. commercial fisheries, particularly the domestic shrimp fishery. It has been to the interest of the shrimp fishery to accent the doctrine of *freedom of the seas for fishing* because the shrimp fishery is classified in part as a distant fishery, as is also true of tuna. This position also explains in advance the apprehension of this fishery as to attachment to any Continental Shelf doctrine.[1]

Our position on the use of deep seas beyond the shelf is not clear, but as noted above, all our commercial and military interests are very wary of any direct and broad-based internationalization of the submerged lands and fishery resources lying beyond the shelf. Without delving into the complex relationship between the form and content of the law and underlying social realities, we may reasonably conclude that the real force behind the two recent international conferences on the law of the sea and the Rhode Island symposium was growing pressure from a rapidly changing technology and therefore the increased capacity to make use of ocean resources. Since these technological developments are overlapping and general in all the principal areas of ocean resources, fish, minerals, oil and military operations, the pressure for readjustment of traditional legal doctrine comes from many sources. In addition it is supplemented by expressions of national self-interest on the part of developing nations.

II. *Attitudes and Problems*

At the conference, it was widely accepted that pressure from these external forces had caused an acceleration in the historically slow rate of change in the law of the sea. A major dispute erupted, however, over whether future changes in the law should precede or follow the course of development of the use of ocean resources. This was, of course, simply an aspect of the disagreement over internationalization. It is fair to say that the issue of internationalization is so complex that neither set of protagonists did it justice. It would also be unfair to describe either position in terms of the relatively simple arguments advanced at this time. Rather, these arguments seem to be more like the opening skirmish in a prolonged debate. It is clear, however, that the burden for any move in the direction of international control will fall on the internationalists.

At present, the internationalists' argument runs along the following lines: The world is in a disequilibrium situation. The two principal disequilibrating forces are the rate of growth of population and the growing disparity in real income between nations. (To the internationalists the vested interests not represented at the meeting were the underdeveloped nations of the world.) The technological superiority of the developed nations means that they will have the power to pre-empt any real net economic gains to be obtained from the use of the oceans. The exploitation of these resources will be on a competitive basis, and since these are open access resources, the exploitation will be wasteful and the net economic yield will be dissipated. Finally, given the tensions in the world, the oceans, like space and Antarctica, should be kept free from military weapons systems. In these circumstances the optimum solution is to turn over the control of these resources to an international organization, presumably the UN or some special agency thereof. This agency, acting as the sole owner, would then license the use of these resources, efficiently capturing the rents created, in the price of the license or through some system of taxation. These rents which are currently lost in the fisheries, would then be available for distribution among all nations. A by-product of this arrangement would be a strengthening of supranational organizations at the expense of national sovereignty.

The direct attack on this position was of the usual kind. Questions were raised about the need for any change prior to a clear demonstration of need, the inadequacy of a body such as the General Assembly of the United Nations to administer efficiently and distribute gains meaningfully, and how it would be possible to safeguard the national interests of the various states and their nationals.

III. *Conclusions*

The arguments pro and con are, as yet, so primitive that the real contribution of the conference was to establish the debate and to indicate some of the inadequacy of the reasoning on both sides. Before any progress can be made it is clear that criteria for internationalization must be developed. There must be some logical, compelling, and specific reasons for taking action. In all probability local and regional agreement will take precedence over broad ocean-wide compacts. In addition, as the broad confusion over the different implications for meaningful economic exploitation of the fugacious fish resources and the sedentary mineral deposits indicated, a further classification of agreements based on resource definition is also in order.

Hard work on the technical nature of and the necessary and sufficient conditions for, agreement on these specifics will focus attention on certain points raised by Burke.[2] For example, the analogy that compares the oceans to outer space. As yet, there are no weapons systems in space. But the oceans, certainly the continental shelves, probably sea mounts, and possibly even the ocean depths are currently being used for military purposes. In these circumstances any general as contrasted with specific, move toward internationalization becomes, as Burke pointed out, a problem in disarmament and an attack on the Navy's position, not simply an attempt to prevent the spread of weapons systems. It will be necessary to understand the presence of this type of constraint in formulating more limited but nonetheless meaningful international agreements on the use of the oceans.

Finally, it is desirable to emphasize the technical difficulties faced by the conference. As Christy suggested,[3] probably the sole international agreement in the fishery, that is considered workable by economists is

313

the fur seal treaty in the North Pacific involving Japan, the U.S.S.R., Canada, and the U.S. In this case the industry is rationalized and the net gains from the resources are distributed among the four participants. The only flaw is that the agreement is partial in the sense that seals are only a segment of the food chain. If, as some biologists suggest, the seals prey on the Pacific salmon, then it becomes impossible to say whether gross, much less net, revenue is maximized by conserving seals. This difficulty of dealing with partial rather than general equilibrium models is but one of the technical issues that must be solved before we may maximize the net economic yield from the oceans.

1. W. R. Neblett, "The 1958 Conference on the Law of the Sea: What Was Accomplished," *supra*, pp. 36–46.

2. W. T. Burke, "Law and the New Technologies," *supra*, pp. 204–27.

3. F. T. Christy, Jr., "The Distribution of the Sea's Wealth in Fisheries," *supra*, pp. 106–21.

CONTRIBUTORS

LEWIS M. ALEXANDER is professor of geography at the University of Rhode Island.

EDWARD W. ALLEN is a member of the firm of Allen, DeGarmo, and Leedy, in Seattle, Washington.

WILLARD BASCOM is President of Ocean Science and Engineering, Inc., in Washington, D.C.

RICHARD BAXTER is professor of law at Harvard University.

WILLIAM T. BURKE is professor of law at the Ohio State University.

WILBERT MC LEOD CHAPMAN is director of the Division of Resources of the Van Camp Sea Food Company Division of the Ralston-Purina Company, in San Diego, California.

FRANCIS T. CHRISTY, JR., is on the staff of Resources for the Future, Inc., in Washington, D.C.

ARTHUR H. DEAN is a member of the firm of Sullivan and Cromwell in New York City, and was chairman of the United States Delegation to the 1958 and 1960 Law of the Sea Conferences at Geneva.

CLARK M. EICHELBERGER is chairman of the Commission to Study the Organization of Peace, in New York City.

NORTHCUTT ELY is a member of the firm of Ely, Duncan, and Bennett, in Washington, D.C.

K. O. EMERY is a member of the staff of the Woods Hole Oceanographic Institution.

ROBERT L. FRIEDHEIM is professor of political science at Purdue University.

L. F. E. GOLDIE is professor of law at the Loyola University in Los Angeles.

BRUCE A. HARLOW is a lieutenant commander in the United States Navy, serving as special assistant on the law of the sea in the office of the Judge Advocate General.

WILLIAM C. HERRINGTON is former special assistant for fisheries and wildlife to the United States Secretary of State.

F. J. HORTIG is executive officer of the California State Lands Commission, in Los Angeles.

BERNARD E. JACOB is professor of law at the University of California, Los Angeles.

RALPH JOHNSON is professor of law at the University of Washington.

MYRES S. MCDOUGAL is Sterling Professor of Law at Yale University.

ALEXANDER A. MELAMID is a member of the faculty of the Center for International Studies of New York University.

JOHN L. MERO is president of Ocean Resources, Inc., in La Jolla, California.

WILLIAM R. NEBLETT is executive secretary of the National Shrimp Congress, Inc., in Key West, Florida.

GIULIO PONTECORVO is a member of the faculty of the Graduate School of Business of Columbia University.

HENRY REIFF is former head of the Department of History and Government at St. Lawrence University, Canton, New York.

GERARD E. SULLIVAN is a member of the Interagency Committee on Oceanography, in Washington, D.C.

316

QUINCY WRIGHT is professor of law at the University of Virginia.

RICHARD YOUNG of Van Hornesville, New York, is a member of the New York Bar and of the Board of Editors of the *American Journal of International Law.*

INDEX